# THE
# SUFFERING
# OF GOD

D0770606

# OVERTURES TO BIBLICAL THEOLOGY

A series of studies in biblical theology designed to explore fresh dimensions of research and to suggest ways in which the biblical heritage may address contemporary culture

*Editors*

WALTER BRUEGGEMANN, Professor of Old Testament at Eden Theological Seminary, St. Louis, Missouri

JOHN R. DONAHUE, S.J., Professor of New Testament at the Jesuit School of Theology, Berkeley, California

*An*
*Old*
*Testament*
*Perspective*

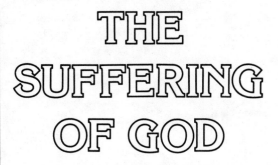

# THE SUFFERING OF GOD

TERENCE E. FRETHEIM

F FORTRESS PRESS    Philadelphia

Biblical quotations, unless otherwise noted, are from the Revised Standard Version of the Bible, copyright 1946, 1952, © 1971, 1973 by the Division of Christian Education of the National Council of the Churches of Christ in the U.S.A. and are used by permission.

COPYRIGHT © 1984 BY FORTRESS PRESS

All rights reserved. No part of this publication may be reproduced, stored in a retrieval system, or transmitted in any form or by any means, electronic, mechanical, photocopying, recording, or otherwise, without the prior permission of the copyright owner.

**Library of Congress Cataloging in Publication Data**

Fretheim, Terence E.
  The suffering of God.

  (Overtures to Biblical theology ; 14)
  Includes indexes.
  1. Suffering of God—Biblical teaching.   2. Bible.
O.T.—Theology.   I. Title.   II. Series.
BS1199.S82F74   1984      231      84-47921
ISBN 0-8006-1538-7

K960C84    Printed in the United States of America    1-1538

To Faith

Partner
Companion
Friend

Mark the first page of the book
with a red marker.
For, in the beginning,
the wound is invisible.

Reb Alce
(Jabes: 13)

Search the Scriptures,
for in them you will find
this God of the loveless,
this God of Mercy, Love and Justice,
who weeps over these her children,
these her precious ones who have been carried from the womb,
who gathers up her young upon her wings
and rides along the high places of the earth,
who sees their suffering
and cries out like a woman in travail,
who gasps and pants;
for with this God,
any injustice that befalls one of these precious ones
is never the substance
of rational reflection and critical analysis,
but is the source
of a catastrophic convulsion within the very life of God.

Karen Drescher
(a former student)

Though thou with clouds of anger do disguise
Thy face; yet through that maske I know those eyes,
Which, though they turne away sometimes,
They never will despise.

John Donne

# Contents

# Editor's Foreword

The tension between biblical theology and systematic (dogmatic) theological formulations is of course well-known and recognized among us. That very tension has made articulation of biblical-theological matters exceedingly problematic. Characteristically, biblical scholarship has escaped the tension in one of two ways. Either we have settled for a consideration of the history of religion, particularly in OT studies. Or we have engaged in exhaustive—sometimes exhausting—reflection on questions of methodology in interpretation. Of course both of these enterprises are not only legitimate, but important. But neither of these, in and of itself, actually gets on with the substantive task of doing biblical theology.

Biblical theology is an attempt to articulate the main theological claims and resources in the text. There is a dearth of examples and models for dealing with the actual substantive matters. In this book Professor Fretheim has provided us with a clear and persuasive example of how biblical theology is to be done. He is, of course, not inattentive to the issues involved in the history of Israel's religion. Nor is he unaware of the complexity of methodological issues. But he has permitted neither of these alternatives to detract or deter him from getting the substantive theological issue: Who is the God who is presented, articulated, and disclosed in the text. Fretheim's book is important formally because he addresses this issue with full awareness that his study leads him deeply into tension with dominant modes of systematic theology. His discussion is important substantively, precisely because he asks a *theological* question, listens to *theological* answers offered in the text, and can entertain those answers as normative for the community around the text, even though those answers are not easily contained in conventional modes of theology.

As concerns the series of Overtures to Biblical Theology, Fretheim takes up the task articulated by Dale Patrick in *The Rendering of God in the Old Testament* (1981). Fretheim considers what God it is that is rendered here, and the result of this rendering for the community which listens to the text.

Fretheim's book takes up classical themes of theology: God's foreknowledge, God's presence, God's form, God's sovereignty. In each case he shows how Israel transforms and subverts the classic themes. He does so not by proposing any general theoretical proposal, but by a close reading of the text. The results are stunning, shattering of much convention, and an invitation to rethink the question. Thus God's *foreknowledge* is not the kind of absoluteness usually attached to the notion of God. The issue of God's *presence* is linked to the troublesome affirmation of God's freedom. The *form* of God's presence is impinged upon by the vulnerability which marks the human analogue. The *sovereignty* of God is open to the reality of pathos. Fretheim shows how the text resists every reductionism and every systematic formulation. While it is well beyond the scope of his work, the implications of his study are enormous for the reformation of our understanding of God.

My impression is that the question of God has most often been bracketed out. It is bracketed out by some who regard the issue as *settled* by conventional formulations, even if those formulations are scholastic. It is bracketed out by others who presume the question of God is *archaic* and surely not pertinent. Against both, Fretheim shows how the Bible treats the question of God as both open and unresolved, and urgent for contemporary life.

The outcome of Fretheim's research is to make clear that suffering belongs to the person and purpose of God. We have had many hints of such a theological claim, but I know of no study which has worked through the biblical material in a comprehensive way as does Fretheim. The effect is that the tension between conventional theology and the Bible is stressed and made visible. The study places into radical question our usual assumptions about God.

The implications of the study, not drawn by the author, run in two important directions. First, the linkages to the NT and a theology of the cross are important and obvious. Second, it occurs to me that such a way of doing theology not only challenges conventional theology but also conventional cultural assumptions that justify our models of humanness and our practices of political and economic power. The subversive force of this theological assertion extends not only to the religious tradition, but to the derivative forms of social power justified by biblical faith. Western preoccupation with dominance and power is no doubt linked to and derived from our imperial "image of God." Clearly when that discernment of God is challenged, the images which take public form are placed in deep jeopardy.

The power of Fretheim's analysis is that he stays free of every ideological inclination and simply lets us see what is in the text. He is a superb reader of the text, able to listen to the claims of the text which surprise and do not fit our schemes. Because his argument stays so very close to the text, it will be difficult to resist his conclusion, even though there are good ideological reasons for resistance. What one finds here is particular attention to many texts. The volume of the text is good, disciplined exegesis of a great many texts. What better way to do biblical theology!

WALTER BRUEGGEMANN

# Preface

This book is written out of a concern to broaden our understanding of the kind of God who is portrayed in the OT. More specifically, I intend to focus on certain images of God which have been neglected in both church and scholarship.

The God of the OT is commonly pictured in the teaching of the church as primarily a God of judgment and wrath, an "eye for an eye, tooth for a tooth" kind of God, who is often vindictive and punitive, seldom gracious and compassionate. God is often depicted in terms of a kind of fatherhood that smacks of a certain remoteness and coldness and sternness, even ruthlessness, a picture that is believed to need decisive correction in the light of the coming of Jesus Christ. This churchly development is at least in part due to scholarly neglect of those OT images which portray God in nonmonarchical terms, not least those which depict God as one who suffers, as one who has entered deeply into the human situation and made it his own.

One not uncommon result of these developments for believers has been the diminishment of the importance of the OT for faith and life. Even more, it has become a stumbling block to others who are on the periphery of the life of the church, or outside of that community altogether. Such persons often choose not to become associated with the church, or only perfunctorily so, because of the kind of God that community's sacred writings seem to hold dear. Such individuals are normally not looking for a comfortable God or a God about whom there is no mystery. They are concerned, however, about intelligibility and coherence with respect to any presentation of God. And they believe in a unitary conception of truth, insistent upon the adequacy of any understanding of God to their individual and social experience. Is such a God available in the OT witness?

The common OT depiction of God may be problematical for many persons because of its excessively masculine character, at least as often presented. Such a virile picture of God may, perhaps unconsciously, lead to a perception of God as one who is able to relate to only part of what it means to be human. God is thus felt, if not understood, to be less than whole. Indeed, we are living in a time when significant shifts are being made in the portrayal of God in the life of the church, not least in the use of masculine-feminine language. The OT depiction of God, while more masculine in character than any contemporary statement ought to be, does contain resources which should be of help in this discussion.

My own interest in this subject is perhaps most determined by my roots in Norwegian Lutheran Pietism. Among other characteristics, this evangelicalism stands over against doctrinal rigidities and lifts up a highly personal relationship between God and people. Though not often articulated in a theoretical way, in practice this has meant an understanding of God who is most intimately involved in the daily life of the people, and in such a way that God is affected as much as people are. For example, I am still amazed at the expectations of the community with respect to the effect that prayer is thought to have on God. Thus, it might be said that the personalism of the God whom I know from my own experience rings true to the God whom I meet in the pages of the OT, but not the God whom I often hear portrayed in the life of the wider church.

In addition, these emphases have been informed by certain other distinctively but not uniquely Lutheran concerns,[1] such as the theology of the cross, with the power of God manifested supremely through weakness, and the *finitum capax infiniti,* that is, the finite is capable of the infinite.

Three other modern developments have helped to fill out this perspective: the work of Abraham Heschel on the pathos of God; feminist theology; and those theological currents which emphasize the unchanging salvific will of God for the world, while stressing the ways in which the divine experience of the world affects not only the world, but the very life of God.

Conversations with many individuals have helped prepare the way for this book. I wish to express my appreciation to students at Luther Northwestern Seminary, to Lutheran pastors in the United States and Canada, as well as faculty seminars in Oxford and Cambridge, who have responded to this material in earlier forms. I am grateful to the Overtures editor, Walter Brueggemann, and to my former teacher, James Barr, for reading the manuscript and offering helpful suggestions for its improvement. A special note of gratitude is due to my colleague, Paul Sponheim, whose encouraging conversations through the years and insightful analysis of the manuscript have sharpened my thinking about these matters in immeasurable ways. I also wish to thank Oxford University for providing library resources, to the Luther Northwestern Seminary Board of Directors for granting a sabbatical leave, and to Lutheran Brotherhood of Minneapolis, Minnesota, for giving assistance along the way. Finally, I express my deep gratitude to my wife, Faith, to whom this book is dedicated; her constant support has been a source of great encouragement to me.

# Abbreviations

| | |
|---|---|
| BDB | Brown-Driver-Briggs, *Hebrew and English Lexicon of the Old Testament* |
| BJRL | *John Rylands Library Bulletin* |
| BTB | *Biblical Theology Bulletin* |
| BZAW | Beihefte zur Zeitschrift für die alttestamentliche Wissenschaft |
| CBQ | *Catholic Biblical Quarterly* |
| HBT | *Horizons in Biblical Theology* |
| HUCA | Hebrew Union College Annual |
| IDBSup | *Interpreter's Dictionary of the Bible* Supplement |
| Int | *Interpretation* |
| IRT | Issues in Religion and Theology |
| JAAR | *Journal of the American Academy of Religion* |
| JB | Jerusalem Bible |
| JBL | *Journal of Biblical Literature* |
| JJS | *Journal of Jewish Studies* |
| JR | *Journal of Religion* |
| JSOT | *Journal for the Study of the Old Testament* |
| JTS | *Journal of Theological Studies* |
| KJV | King James Version |
| NEB | New English Bible |
| NT | New Testament |
| OBT | Overtures to Biblical Theology |
| OT | Old Testament |
| OTL | Old Testament Library |
| PHOE | *The Problem of the Hexateuch and Other Essays* |

| RS | *Religious Studies* |
| RSV | Revised Standard Version |
| SJT | *Scottish Journal of Theology* |
| TEV | Today's English Version |
| THAT | *Theologisches Handwörterbuch zum alten Testament* |
| THST | *Theological Studies* |
| ThWAT | *Theologisches Wörterbuch zum alten Testament* |
| TT | *Theological Studies* |
| VT | *Vetus Testamentum* |
| VTSup | *Vetus Testamentum Supplement* |
| USQR | *Union Seminary Quarterly Review* |
| ZAW | *Zeitschrift für die alttestamentliche Wissenschaft* |
| ZTK | *Zeitschrift für Theologie und Kirche* |

# CHAPTER 1

Introduction

## WHAT KIND OF GOD?

It is not enough to say that one believes in God. What is important finally is the *kind* of God in whom one believes.[1] Or, to use different language: metaphors matter. The images used to speak of God not only decisively determine the way one thinks about God, they have a powerful impact on the shape of the life of the believer. They may, in fact, tend to shape a life toward unbelief.

In his autobiography, the American journalist and critic Thomas Matthews, a preacher's kid, writes:

> Try as I may, I cannot altogether shake off my habitual awe of the church nor completely dissociate it from the far more fearful God to whom the church makes its ritual obeisance. I still think of God—no, not think, but apprehend, as I was trained as a child to envision him—as a watchful, vengeful, enormous, omniscient policeman, instantly aware of the slightest tinge of irreverence in my innermost thought, always ready to pounce if I curse, if I mention him in anger, fun or mere habit (though with ominous patience he might hold his hand for a time). . . . But how can that kind of fear of that kind of God be the beginning of wisdom?[2]

All too often the sole focus of the ministry of the church has been on *whether* one believes in God. Insufficient attention has been given to the kind of God in whom one believes, often with disastrous results. Witness any number of atrocities, from the Inquisition to Jonestown, committed in the name of God by those who believe in God. Moreover, to define God solely or primarily in terms of activity can get one into comparable difficulties. The God of Jonestown was a creator and redeemer God who had a clear plan and purpose, moving

1

the people toward a specific goal. The question of the kind of God in whom one believes is not only important, it is crucial. It is a question of images. Metaphors matter.

The OT tells us that the people of God were often guilty of worshiping idols, of making up their own god, of creating gods, or even Yahweh, in a certain image. We oversimplify this matter if we think of such images solely in terms of wood or stone; the plastic image conveyed a particular way of understanding these gods or Yahweh. And, we have learned over the years that idolatries do not need the plastic form to qualify as such. One can move directly to mental images which construct a false image of God and have the power of wreaking havoc in people's faith and life. Metaphors matter.

This issue can be approached from a different perspective. The preaching and teaching of the church have commonly been so focused on a certain portrait of Jesus that many of the biblical images for God have been neglected, and stereotypical images have been allowed to stand unchallenged. It is almost as if faith in Jesus were thought to take care of the picture of God automatically; thus, one need pay no special heed to it. But this assumption has commonly created inner tensions for the faithful, perhaps even intolerable tensions; for the picture of Jesus presented often stands at odds with the commonly accepted picture of God. Attributes such as love, compassion, and mercy, accompanied by acts of healing, forgiving, and redeeming, tend to become narrowly associated with Jesus, while the less palatable attributes and actions of holiness, wrath, power, and justice are ascribed only to God. What tends to fill the mind is God as Giver of the Law and Judge of all the earth. If God is not the cause of all the ills in the world, God is still seen as the one who is to blame for not really doing anything about them. It is the goodness of God that is ignored, not the goodness of Jesus. One can almost hear someone say: "If only Jesus were here, he would do something about all our troubles!" People often seem to have a view which suggests that Jesus is friend and God is enemy. An understanding of the atonement gets twisted so that Jesus is seen as the one who came to save us from God.

One wonders whether the creeds of the church have not in some ways contributed to such perspectives. God the Father gets one line of the Apostle's Creed, and (unlike the Nicene Creed) the fatherhood of

God is not separated from almightiness; the emergent image is one of an authoritarian Father—an impression somewhat at odds with the biblical metaphor. Moreover, the saving and blessing activity of God is not directly suggested. Repeated Sunday after Sunday, one wonders about the Creed's effect on the understanding of God. When this influence is combined with a common tendency to ignore the reading of OT lessons, and an absence of regular preaching on OT texts, people tend to continue with their stereotypical images of God, which become even more deep-seated in the process.

Such perspectives regarding God and the relationship between God and Jesus, even if exemplified in nothing more than a tendency in language and thought, have probably commonly led to a kind of "Jesusology," in both naive and more sophisticated forms.[3] God remains at a distance as someone to be feared, while Jesus lives tenderly in one's heart. Or, when combined with an idea that God is really unknowable, one is led to a notion that Jesus is finally all we have, and commonly only in a very human form: Jesus, not Jesus Christ. A very close correlation can be seen between the idea of a God who is "wholly other," totally removed from the world, and "God is dead" proclamations, whether the last phrase be understood literally or figuratively. This tendency is reinforced by secularistic trends which have made the activity of God in the world problematic, while Jesus continues to be seen as an actual historical figure; hence one can talk about his spirit living on in the hearts of the faithful with less difficulty.

From another perspective, the mission of the church can be seriously hindered by misconceptions, particularly among those whose difficulty with the church is due to a certain image of or questions about God. The message of the church may be so narrowly focused that it simply does not address the question of God's nature for such individuals, and the proclamation of divine love may indeed pass them by. Anyone seriously concerned with mission or evangelism must be concerned about people's questions, including their questions about God. They often have to be answered before the gospel of Jesus Christ can receive a hearing. Thus, a much more concerted effort to deal with the God of the OT needs to be engaged in by the church at all levels, if it is to reach out to those who have intellectual difficulties with this matter.

Considerations about the relationship between God and Jesus, according to the NT, should assist us in our deliberations, the Gospel of John in particular:

> I and the Father are one.
> (10:30)

> The word which you hear is not mine but the Father's who sent me.
> (14:24)

> All that the Father has is mine.
> (16:15)

> He who has seen me has seen the Father.
> (14:9)

It would appear that, whatever one might say about classical doctrinal formulations, Christian preaching and piety fail to take such statements with sufficient seriousness. It would be unfair to say that there is no talk about the love, grace, and mercy of the Father in the event of Jesus, but the fatherhood of God more generally seems to be seen narrowly in terms of authority and even domination. Such NT statements, however, insist that in Jesus Christ we are in the fullest possible sense looking at the heart of God the Father, the God of the OT. The coming of God in Jesus Christ is indeed the coming of God in a quite concrete way in the entire life of a human being. That is the special force of the NT message: God, unsurpassably enfleshed in the human being, Jesus of Nazareth. The claim would seem to be clear: The point of fulfillment is not alien to the promise, nor to the presence and activity, of the God of Israel. There is a decisive continuity in the history of the God of the OT and the God and Father of our Lord Jesus Christ. Those central touchstones in the life of Jesus—Incarnation, Ministry, and Cross—are neither foreign to, nor a departure from, the portrait of God revealed to us in the pages of the OT. I intend to show how I believe this to be so.

The relationship between the two testaments is more than simply verbal, with words of promise or prophecy finding their fulfillment in the life, death, and resurrection of Jesus Christ. It is more than typological, with patterns of speech and action having points of continuity across the testaments. It is more than historical and theological, with all the family resemblance that can be discerned by probing into roots and ideas. There is also a decisive continuity in the history of God, who is the same yesterday, today, and forever. An important way to discover that continuity is through an analysis of key metaphors for God. The metaphorical continuity between the Testaments has a considerable capacity to reveal what kind of God it is who is involved in this history. It leads not to information about God, in a narrow sense, but to a knowledge of God in a more holistic sense, a kind of participation in what the journey has meant for God. It gives some sense of identification with what the story of God has been like. And for one who "experiences" the metaphors across the Testaments, the history of God is seen to be coherent, consistent, and marked by certain constants that are finally unsurpassably exemplified in the life and death of Jesus Christ. "He who has seen me has seen the Father" can, in at least one significant sense, be turned around to say: "He who has seen the Father has seen the Christ."

## ANTHROPOMORPHIC METAPHOR

Having noted the central importance of metaphor in any study of the God of the OT, a sketch of the meaning and use of metaphor which informs this discussion needs some attention.[4] A basic definition of metaphor is in order, first of all. Black's formulation is helpful:[5] "A memorable metaphor has the power to bring two separate domains into cognitive and emotional relation by using language directly appropriate to the one as a lens for seeing the other." In other words, a conventional understanding of a matter (e.g., a body, a parent) becomes a window through which we can gain insight into another matter, usually less well known (e.g., the church, God). A metaphor always has a duality of association: the surface associations, drawn from life as experienced, and the analogical association. But insight into the latter can be attained and, indeed, retained only by reflecting on the former in relationship to it. Such insight comes, not only through observing what is similar between the two terms, but also through that which is different. Crucial to a proper understanding of a metaphor is the recognition of both similarity and difference.

It has been rightly stated that virtually all of the language used in the Bible to refer to God is metaphorical; the word "God" would be an exception.[6] Occasionally such language is drawn from the natural world, both animate (God is an eagle, Deut. 32:11) and inanimate

(God is a rock, Ps. 31:2–3). The vast majority of the metaphors for God in the OT, however, are drawn from the sphere of the human: (a) form, with its function (mouth, speaking, Num. 12:8); (b) emotional, volitional and mental states (rejoicing, Zeph. 3:17); (c) roles and activities, within the family (parent, Hos. 11:1) or the larger society (shepherd, Ps. 23:1). The natural metaphors are important, particularly as they demonstrate an integral relationship between God and the nonhuman created order, with continuities seen between God and that world. My primary concern here, however, is with the anthropomorphic metaphor,[7] speaking of God in language drawn from the human sphere.

Anthropomorphic metaphors have tended to be depreciated, even denigrated, in the history of Judeo-Christian thought and OT scholarship in particular.[8] This attitude can be traced from Philo of the first century (for the benefit of those whose "natural wit is dense and dull, whose childhood training has been mismanaged")[9] to contemporaries such as H. H. Rowley ("mere accommodations to human speech, or vivid pictures used for their psychological effect rather than theological in significance").[10] Yet, there have always been those who have sensed a deeper importance in this material, for instance, E. Jacob: "A line not always straight, but nonetheless continuous, leads from the anthropomorphisms of the earliest pages of the Bible, to the incarnation of God in Jesus Christ."[11]

It is ironic that OT interpretation should have problems with these concrete ways of depicting God. To understand this language in a purely figurative sense would mean that it is thought finally to stand over against the concreteness and realism commonly said to be characteristic of OT thought. A figurative interpretation buys abstraction at the expense of concreteness. A further irony can be noted in the fact that anthropomorphic metaphors predominate in Israelite talk about the deity in a way that is not the case elsewhere in the ancient Near East (cf. the use of animal-human hybrids).[12] This preponderant tendency is thus a point of distinctiveness in the OT understanding of God, which many would try to explain away.

It is also ironic that Christians should have trouble with this language.[13] In the incarnation, God has acted anthropomorphically in the most supreme way. The NT, far from being the culmination of a progressive spiritualization in the understanding of God, speaks of

God unsurpassably enfleshed in the human. Apart from the Christ-event, the NT continues to speak of God in terms of such metaphors. This continuity is consonant with developments within the OT itself, where one is struck by the constant use of such language. There are no anti-anthropomorphic tendencies to be discerned; even in dreams or visions or glimpses into heaven God is spoken of in such ways.[14] Such later passages as Isa. 42:14; 63:1–6; and Dan. 7:9 contain some of the more daring anthropomorphic metaphors in the OT.

One of the most basic issues relating to the understanding of metaphor is the relationship between metaphor and essential definition. We need to steer between Scylla and Charybdis in dealing with this matter.

On the one hand, there is the danger of positing no real or essential relationship between the metaphor and God as God really relates to the world. Thus, people speak of "mere" metaphor, or consider it to be only illustrative or decorative of thought, to be dispensed with as one moves on to more abstract definitions. But, as with all metaphors, while there is no one-to-one correspondence, the metaphor does say some things about God that correspond to the reality which is God, while saying other things as well. To use the language of J. Janzen: "For all their manifold richness and overtone and allusion, metaphors at their center do imply one thing and not another; and the most natural procedure is to take the metaphor as adumbrating an essential character which is analogous to the metaphoric vehicle, and not contrary to it."[15] The metaphor does in fact describe God, though it is not fully descriptive. The metaphor does contain information about God. The metaphor does not stand over against the literal. Though the *use* of the metaphor is not literal, there is literalness intended in the relationship to which the metaphor has reference. God is actually good or loving; God is the supreme exemplification of goodness and love. One must say that such metaphors reveal that God is literally related to the world, unless one is prepared to say that God is literally not in relationship to the world.[16] The metaphors do reveal an essential continuity with the reality which is God; to use J. Martin's apt phrase, the metaphors are "reality depicting."[17]

On the other hand, there is a danger of suggesting that a literal correspondence exists between metaphor and reality in every respect. In popular theology this will often entail a portrayal of God in terms, say, of an old man with white hair (cf. Dan. 7:9). While the tendency in the first danger is to make God so wholly other as to make relationship, let alone knowledge, impossible, the danger here is to reduce God to human frailty; both directions lead to idolatry. On this point, the discontinuities inherent in the metaphor need to be lifted up. Anthropomorphic metaphors ought not be conceived in terms of pictures, replicas, scale models, copies, or the like. The variety of biblical metaphors should prevent us from such literalism: for example, to combine the husband-wife and the parent-child metaphors in literal fashion will create problems! There is always that in the metaphor which is discontinuous with the reality which is God. God outdistances all our images; God cannot finally be captured by any of them.

Steering between these two poles, how does one move from metaphor to essential definition? By interpreting "along the metaphorical grain" and not contrary to it, by "following the thrust of the analogy."[18] If one moves against the natural implication of the metaphor, one is misinterpreting it. At the same time, while the metaphor primarily generates insight into the divine reality at the basic thrust of the analogy, it also does so more indirectly at those points where it is discontinuous with the reality which is God.

Let me illustrate this last point with some of the metaphors central to this study. To speak of God as one who repents, with the basic ideas of reversal and change, does have some basic points of continuity with the way God actually relates to the world. Yet, there is no one-to-one correspondence between the way people and God repent. Or, to speak of God as one who suffers is to take with utmost seriousness the continuity inherent in certain metaphors (e.g., God as mourner). At the same time, God does not suffer in exactly the same way as humans do, and to try to get at that is important. Or, to use temporal categories for God is to interpret along the grain of certain metaphors (e.g., God as planner); yet, the dissimilarities are also important, that is, God is not subject to the ravages of time.

We now need to inquire into the importance of the great number and variety of the anthropomorphic metaphors for God in the OT, and issues of their relative value. One of the dangers for the people of God in any age is that they will be content with a rather limited fund of metaphors. Thus, for example, the court of law metaphor has become predominant in the thinking of some people regarding God, with other metaphors being subordinated to this or blocked out altogether. The particular danger is that the power such metaphors have in the shaping of thought and life is not always recognized. Metaphors work not simply at cognitive levels, but at the levels of emotion and will as well. To understand this phenomenon is to focus on the very issue we have been raising. The metaphors with which one lives shape one's life. The predominance of the law court in our operative fund of metaphors may effectively cut us off from a side of our experience of God, shaping our religious attitudes and sensitivities adversely. It is not a matter of exchanging one metaphor for another, but of evaluating our operative metaphors and working to extend that list. This is one of my basic concerns: to lift up certain neglected metaphors so that our operative fund of them will be more congruent with the biblical witness and our experience of God in the world. While even a multitude of metaphors will not in itself guarantee this objective, their availability can provide greater balance in our understanding of God as they shed light on, and even correct, one another.

The tendency in OT scholarship has been to forfeit many such metaphors, primarily by collecting a large number of them and drawing a few general conclusions (e.g., God is personal, living),[19] rather than examining each in turn for the insight it might generate. Thus, for example, one needs to ask what speaking of God's eyes and ears (2 Kings 19:16) adds to the understanding of the relationship of God to world that living, seeing, and hearing do not.[20] Such language makes the idea that God receives the world into himself vivid and concrete. God's experience of the world is not superficial; God takes it in, in as real a way as people do who use their eyes and ears. At the same time, in ways that people do not, God takes it *all* in (Jer. 32:19), and not with fleshly eyes (Job 10:4).

Nevertheless, while examining each metaphor in its specificity is important, the general conclusions drawn continue to be significant. In addition to revealing God as living and personal, they testify to the intimate relationship between God and world. The continuities between God and world are at the heart of every such metaphor. Images drawn from personal life—home, fields, and shops—are those used to speak of God. This frame of reference serves to anchor the experience of God in human experience, especially the public arena. As a result, talk about God is strikingly "secular," inextricably interrelated to an amazing array of those things which characterize the world, yet without collapsing God and world into one another. The metaphor is continuous with both God's presence in the world and God's self-revelation.

While discerning the variety of metaphors in both their specificity and generality is important, not all have the same value. This is true at two related levels. First, we need to recognize what might be called the "varying degrees of correspondence"[21] between the two terms of the metaphor. One might speak of degrees of revelatory capacity. There are those with a low capacity (God as dry rot, Hos. 5:12; God as lion, Hos. 5:14; God as whistler, Isa. 7:18), with a moderate capacity (God as rock, Ps. 31:2–3; God's arm, Isa. 53:1), and with a high capacity (God as parent, Hos. 11:1).[22]

Those of low correspondence are not communal property and tend to be used for their surprise or shock value, especially in Hosea. Those with high correspondence are communal, having found a staying power in the life of the community of faith over a longer period of time. Most common among these are the interpersonal metaphors, though those drawn from the human relationship to the nonhuman (e.g., farmer) are also often rich, largely because the God/human relationship is primarily in view (Isa. 5:1–7).

Why are these metaphors so central?[23] They have a richness of association in human experience; they are true to life, revealing a certain fitness with respect to that experience. They have a capacity to capture, organize, and communicate our experience and understanding of God; to focus our thinking, feeling, and living. They can often be extended to capture many facets of an experience (e.g., family interrelationships). They lend themselves to "a two-way traffic in ideas."[24] For example, the father metaphor moves not only from human fatherhood to God, but doubles back and helps shape the human father into the likeness of God. But, the understanding of the human as created in the image of God (Gen. 1:26) is of central importance here. These metaphors are especially important because Israel believed that "the pattern on which man was fashioned is to be sought outside the sphere of the created."[25] Rather than accommodating God to the level of the human or raising human characteristics to the nth degree, the human is seen to be fashioned in the likeness of God. Hence, the human is seen in theomorphic terms, rather than God in anthropomorphic terms.[26] Thereby, the essential metaphorical process is revealed to us. The "image of God" gives us permission to reverse the process and, by looking at the human, learn what God is like.

This brings us to our second point on the relative value of such metaphors: the idea of a controlling metaphor. One of the more important issues here is how to determine whether a given metaphor is appropriate, is being misused, or has been exhausted. It is clear from a survey of the OT metaphors for God that some elements of the human experience are not considered appropriate, even in part:[27] death, sexuality, embitterment, lack of wisdom, and capriciousness, as well as certain roles (e.g., criminal), to name a few. These and others can be eliminated because certain metaphors function to delimit metaphorical possibilities. The bulk of these controlling metaphors are probably to be found in passages like Exod. 34:6–7. Through the years they have gained a special place in the community. (See chap. 2.)

Such controlling metaphors also function in other ways. They not only serve a limiting purpose, but as metaphors among metaphors, not unlike a "canon" within the canon, they are able to bring coherence to a range of biblical thinking about God; they provide a hermeneutical key for interpreting the whole. The sovereignty of God and the grace of God are two obvious examples in the history of biblical interpretation.

Finally, we note the qualifying function such controlling metaphors have. For example, the metaphor "father" in and of itself is not capable of constant meaning or value to those who hear it or use it. The use and meaning of metaphors is heavily dependent upon historical-cultural factors, especially those of our individual experience. The meaning of a metaphor varies from culture to culture, and even from individual to individual within a single culture. A child, for instance, with a brutal or incestuous father will hear the word "father" for God with far different ears than I will. Certain common metaphors for God may, in fact, be closely related to the worst experiences in the lives of people. While this argues for the importance of using a variety of metaphors in our talk about God, it also means that every metaphor finally needs to be qualified by the controlling metaphors of the community of faith. Thus, God is not simply father; God is a certain kind of father. God is a loving father, always (Hos. 11:1). And God is not simply mother; God is a certain kind of mother. God is a mother who will not forget her children, ever (Isa. 49:15).

In what follows I will first of all comment on some of the basic perspectives on God in current OT scholarship (chap. 2). Next I will address the relationship of God and world (chaps. 3–5). These chapters are basic to all that follows. Any discussion of divine suffering presupposes a certain understanding of the God-world relationship. Then I look at theophany and the human form of God (chap. 6), as well as certain neglected anthropomorphic metaphors associated with suffering, ones which I contend are integral to the OT understanding of God (chaps. 7–9). Finally, I look at the prophet, who embodies this God in the world in a special way, providing a special connection to NT perspectives (chap. 10). The suffering of God is the predominant theme throughout all these chapters.

My approach is synchronic rather than diachronic, though observations on the latter will be made from time to time.[28] Attention will also be paid to "the assumptions presupposed in the texts, and not only to the contingent messages of the texts."[29] I am very much aware that the texts chosen to be explored are limited in scope, and that other perspectives may be discerned within the OT.[30] At the same time, many other OT texts could also be profitably examined from the point of view offered here.

# CHAPTER 2

# God in
# Old Testament
# Theology

The understanding of God in current OT studies will preoccupy us not least because it is important to place this discussion within the larger context of contemporary theology, however briefly. Consciously or not, biblical-theological studies of God have always been forged in the light of prevailing theologies in synagogue and church. At times such biblical studies stand over against contemporary formulations; at other times they move in tandem with one another in mutual support. It is important for such studies to be as explicit about this relationship as possible. From another perspective, contemporary constructive theologies are often dependent upon a study of the Scriptures standing in some independence of biblical scholarship; insights into biblical perspectives are thus often available in this literature. Ongoing conversations among the theological disciplines are important if the fullest possible range of thought about the Bible is to be brought to bear upon such matters as the God-question.

## A METAPHORIC SHIFT

If some of the metaphors for God are neglected, or are not in balance in relation to one another, God's story tends to become incoherent. This has occurred in significant ways in recent generations, so that a *metaphoric shift* seems in order: not so much a shift away from certain metaphors to others, but a renewed recognition of those metaphors which have been neglected, with a consequently more appropriate weight given to those which have endured. A close look at some of these *neglected metaphors* will occupy much of our attention in this book.

In contemporary theology, such a metaphoric shift is already well underway. That this movement is having an impact upon the wider life of the church is clearly evident. Twenty years ago, S. Ogden could rightfully claim that "the reality of God has now become the central theological problem."[1] This focus was perhaps most evident to the general church public in J. A. T. Robinson's *Honest to God.*[2] In the intervening years, books on God have emerged in considerable numbers across a wide theological spectrum. Even if one were to discount the more extreme positions articulated from time to time, it seems evident that the emerging image of God is somewhat different from that which has been more traditionally espoused by the church. Some of the more visible trajectories in this metaphoric shift might be noted briefly.

The women's movement has exposed the decisively male orientation in the traditional understandings of God in the church and its theology, including biblical interpretation.[3] The powerful impact that the seemingly innocent use of exclusively male language has had on both thought and life has been amply demonstrated. There can be little doubt that such diction has led, perhaps often unknowingly, to a diminishment of the role of women in church and society. Among the issues being explored are the images used to speak of God; and the OT, with its predominantly masculine metaphors, has been seen to be an integral part of the problem. The extent to which the biblical viewpoint ought to have a normative role, if any, in the shaping and use of such images is a substantive issue. Suffice it to be said here that the feminine characteristics of God are being lifted up for our attention in striking ways, given the concentrated look at those metaphors for God which have their roots in experiences unique to women, including those contained in the OT. As a result, masculine images for God are being given a relatively nuanced interpretation.

This metaphoric shift is also evident in other movements, such as Black Theology or Liberation Theology.[4] There is little doubt that the church and church-influenced societies often highlighted certain understandings of God and used them to justify socioeconomic stratifications as divinely ordained, often leading to subjugation and, indeed, even slavery. Again, the issue of the images for God is in the forefront of the discussion. Those metaphors offering justification for the domination or regulation of others, or capable of such an interpretation (e.g., God as King or Father), have been shown to have received an imbalanced consideration, adversely affecting the shape of human society. But now, in the wake of a new consciousness, those images for God associated with the liberation of the poor and oppressed are seen to be prominent in the Scriptures, perhaps especially in the OT, and are beginning to receive proper attention.

One should also note the effect of certain catastrophic events in recent world history upon traditional understandings of God. By virtue of an imbalanced and incorrect interpretation, biblical metaphors for God—not least those from the OT which speak of God the Warrior—may have at least in part contributed to warmongering tendencies in human society, which have led to a perpetration of incomprehensible evil. In addition, those traditional images for God which suggest that God is unmoved by the resultant world suffering have made it difficult to portray God as good, omnipotent, or credible in the face of such horrors. As MacLeish's J. B. puts it: "If God is God he is not good; if God is good he is not God." One way of responding to such issues has been an exploration of images for God. Thus, in the aftermath of World War I, some scholars were preoccupied with the issue of the impassibility of God.[5] Although the concern was not sustained, World War II and the Holocaust in particular have prompted a renewal of interest in the pathos of God, as well as other metaphors closely associated with issues of theodicy. For instance, Jürgen Moltmann's *The Crucified God*[6] represents an elevation of certain metaphors for God long associated with Jesus only.

Finally, we are living in a culture decisively shaped by developments in science and technology, as well as in such social sciences as sociology and psychology, with concomitant secularistic tendencies. With explanations for cosmic activity now freely available from human discoveries and resources, the place of God in the life of the world has become increasingly problematic for many. Atheism abounds as never before. For many God is God only for the gaps in life, and God is being crowded out of those spaces as well. In the face of such developments, what sense can be made of such traditional images of God as one who acts in history and nature, of God the miracle-worker, of divine providence? Numerous attempts have been and continue to be made in theology to come to terms with this pervasive phenomenon, from escapism to embrace, from entrenchment to experimentation.[7] Many affirmations of God's nature taken for granted until recently have been dismissed or radically redefined. With OT perspectives on God so closely related to these issues, one wonders as to the importance the OT might continue to have.

These and other developments in theological work have occasioned a new look at virtually every traditional metaphor for God. Widely discussed are such issues as divine eternity—temporality, freedom, immutability, foreknowledge, impassibility, omnipotence, aseity, immateriality, and immanence-transcendence. Apart from the convictions of discrete schools of thought, certain modifications in the traditional understandings of such divine images are becoming widely accepted (e.g., divine temporality).

In the ongoing work of the evaluation of traditional and emerging images for God, certain criteria are available,[8] including the following: (1) adequacy to common human experience; (2) intelligibility and coherence; (3) faithfulness to the biblical witness and the tradition in which a given image stands.

1. It seems clear that many traditional images of God in church and theology are seen to be divorced from common human experience. They no longer function for many people. They seem to float above the maelstrom of actual life or are narrowly associated with one or another segment of society. Thus, the relation of God to real people and actual experience is slowly but surely having the life taken out of it. I believe that the OT has significant metaphoric resources which can be appropriately interpreted in order to accommodate this criterion.

2. The criterion of intelligibility and coherence is relevant, especially with reference to the significance of metaphor (cf. chap. 1). A longstanding issue in theology is the relationship between metaphor and essential definition. As I have shown, the images used for God really do say something about God; they are not merely illustrative or decorative.[9] This has significant implications for the issue of coherence.

3. The idea of faithfulness to the biblical witness is an area needing special attention from OT scholars. Are current developments in theology regarding God congruent with biblical understandings, or are they a departure from those fundamental moorings?

This exploration of OT understandings of God will attempt to touch base with these current concerns.

## CONVERGENCE AND PLURALISM

In a limited review of the literature on the current discussion of the God-question in theology, I am struck by the frequent references to the OT, either in support of a given perspective or as something against which a particular perspective is developed. It is equally striking how seldom the work of OT scholars is taken into account. It would appear that, as with the Karl Barth of *The Epistle to the Romans,* theologians are once again doing their own exegesis. Apparently, they think that biblical theological resources are simply not available for the task, or that those which are available are so adverse to their own theological tendencies that they are deemed to be of little assistance. Thus, they proceed on their own with the biblical material. Is such a development justified?

As one surveys the landscape of OT scholarship on the understanding of God, the portrait of God which normally emerges bears a striking resemblance to the quite traditional Jewish or Christian understanding of God regnant in synagogue or church. Save for matters relating to historical development (e.g., from henotheism to monotheism) one can read back and forth between church dogmatics textbooks and most God-talk in OT studies without missing a beat. Thus, for example, God is understood in terms of traditional categories: freedom, immutability, omniscience, and omnipotence; if not explicitly stated, they are commonly assumed. I cannot ever recall a commentator on an OT text dealing with the future, suggesting that God's knowledge of the future is limited, and that consequently the text should be interpreted with that in mind.

This consensus can work negatively when the reigning traditional theology inhibits exegesis or issues in some, perhaps unconscious, efforts at harmonization with such a theological perspective. Thus, for example, the nearly forty references to divine repentance in the OT, the preponderance of which occur in later texts, receive little or limited attention in commentaries and other studies. Or, one might cite the general depreciation of the importance of anthropomorphic materials. Given the utter lack of any inner-biblical warrant for such negative judgments, the norm must be found in the theology of the commentator who, in this case at least, is largely reflective of the traditional theology of the church or synagogue, though not of some popular conceptions of God.

One wonders why this bias exists, particularly given the long history of efforts to free biblical studies from the straitjacket of church dogmatics. An answer to this question is not easy to come by, but the following considerations are suggestive of directions in which we might look.

A review of nineteenth- and early twentieth-century OT theologies reveals less congruence with prevailing understandings of God in the church. This is probably due largely to the perception of a historical development from the more primitive to more sophisticated understandings of God.[10] But, primarily as the result of significant religio-historical studies, and particularly in comparison with ancient Near Eastern materials, the distinctiveness of earlier OT theological understandings has been demonstrated.[11]

Thus, there has emerged much greater continuity across the OT with regard to theological matters. Although development in the OT understanding of God continues to be affirmed, a basic substratum in the understanding of God remains essentially constant (e.g., God is personal). This has resulted in a gradual *convergence* between what the OT is believed to say about God and that view which prevails in the Christian tradition.

At another level, particularly under the impact of tradition-historical studies, OT traditions are seen to reflect differing theological emphases, nuance their God-talk in various ways, or stress different images for God. The comprehensive statement of Gerhard von Rad in particular has demonstrated the diversity of theological formulation in the OT.[12] Hence, an emphasis upon theological *pluralism* has also emerged.

At the same time, one of the more striking things to be noted about this pluralism of OT talk about God is that it is well within the traditionally allowable parameters of things Christian. For example, while it is not uncommon to observe that the God of the apocalyptic literature is characterized in ways that are somewhat different from that of the prophets (e.g., more transcendent), the range in thinking is within the acceptable scope found in the varieties of traditional

Christian theology. Thus, Christian traditions which vary with respect to certain understandings of God can find biblical justification for their differences in content and emphasis. In fact, it may be said that the theological pluralism within the Christian community had its origin in the pluralism of the biblical testimony regarding God, and each tradition continues to highlight those materials which best support its particular emphases. With regard to God-talk at least, whether one speaks of convergence or pluralism, the results seem to be quite traditional.

Recently, however, two directions of thought may be noted which seek to diminish this theological pluralism. First, canonical criticism may foster further convergence, which in turn threatens pluralism.[13] Simply put, the entire OT is to be interpreted from the perspective of the final redactors. Whatever earlier developments in theological understanding may be observed within and behind the present text, the whole has been simplified in terms of this latest theological perspective. And it is this "canonical" perspective which is authoritative for the church. While I will not enter into a critique of this point of view here,[14] such a perspective fails to recognize adequately that the pluralism of OT theologies has in fact issued in a pluralism of Christian theologies, despite a finally shaped canon, just by virtue of giving greater attention to this or that aspect of the OT. This pluralism of OT interpretation is already evident in the NT, which issues in a new pluralism of its own.[15] Even if the latest redactors of the OT interpreted the whole OT in terms of a unified perspective, the fact of theological pluralism in the NT and the church means that a truly canonical approach ought to be as concerned with theological diversity as unity, as well as being especially open to new insights which might have their roots in a heretofore undiscovered dimension of this pluralism. *Pluralism has been canonized.*

A second, perhaps more common direction also moves toward convergence and away from pluralism but through a kind of canonical reductionism. The concern here is to remove certain materials from the OT theological repertoire. One can point to efforts by OT theologians to evaluate theological materials negatively and to deny them a place in an OT theology. These are usually some of the more difficult passages theologically; for example, those dealing with God the Warrior in holy war texts or God the Avenger in the imprecatory psalms.[16] While the criteria used are not always clear or consistently applied,[17] it would appear that a primary concern is to trim the OT theological resources in such a way as to move toward convergence with an acceptable Christian theological perspective. The difficulty here, of course, is to find acceptable criteria—particularly in the absence of any inner-OT, or inner-biblical warrant—that a given theological perspective has been made obsolescent by theological developments. Indeed, if *theological development has been canonized,* then the task is not to eliminate whatever earlier or less sophisticated forms of theology may be discovered, but to recognize the important role such materials continue to play in the ongoing task of working toward clarity in theological understanding. Thus, earlier forms of theology in the history of Christian thought continue to play an important role in the ever contemporary task of theological formulation. More generally, if one begins with the assumption that theological pluralism is a good thing, as something to be highlighted and not hidden, then this entire direction becomes problematic.

Thus far, it seems clear that OT scholarship is strongly informed implicitly or explicitly by a move toward theological convergence with traditional Christian or Jewish theological formulations. Where theological differences within the OT are recognized, and even stressed, these seem to be reflective of already existing and acceptable varieties within the theological tradition. In general, scholarship is moving in new directions theologically—at a rather slow pace. While new and important theological studies continue to emerge, the discipline does not seem to be committed to such matters. The tendency, then, is to stay with the insights which have been generally accepted. Moreover, in spite of interdisciplinary advances in some areas of OT study, such are not common in theological work. In sum, a certain reticence in responding to many of the new probings in contemporary theology, particularly as regards the understanding of God, is evident.

## DIRECTIONS

Two specific types of concerns on the God-question in recent scholarship now need attention:

First, very briefly, there have been studies critical of prevailing theological tendencies in previous scholarship, some of which relate to the understanding of God. The most visible of these developments relates to criticism directed against various aspects of the "biblical theology" movement.[18] Considerable critical distance has been gained on the "Heilsgeschichte" approach to the OT. It is no longer possible to speak in any simple way about the "God who acts in history" or "revelation in history." This direction has been given support by both specialized studies[19] and more general, constructive reflections.[20] Relative to the understanding of God, this development has ameliorated a narrowness in the way in which God was perceived to be related to the world; it has revealed the need for a more comprehensive probing of the God-world relationship (cf. chap. 3).[21]

Second, I must note developments within OT theology as a specific discipline, particularly the presentation of OT material about God.

Most OT theologies have taken a systematic approach, developing sections dealing with key divine actions and attributes. Eichrodt,[22] for instance, presents the material in terms of "Affirmations about the Divine Being" (God is personal, spiritual, one) and "Affirmations about the Divine Activity" (God's power, love, wrath, holiness, etc.). While Eichrodt includes no justification for this division, his theological instincts are certainly correct. While one might quarrel with the specifics (e.g., love), a distinction does need to be made between that which is true about God in every relationship with the world, and those aspects of the divine life which are affected by this relationship in one way or another (e.g., being provoked to anger). While historical developments in Israel's understanding of God are certainly not necessarily neglected in this approach, especially in Eichrodt, this approach tends to be synchronic. Such a treatment of the material about God is certainly legitimate: it is paralleled by directions which Israel itself took in thinking about God.[23]

The other major approach to OT theology is that of G. von Rad,[24] in whose work one finds the materials about God presented in terms of the history of tradition. To oversimplify, this entails the integration of the OT's conceptions of God into treatments of the overarching theological concerns of specific traditors (Isaiah, Priestly writer, etc.) in their historical contexts. Although at times von Rad departs from his own approach to present such materials in a more systematic way (e.g., on the righteousness of God), this is in line with his understanding that "the presentation of the 'ideas, thought and concepts of the

Old Testament which are important for theology' will always form part of the task of Old Testament theology."[25]

While von Rad's approach results in a somewhat piecemeal treatment of God issues, there are certain perspectives on God that pervade his entire presentation, regardless of the tradition with which he is working; and they must be assumed by him to be characteristic of the entire OT portrayal of God (e.g., God is personal). These perspectives, in fact, unify his entire work; they function as essential presuppositions for what he has to say theologically about a whole host of matters. He essentially admits this in places,[26] but a more forthright approach at this point would have been helpful. While not to be put forward as a center for OT theology proper,[27] certain basic perspectives regarding God inevitably come to play a pervasive role in any OT theological study, regardless of the method used. Some way should be found to state them as clearly and forthrightly as possible.

In some ways, C. Westermann's recent work on OT theology[28] seeks to utilize the best in both of the approaches we have noted, and is especially attentive to this last point. Because Westermann has rightly seen the central place Israel's understanding of God must have in any OT theology, one needs to pursue his observations in greater detail.

For Westermann, "OT theology acquires both a systematic and historical aspect" (pp. 11–12). Yet, these aspects are secondary to the primary structure of an OT theology: "The theology of the Old Testament remains determined throughout in every respect by the outline of a story" (p. 11). Thus, "The structure of an Old Testament theology must be based on events rather than concepts" (p. 9), and hence cannot be "reduced" to comprehensive terms such as salvation, covenant, etc. Thus also, an OT theology must consist basically of a portrayal of "a history of God and man" centered in the divine actions of saving and blessing, in which inheres the Word of God, which the people experience, and to which they respond.[29] The systematic aspect emerges from the talk about God which remains constant throughout the entire OT; he sees this primarily in the God-world interaction—inclusive of speaking and acting on both sides—as well as the oneness of God. The historical aspect emerges from the fact that "this God of whom the Old Testament speaks has bound himself to the history of his people" (p. 12).

Three matters in particular call for discussion. First, while the use of the phrase "history of God" is a salutary development, Westermann must be using the word "history" in an unusual sense. When he refers to the history of people he speaks of change and contingency, but with God it is only a matter of "singularity and uniqueness" (p. 12). But to use the word "history" for God, unless it is to have an esoteric meaning, must also entail change and contingency for God. If God has indeed "bound himself to the history of his people," and Westermann is on solid ground at this point, this can only be understood in a perfunctory sense, unless God is understood to have made that history his own in a very real sense.

Second, the priority given to the concept of "story."[30] A basic problem with this currently popular category is its isolation from the "constants" of which Westermann speaks, the generalizations which make sense of the story. He seems to recognize this when he says that the constants make "this incomprehensibly rich profusion of events between beginning and end into a context, a connected history" (p. 32). Only such generalizations, irreducible to story form, enable one to discern continuities, or something strange or new, and to realize when an objective has been reached.[31] For example, the Exodus story is comprehensible to Israel only on the basis of certain generalizations revealed to Moses (Exodus 3), which in turn had fundamental continuities with a prior story and prior generalizations. Thus, story and generalization must be kept inextricably interwoven; together they determine the structure and form of an OT theology. This calls into question Westermann's contention that "events rather than concepts" must constitute the basis of the structure of an OT theology; it is both/and, rather than either/or.

Finally, there is the matter of constants. We have noted the key items that Westermann has isolated. The basic question is this: on what grounds are these isolated, rather than others? The only cited "affirmation about the divine being," to use Eichrodt's language, is "the oneness of God." Why not, for example, "God is personal" or "God is love"? If, as Westermann seems to believe, the "oneness of God" is one of those deep, underlying assumptions about God which suffuses all descriptions of his activity, why are these others not noted? His subsequent discussion about a God who saves and blesses certainly presupposes these, and perhaps others.

STORY AND GENERALIZATION

To return to our question: How is one to determine which constants suffuse the story, which generalizations are necessary for the story to be coherent and intelligible, and hence would need to be considered as a part of the most basic stratum of OT theology? One should begin at those points in the text where the authors themselves incorporate generalizations which serve to give basic internal directions as to how the story is to be read, as well as overall coherence. The various stories in and of themselves could provoke all kinds of reactions in the reader, but there are occasional reflections given which bring a focus to what the story is all about, and make truth-claims which decisively limit the number of possible interpretations. While it might be said that there are a variety of such generalizations (e.g., regarding the nature of the human or the world), we are concerned here with those underlying assumptions about God which are occasionally expressed.

In short, it is not enough to say that God is the one who saves and blesses in these stories; what is crucial is the *the kind of* God who is understood to be saving and blessing. A capricious God can save and bless. Even an impersonal God could engage in such activities. Is such divine activity motivated by love, or are there other factors? It has been demonstrated that there is nothing special about Israel's believing that God acts in its history, except that it may have done this more often and more consistently than other peoples. There is, moreover, no uniqueness to be found in the fact that its God was believed to be a saving and blessing God, though these are important words to preserve in any "OT Theology." It is the truth-claims that Israel makes regarding *the kind of* God who was active in its life that provide a crucial interpretive clue to the story, and insist that it be read in a certain way, delimiting possibilities of meaning.

Scholarship of the recent past has been especially attentive to a certain type of reoccurring material which has been thought to supply an interpretive clue to the reading of Israel's story—namely, the so-called historical recitals (e.g., Deut. 26:5–9; Josh. 24:2–13).[32] These recitations of God's mighty acts have been considered reflective of the very heart of Israel's confession of God. Whatever role such materials may have played in the formation of Israel's early traditions, and whether understood primarily in terms of individual acts or a "continuous process,"[33] these materials should continue to inform any portrayal of Israel's theology in a significant way—in *all* their forms, including those with a creation component, e.g., Neh. 9:6–31; Psalm 136; Jer. 32:16–23. But, if they alone occupy the center of attention, these recitals and comparable materials will lead to a biased presentation of any "OT Theology." For underlying these materials is a certain understanding of *the kind of* God who has been engaged in such activity on Israel's behalf.

Alongside these recitals, and sometimes integrated into them (e.g., Deut. 7:6–11; Jer. 32:16–23; Neh. 9:6–31; Psalms 106, 136), is another type of reoccurring material.[34] Its earliest and fullest articulation is probably to be found in Exod. 34:6–7:

> The Lord passed before him, and proclaimed, "The Lord, the Lord, a God merciful and gracious, slow to anger, and abounding in steadfast love and faithfulness, keeping steadfast love for thousands, forgiving iniquity and transgression and sin, but who will by no means clear the guilty."

This confessional statement occurs many times in various, usually abbreviated, forms,[35] and in numerous echoes[36]—throughout the OT. It also appears in a variety of traditions and types of literature.[37] While its origins are obscure, there is no reason to suppose that it is not relatively early, at least pre-Deuteronomic. It also bridges the exile. No other statement can be said to occur so often in the OT.[38]

One cannot help but wonder whether such a common OT statement has been ignored because it has a certain abstract, even propositional, character. For those who maintain that the OT is concerned with events rather than concepts, who believe that Israelite thinking does not bother with the abstract, these common biblical affirmations regarding God come as something of an embarrassment; hence, it has been convenient to pass them by. But, it may now be time to give appropriate attention to these generalizations without worrying about falling back into older ways of dogmatic theology. These materials are important for balancing any concern for the historical, or any concern for the OT as story.

An illustration of our concern might be seen in P. Hanson's *Dynamic Transcendence*. One of the more striking things about this study is its comparatively rare reference to God as one who is faithful, loving, gracious, merciful, righteous, or their semantic equivalents. The most common language Hanson uses has to do with the divine plan and purpose, as well as God's creative and redemptive activity. Such language, however, is elusive to interpret without explicit reference to the kind of God who is involved in such plans and activity. Hanson does cite Exod. 34:6–7 once (p. 57), but neither it nor its concerns play any apparent role in his understanding of the confessional heritage, which supplies "the perspective from which a particular event could be recognized as a purposeful part of a divine plan" (p. 32). It is important to emphasize that any discussion of the heritage's norming function needs to consider the crucial role such an understanding of God plays in the evaluative task.

In addition to their function in delimiting possibilities of meaning in the materials in which they are embedded, such generalizations provide continuity for any theological presentation of the OT. The historical events of the recitals do not provide continuity in the same way.[39] In fact, there are a number of indications, particularly in the literature which overlaps the fall of Jerusalem, that Israel is to forget the salvific events of the past; indeed, they have lost their salvific value:[40]

> Therefore, behold, the days are coming, says the Lord, when men shall no longer say, "As the Lord lives who brought up the people of Israel out of the land of Egypt."
> (Jer. 23:7; cf. 3:16, 16:14–15)

> Remember not the former things,
>     nor consider the things of old.
> Behold, I am doing a new thing.
>             (Isa. 43:18–19)[41]

Passages from Ezekiel 20 and Hosea 2 (cf. 8:13; 11:5, etc.) suggest that God in effect takes back the salvific significance of the important events of Israel's past; Israel must now look to the future for such divine action.

That which provides for the continuity between the past events which no longer have salvific value and the future events that do are certain basic convictions regarding God. In the hiatus between old and new, that which the people can fall back on in a special way are affirmations such as Exod. 34:6–7 or Isa. 40:28 or 44:6. It is just such theological generalizations which are important in enabling Israel, not only to see the continuity in its own story, and interpret it in appropriate ways, but to be carried through those times when the story seems to have broken off. They enable Israel to perceive that, though its own story may be interrupted, God's story continues. God's loving and gracious purposes and his faithfulness to promises made will persist, though Israel's perception may be clouded at times.

The Book of Lamentations, which never appeals to salvific events in Israel's past, makes this point very well (3:20–32):

> My soul . . .
>     is bowed down within me.
> But this I call to mind,
>     and *therefore* I have hope:
> The steadfast love of the Lord never ceases,
>     his mercies never come to an end;
> they are new every morning;
>     great is thy faithfulness. . . .
> For the Lord will not
>     cast off for ever,
> but, though he cause grief, he will have compassion
>     according to the abundance of his steadfast love.

In the midst of the great gulf between the past and the future, the only hope is in a certain kind of God (cf. Psalm 79). Second Isaiah is filled with comparable generalizations regarding the kind of God who is active in this way (e.g., 40:28; 44:6).

It might be suggested that Israel knows God as this kind of God only because of what God has done in its history. In many ways this is true; Israel's confession of God as merciful, gracious, and so forth, is shaped in significant ways by what Israel has experienced of God in history, and the continuities observed in such events. At the same time, what Israel confesses of its God is based not only on inferences drawn from the events of the recitals but also on prior as well as succeeding understandings and experiences of various kinds. For example, Exod. 34:6–7 is represented not as an inference drawn from recent events, but as a direct revelation of God in a theophany. In fact, this confession is tied up contextually not to the Exodus event, but to the sin of the golden calf. Thus, it could be said that it is the way that God does *not* act, in response to human sin, that is as revealing of his nature as the more spectacular salvific events.

Insight into the nature of God comes to Israel through the years via an amazing array of avenues; of these, the key events may be said to be primary, particularly if one includes the reflection upon those events, so that "revelation" is not narrowly associated with the event itself. In any case, Israel then uses that *understanding* of the nature of God, and not just what prompted the understanding, as a norm to make judgments about the way God is involved. If all Israel could have said was that God had acted, even acted in creative and redemptive ways, then hope would have been an occasional thing; for who knows what God will act like the next time? The crucial importance lies in knowing what kind of a God it is who has been, is, and will be acting. God is faithful, loving, gracious, and righteous; hence, there is hope.

To summarize my response to the three issues raised: First, regarding the nature of the discussion of God in OT theology, it must be as attentive to the generalizations as to the history/story. It is the former which makes the latter intelligible and coherent.

Second, regarding the theological constants which should inform and undergird such theological discussions, the OT provides a number of reoccurring confessional statements concerning the nature and activity of God which should determine these in a basic way. Thus combined, they would say something like this: the God who saves and blesses is always faithful, loving, gracious, and righteous. Thus, it can be said that Israel was both synchronic and diachronic in the way in which it developed and presented materials about God.[42]

Third, this discussion must be set in the context of my comments on pluralism. That these two types of confessional statements are integrated in later literature, and in a variety of forms cutting across diverse types of literature, suggests that they represented some unanimity amidst the theological pluralism, perhaps even a kind of "canon" within the canon. Just as the historical recitals determined those events in Israel's history which were constitutive of its present existence, and thus separable from all other events as crucial for faith, so also the generalizations about God provided the appropriate interpretive clue for the determination of the meaning of that history.

In any move in this direction, however, it is important to note that there was no necessary form which the words had to take. Both types of statements occur in various forms in different contexts; they are always developing. Thus, creation materials appear in the later recitals, and the repentance of God motif is added to the affirmations about God. Yet, wherever they are found, there is a definite family resemblance. This would suggest, however, not that the crucial affirmations were an elusive matter; rather, they pointed to a confessional configuration, which was not finally reducible to formulas but remained open to new knowledge and experiences of God. As such, they did not lead to a monochromatic set of beliefs; yet they were sufficiently definitive to delineate the parameters within which a legitimate pluralism could operate. It is quite probable that the affirmations function this way for the author of the Book of Jonah (cf. 4:2). From another perspective, the Book of Psalms—like the service books and hymnals throughout the ages, it presents the faith in its leaner forms—appeals to the content of these confessions with amazing regularity. Whether in lament or praise, the essence of the matter, finally, is the kind of God Israel worships. All of this seems to say that diversity can become *theologically* significant only if placed within a context of that which makes for unity.

## THE OLD TESTAMENT GOD AND CONTEMPORARY ISSUES

Among the contemporary issues noted previously, the various liberation movements have had the greatest impact on OT scholarship. Such studies are now wide-ranging, encompassing sociological, religio-historical, and theological work, as well as close exegetical study and thematic analyses, with a view to a fully critical, inclusive hermeneutic.[43] The discussions have moved beyond a concern simply to locate and explicate those OT materials which would support the metaphoric shift (e.g., the feminine metaphors for God). No simple, univocal perspective on these matters and associated images for God is available in the OT; the data is diverse and the issues complex. Thus, the images of God are as variable as life and reflect the experiences of all: God is both mother and father, king and fellow-sufferer. Within the span of a few verses, we can see God raising up the poor from the dust and giving strength to the king (1 Sam. 2:

1–10), comforting like a mother and wielding the sword of the warrior (Isa. 63:13–16). God is imaged in terms of form and reform, stability and disruption, consolation and wrath.

These polarities exist in a dialectical relationship with the general culture, as well as developing in interaction with historical events. The faith-culture issue is spread out between the two interpretive poles of the "overagainstness" of faith to cultural realities, the general perspective of the "biblical theology" movement, and seeing "cultural and social realities as the matrices for spawning correlative beliefs about God."[44] Generally, it may be said that the images are taken over from the general culture, yet transformed by being brought into the orbit of Israel's peculiar understanding of God. At the same time, they retain certain cultural particularities and help shape developing ideas about God. Speaking of God as Father, for instance, inevitably reflects the understanding of fatherhood in the general culture, while the existing theological heritage gives new shape to the meaning of the image when applied to God.

Regarding historical developments, the basic vision of egalitarianism is commonly apparent from an early time, essentially rooted in but also contributing to a certain understanding of God. God is not conceived to be either a sexual being or tolerant of injustice. Nevertheless, while Israel might be viewed as a social mutation in the ancient Near East, the impact of its peculiar faith on culture and social practice took time. Or, from another perspective, egalitarian perspectives in both religion and culture were soon lost in the oppressive tendencies of monarchical structures, but surfaced again from time to time. In any case, no simple development in the faith-culture interaction can be discerned. One can discern positive changes in attitude toward women and slavery in the development of the Book of the Covenant (Exodus 20—23) and in Deuteronomy (cf. chaps. 10 and 15), no doubt rooted in reflection upon the inherited traditions, in which a certain understanding of God was integral. One can see that, in interaction with the theological heritage, certain sociopolitical realities bring into prominence certain images of God from time to time: the liberation images during the time of the Exodus, Hosea's marriage imagery in the contest with the fertility cults, the feminine images in the despair of the exile. Whatever the details, the process itself is theologically important; for it shows how the theological heritage, in continual interaction with sociopolitical realities, calls into question honored images and practices, moving the people on to new understandings of God and new vistas of that shape of life which faith in such a God implies.

This renewed attention to neglected biblical images for God, and Israel's struggles related thereto, should assist the church in restoring balance to its understanding of God, while at the same time instilling a wariness of simplistic directions of thought.

Two additional notes may be sounded for continued attention. First, in the midst of all that makes for process and polarity, there is that which is quite undialectical and utterly constant. Certain metaphors for God have a priority over others. There is, in fact, a divine constancy throughout the use and abuse of these metaphors that is not grasped by developmental and dialectical language. That which provides for the most fundamental continuity through the centuries is not the story of ever-lapsing Israel, nor the heritage of faith which is always being reformulated; it is the history of a certain kind of God who will always, come what may, execute justice and love the sojourner (Deut. 10:18). God's salvific will is never diminished; God's righteousness is never compromised; God's steadfast love endures forever. Psalm 136, in which the latter phrase reoccurs as a litany, shows that, from form to reform and back to form, from creation (vv. 5–9) to redemption (vv. 10–15), and from historical acts (vv. 16–22) to general blessings (vv. 23–25), God's actions will always be motivated by an unshakeably constant and loving purpose. In other words, OT God-talk will always need to be cognizant of two dimensions of the divine: (1) Those images of God which are unfailingly non-contingent; God will be this kind of God wherever God is being God. God is love; God is faithful. (2) Those images of God which move around with people and their stories, and are affected by them. Thus, the wrath of God (cf. Ps. 30:5).

Second, one needs to be sensitive to what is implied by using such images for God. What does it mean to speak of God as one so enmeshed in the life of the world? It is, after all, a matter of taking such divine relatedness with utmost seriousness. If God is *really* so immersed in that which makes for change and contingency, what does that say about God, and these various images for God? If God, indeed, becomes a Warrior in a given situation, what effect does that have on God? Given such an image, what does it *cost* God for God to *be* God? Freedom and immutability are two things which come quickly to mind. In other words, what do these various images say not only about the community of faith which used them, but about the history of the God of whose actions they are an actual reflection?

In relation to the other contemporary issues, OT studies are more isolated, though a number of them are of considerable importance. Thus, one can point to the very significant achievement of Heschel's *The Prophets*,[45] dedicated to the victims of the Holocaust. One finds here a remarkable account of the pathos of God. It has had little apparent effect on OT studies since its publication, though it is one of the OT studies most commonly cited by contemporary theologians.[46] In sum, only a few studies appear to have been directed specifically to the issue of divine (im)passibility with the various associated anthropopathisms. The issue of human suffering has occasioned some studies of the issue of theodicy,[47] though the implications of this scholarship for more general OT understandings of God remain to be fully explored.

While consideration of the God-world relationship has always been an integral part of the standard theologies (particularly so in Eichrodt, following O. Procksch),[48] such discussions have tended to be isolated from other dimensions of OT theology. But now, because a certain narrowness in approach to God issues occasioned by the "biblical theology" movement has been overcome, new perspectives are emerging. One of the byproducts, of course, has been an increased interest in wisdom literature. This has meant the lifting up of the importance of the human in the divine economy,[49] which has important implications for the God-question, as well as God's extra-Israel relationship to the created order. Issues relating to the divine providence are receiving new attention, perhaps most evident in the work of Westermann on blessing,[50] while the importance of creation theology in Israel is now being approached from new angles of vision. The recent article by R. Knierim,[51] with its review of literature and constructive proposal, is of special importance. Furthermore, discussions of theophany also carry significant implications for Israel's understanding of the relationship between God and world, as recognized long ago by Eichrodt.[52]

Moreover, the increased focus on matters sociological and anthropological in OT studies[53] has the potential of touching base with contemporary theological efforts to discern the reality of God in ordinary human experience,[54] not to mention studies of the correlation between sociopolitical realities and developing images of God.[55]

Finally, one should note the significant work of those engaged with issues raised in particular by process theology.[56] These studies promise important new developments in the understanding of the God of the OT, perhaps especially in a shift away from traditional formulations regarding the divine attributes.

The following chapters are an effort to contribute to this emerging discussion. While they lend support to the theological pluralism in the OT, there may be sufficient evidence to suggest that the understanding of God detailed at some points is a part of the basic substratum of OT thought about God.

# CHAPTER 3

# God and World:
## Basic Perspectives

Israel's understanding of the relationship between God and world has not often been the special focus of OT theological work.[1] Attention has largely been centered on the relationship between God and history, Israel's history in particular. Yet a logically prior question is God's more general relationship to the world. God's relationship with Israel, and indeed with historical processes more generally, presupposes a certain way in which God is related to the world. God's redemptive purposes in and through Israel presuppose the reality of the world as the creation of God and the world in need of reconciliation; God's activity in the history of Israel is for the sake of the world. Even more, it assumes certain very specific matters regarding the God-world relationship: For example, that God can speak and people can hear, that genuine dialogue between God and people is possible. Here I will explore some basic aspects of this relationship, in the light of which the remaining chapters of the book are developed, and, in turn, fill out this understanding.

It is clear that two possible understandings of the God-world relationship can be eliminated immediately as far as Israel is concerned.[2] One would be pantheism: from this viewpoint, God is identified with the world; everything in all creation is seen to be pulsing with the divine. For Israel, God and world are not collapsed into one another; the world was created by God and is to be distinguished from God. At the other extreme would be dualism, where God and world would be viewed as independent of one another, and indeed opposed to one another. But, for Israel, the world is dependent upon God and the creation is "very good," not anti-God in principle or in actuality, however much evil may be said to have permeated its life.

The problem is to determine where, between these two poles, Israel's understanding of the God-world relationship lies. Two images might be suggested: the monarchical and the organismic. The former is certainly the image that prevails in contemporary OT interpretation. Among other matters, this point of view emphasizes the discontinuity between God and world, considering such items as divine sovereignty, freedom, immutability, and control to define the basic character of the God-world relationship. God is a radically transcendent Lord who "stands outside" (apart, above, beyond) and holds the whole world in his hands. The organismic image, on the other hand, is seldom represented in theological discussions of OT material. From this perspective, a greater continuity, indeed intimacy, between God and world is discerned in the texts, in what might be termed a "relationship of reciprocity."[3]

It may be that, given the theological pluralism of the OT, both images are appropriate, depending on the passage one is citing. Yet it is our conviction that the predominant OT perspective on this issue is organismic. At the least, this is the image which needs greater exploration in OT interpretation. It is our concern to feature the organismic image in the interest of increased balance in elucidating the OT understanding of the relationship between God and world.

A few specific examples of such an approach are in order: The world is not only dependent upon God; God is also dependent upon the world. The world is not only affected by God; God is affected by the world in both positive and negative ways. God is sovereign over the world, yet not unqualifiedly so, as considerable power and freedom have been given to the creatures. God is the transcendent Lord; but God is transcendent not in isolation from the world, but in relationship to the world. God knows all there is to know about the world, yet there is a future which does not yet exist to be known even by God. God is Lord of time and history, yet God has chosen to be bound up in the time and history of the world and to be limited thereby. God is unchangeable with respect to the steadfastness of his love and his salvific will for all creatures, yet God does change in the light of what happens in the interaction between God and world.

As a way of giving greater prominence to the organismic images, I will make two affirmations and explicate them in terms of specific examples.

## GOD'S RELATIONSHIP TO THE WORLD
## IS REAL AND HAS INTEGRITY

A survey of OT studies which speak of God-world, God-Israel, or God-individual would reveal that the most common word used is "relationship" or related words. *Relatedness* is perhaps the most basic category with which scholars work in speaking of such matters. Virtually any God-world metaphor one could name from the OT assumes this most basic of metaphors: king-subject; husband-wife; parent-child; shepherd-sheep; redeemer-redeemed. Not every metaphor speaks of the relationship in the same way, or lifts up the same concerns with equal prominence, but relatedness is basic to the use of such language; it is a root metaphor which undergirds all of these more concrete metaphors.

In this light, the key questions to be asked are these: What if the word "relationship" were taken with utter seriousness? What does it take for a relationship to be real? What does it mean for a relationship to have integrity as a relationship, which is presumably the only kind of relationship God could have, for God is certainly the supreme exemplification of what is entailed in relatedness? What does it mean for God to be faithful in a relationship which is real? Once having entered into such a relationship, is God bound to it, no longer free to become unrelated?

As in any relationship of integrity, God will have to give up some things for the sake of the relationship. Thus, God will have to give up some freedom. Any commitment or promise within a relationship entails a limitation of freedom. By such actions, God has decisively limited the options God has for speaking and acting. God has exercised divine freedom in the making of such promises in the first place. But, in having freely made such promises, thereafter God's freedom is truly limited by those promises. God will do what God says God will do; God will be faithful to God's own promises, and that is a limitation of freedom. God's freedom is now most supremely a freedom *for* the world, not a freedom *from* the world.

Moreover, any relationship of integrity will entail a sharing of power. Each party to the relationship must give up any monopoly on power for the sake of the relationship. Neither party to the relationship can be overwhelmed for the relationship to be a true one.

For the sake of the relationship, God gives up the exercise of some power. This will in turn qualify any talk about divine control or divine sovereignty. Total control of the other in a relationship is no relationship of integrity.

## GOD IS INTERNALLY RELATED
## TO THE WORLD

Two of the most basic perspectives on God's relationship to the world have to do with space and time.

### *God and Space*

That God is internally related to the world may be seen, first of all, in terms of spatial realities.[4] While the OT does not have a specific word for world or cosmos, the language of "all things" (e.g., Isa. 44:24; Jer. 10:16) and/or "heaven and earth" (e.g., Pss. 89:11; 146:6) has reference to the totality of the world as a unity in which everything has its proper place and function.[5] At the same time, the regular use of "heaven and earth" testifies to a "bipartite structure" within the unified created order; there are thus "two fundamental realms within creation."[6] "The heavens are the Lord's heavens, but the earth he has given to the sons of men" (Ps. 115:16).

Here the heavens are an integral aspect of the *world as created*. Using a variety of construction language, God is said to have built his own residence, "the living space of God," into the very structures of the created order.[7]

> Thou . . .
> who hast stretched out the heavens like a tent,
>> who hast laid the beams of thy chambers on the waters.
>>> (Ps. 104:1–3; cf. Isa. 40:22; Amos. 9:6)

The heavens (or semantic equivalents) thus become a shorthand way of referring to the abode of God *within* the world, "a distinct realm in cosmic space"[8] (e.g., Pss. 2:4; 11:4; 103:19; 104:13; 1 Kings 8:30–52). From this "lofty abode" God looks down or hears or speaks (e.g., Exod. 20:22; Deut. 26:15; Pss. 18:9; 102:19; Jer. 25:30). God is commonly said to move from God's own realm to earth (e.g., Gen. 11:5–7; Ps. 18:9). Nevertheless, this is a movement from *within* the created order, and hence must be conceived in terms different from what would be the case if God's movements were from without the world to within.

"Yahweh's place is in the world," and we might add, only in the world.[9] Where there is world there is God; where there is God there is world. There is no God "left over" in some sphere which is other than world. God, who *is* other than world, has wholly immersed himself in the world (cf. Jer. 23:24). Thus, whatever may have been the case before the creation of the heavens and the earth, since the creation God has taken up residence within that creation, and thus works from within the world, and not on the world from without.

Two other texts may represent a somewhat different understanding of this issue, but it does not seem likely. The first is 1 Kings 8:27 (with parallels in 2 Chron. 2:6; 6:18), "heaven and the highest heaven cannot contain thee." What this phrase might entail is uncertain; but it likely means little more than the view represented in Jer. 23:24, "Do not I fill heaven *and earth*?" That is to say, the earth, too, must be included in God's domain (cf. Deut. 10:14; Neh. 9:6). Given the polemics against any idea that the temple ("this house") could contain God, it has reference to the fact that no *specific place* within the world has the capacity to contain God, not even God's own heavenly abode. In any case, the passage does not testify to any notion that God works on the world from without; the context is filled with references to God's working from within (vv. 30, 32, 43, 49, etc.).

The other passage is Ps. 102:25–27 (cf. Heb. 1:10–12), the interpretation of which is also uncertain. The crux of the matter is whether the world experiences the ill effects of time and needs renewal (cf. Isa. 65:17–25; 66:22), or will actually vanish.[10] Most OT texts state that the earth and the heavens are established in perpetuity (cf. Pss. 78:69; 93:1; 104:5; 148:6; Eccles. 1:4; Jer. 31:35–36), while a few seem to suggest otherwise (cf. Isa. 34:4; 51:6).[11] The basic point of Psalm 102 seems to be that God is not subject to the ravages of time as is the finite world, and is not in need of renewal. In any case, for the time of this world, God works from within it, and given the new heaven and earth, God will never be without a world. That God upholds this world and will see to its renewal means, of course, that God is Lord of the world though God is immersed in it.

To move to a related issue, of what import is the bipartite structure of heaven and earth? The heavens are a sort of "consecrated zone"[12] within the created world, thoroughly imbued with the presence and will of God; the earth, however, is that worldly realm where God's will is contested.[13] God's will is done in heaven in a way that it is not on earth (cf. Matt. 6:10). Thus, the cosmic bipolarity of heaven/earth within the one world has a theological significance. To use R. Knierim's language:[14] "History appears to have fallen out of the rhythm of cosmic order, whereas the cosmic order itself reflects the ongoing presence of creation. It remains loyal to its origin. . . . And it knows about it." Pss. 19:1–6, 103:19–22, and 148:1–6 are cited as examples of how "the cosmic space proclaims daily and without end the glory of God, and itself as his handiwork."[15]

It is important not to overstate this separateness, however. God does move freely back and forth across the realms of the world, while heaven is "unreachable from the earth."[16] Yet, unreachability ought not be interpreted in terms of unaffectability. The prayers of the people are heard in heaven (cf. 1 Kings 8) and, as we shall see, God is affected in many ways by what happens on earth. God is not untouched in heaven, nor are the heavens untouched. Passages such as Jer. 4:23–28 and Joel 2:10 indicate that the heavens have been affected by human sin and its judgmental aftermath; hence there is need for a new creation and not just a new people.

The theological significance of Israel's cosmology thus goes beyond seeing heaven as a symbol of God's exaltedness; the various cosmological features say something very important about the God-world relationship in more comprehensive ways.[17] While it is a truism to say that Israel's cosmology was different from ours, the fact that the understanding of the cosmos was given such theological import by Israel lays a significant foundation for the contemporary theological task in this area.[18]

Knierim indicates that this interpretation of Israel's cosmology has implications for the understanding of God's presence: in the cosmic order, "Yahweh is present in a way different from his presence in history;"[19] God is present in a more intensified way. It is thus important for us to explore in greater detail aspects of Israel's understanding of God's presence in the world, particularly on earth.

### God and Time

It is almost universal in OT scholarship to maintain that "Yahweh's time is different from the time of the world-order."[20] Is this so? That

God was God before the creation of the *ordered* world is clear (e.g., Ps. 90:2), as is the understanding that God endures in a way that the world does not (e.g., Ps. 102:26–27). Yet many other texts suggest that, at least since the creation of the heavens and the earth, God has been related to the world from within its structures of time as well as those of space.

Let it be clear from the outset that we are not directly concerned with defining time (and eternity) here, nor discussing their relationship to one another;[21] our concern is with Israel's understanding of God's relationship to temporal realities. There is probably no explicit concern in the OT for defining or relating time and eternity; yet there are materials which speak of God's relationship to time which, in turn, carry some implications for the understanding of eternity. Whether Genesis 1 conceives of time itself as beginning with the ordering of creation, or only time as being ordered ("evening and morning"), is uncertain. (There would seem to be evidence, however, only for the latter. But, whatever one's view, our concern is with God's relationship to temporal realities since the creation.[22] Following Barr's dictum,[23] we are concerned here with OT *statements* about God's relationship to time, and, it might be noted, with statements which fall largely outside the purview of his study. I would also suggest that, in showing how God is rendered as actor in the OT, D. Patrick's book, *The Rendering of God*,[24] could be correlated nicely with this material.

First of all, note those passages where God is the subject of verbs relating to devising or planning. God makes plans for both judgment and blessing:

> Thus says the Lord, Behold, I am shaping evil against you and devising a plan against you.
>
> > (Jer. 18:11; cf. 26:3; 49:20, 30;
> > 50:45; Mic. 2:3; 4:12)

> For I know the plans I have for you, says the Lord, plans for welfare and not for evil, to give you a future and a hope.
>
> > (Jer. 29:11)

Certain contexts make it especially clear that there is a temporal distinction between the divine plan and its execution:

The Lord has both planned and done
    what he spoke concerning the inhabitants of Babylon.
                  (Jer. 51:12; cf. 4:28; Lam. 2:17;
               Isa. 22:11; 37:26; Zech. 1:6; 8:14)

When these materials are correlated with the language of divine repentance (e.g., Jer. 18:7–9) and instances of divine consultation with prophetic leaders (e.g., Gen. 18:17–22; see chap. 4) it is clear that the time between the divine plan and its execution is an important period, not only for the people but for God. The interaction between God and people will determine whether the plan is put into effect.

This common language of planning assumes that temporal sequence is important for God—past, present, and future are meaningful categories. There is temporal succession, a before and after, in the divine thinking. Temporally, God is internally related to the world, that is, from within its structures of time, and in such a way that there are now no other options for God.

Just as God anticipates and plans for the future, so God also recalls the past. God has memories as well as hopes. While it may be said that God has "total recall" of the past, God as the subject of the verb "remember" indicates that the past is truly past to God (e.g., God remembers the covenant, Exod. 2:24; 6:5; Lev. 26:42; Jer. 14:10, 21). God is also said not to remember nor to forget certain matters (e.g., sins, Isa. 43:25; Jer. 31:34; people, Ps. 88:6; Hos. 4:6). Such passages indicate a change of status with regard to such matters for God; what was once remembered is now forgotten as far as having any effect on the relationship. For such passages to make sense, however, God cannot be said to remember and forget simultaneously; such divine actions must thus be viewed in terms of a temporal flow of events.

Perhaps the clearest materials on this matter are those relating to the divine anger. In the most common OT credal statement, God is said to be slow to anger (Exod. 34:6, etc.). Elsewhere, God is said (not) to restrain his anger (e.g., Ps. 78:38; Isa. 48:9; Lam. 2:8; Ezek. 20:22) and to hold his peace (e.g., Isa. 57:11; Ps. 50:21). Another type of reference to God's anger comes in Deut. 32:21:

They have stirred me to jealousy . . .
    they have provoked me with their idols.
    (cf. Ps. 78:58; 106:29; Isa. 65:3; Jer. 8:19)

Elsewhere we are assured,

He will not always chide,
>nor will he keep his anger for ever.
>>(Ps. 103:9; cf. Isa. 57:16;
>>>Jer. 3:12; Mic. 7:18)

His anger is but for a moment,
>and his favor is for a lifetime.
>(Ps. 30:5; cf. Ezra 9:8; Ps. 85:3)

For a brief moment I forsook you, . . .
In overflowing wrath for a moment
>I hid my face from you,
but with everlasting love I will have compassion on you.
>>(Isa. 54:7–8; cf. Isa. 26:20; Exod. 33:5)

These references to God's wrath are coherent only if placed along a time line, so that one can speak of delay, a time of provocation, a time of momentary execution, and a time when such wrath comes to an end. "I will be calm, and will be no more angry" (Ezek. 16:42). God's anger is thus expressly described as historical anger. God is not always angry. The divine anger has its time, and a time when it is not (see Jer. 18:23, "the time of thine anger," cf. 6:15; 23:20).

Such passages would also relate to God's knowledge of the future. It is sometimes said that one does indeed need to speak of temporal sequence for God, but that God knows the future as well as past and present. But the anger passages make necessary some qualification of such a notion. For God to say, for example, "I know that I will be provoked to anger by the sin of David with Bathsheba," runs into tough moral ground. God should immediately be angry at the point of God's *knowledge* of the sin, and not just at the point of its occurrence. But the texts say that God was provoked to anger at a particular historical moment, and not that some previous divine provocation was realized.

Two other types of passages show how Israel understood God to be bound up in temporal realities. Note, first of all, that temporal language is used in connection with appointed or set times for the divine action. Outside of "the Day of the Lord" texts (e.g., Lam. 2:22), the following should be cited:

"In a time of favor I have answered you,
>in a day of salvation I have helped you.
>>(Isa. 49:8)

It is time for the Lord to act.
(Ps. 119:126)

It is the time to favor her,
the appointed time has come.
(Ps. 102:13; cf. Exod. 9:5;
Job 24:1; Ps. 69:3; Isa. 60:22)

Second, there are a number of references to God's days or years: "Thy years have no end" (Ps. 102:27; cf. v. 24; Job 24:1; 36:26).

That God's years are different from human years might be inferred from a passage such as Ps. 90:4 (cf. Job 10:5; 2 Peter 3:8):

For a thousand years in thy sight
are but as yesterday when it is past,
or as a watch in the night.

This passage does not mean, however, that one thousand of God's years are equal to one human day or part of a day. Rather, given the unending divine years compared to the short span of a human life, one thousand of God's years are *like* one human day (see TEV).[25] Moreover, the larger context of this passage suggests that the difference between God's temporality and that of the human is not simply quantitative; it is also qualitative. As for human years, "their span is but toil and trouble; they are soon gone, and we fly away" (Ps. 90:10). But with God, it is different. God remains the same; God does not waste or wear away like the grass or a change of clothes (cf. Ps. 102:26–27). God is immune from the ravages of time: time is no threat to God. God's thoughts, name, faithfulness, and kingship remain constant "to all generations" (Pss. 33:11; cf. 102:12; 119:90; 135:13; 145:13; 146:10). The experience of temporality is thus supremely exemplified in the divine life; God's experience in time is *as God*. If this both quantitative and qualitative difference is what is constitutive of eternity, and whatever in addition it might entail, the eternal life and infinitude of God are seen to be compatible with being caught up in the temporal flow.

The God of the OT is thus not thought of in terms of timelessness. At least since the creation, the divine life is temporally ordered. God has chosen to enter into the time of the world. God is not above the flow of time and history, as if looking down from some supratemporal mountaintop on all the streams of people through the valleys of the ages. God is "inside time," not outside of it. Yet there never was nor will there ever be a time when God is not the living God. There is no moving from birth or toward death for God. God's life within the flow of events is qualitatively supreme; God's salvific will remains unchanged; God's faithfulness is never compromised; God's steadfast love endures forever.

The OT witnesses to a God who truly shares in human history as past, present, and future, and in such a way that we must speak of a history of God. God has so bound himself in relationship to the world that they move through time and space together. God is the eternal, uncreated member of this community, but God, too, will cry out from time to time: "How long?" (e.g., Jer. 4:14; 13:27; Hos. 8:5).

There is indeed a divine *self*-limitation to the order of creation. Yet, it needs to be realized that to insist that God is not so limited is to limit God in other ways. God would not be able to make free, spontaneous decisions in the light of the spontaneities of human action. God would also be deprived of the experience of novelty or of the joy of discovery. God's activity in the world would become a kind of production, a mere drawing out of what God has always determined. If it is not too flip, God thereby would become an already programmed computer. The truly personal dimension of the divine life would be sharply diminished. This self-limitation, of course, affects God's knowledge of the future.

# CHAPTER 4

# God and World:
# Foreknowledge

Rarely do OT studies speak directly to the question of divine fore-knowledge.[1] This is probably due to the paucity of specific textual evidence which can be cited to support such an idea. But there are a variety of texts which point to a divine limitation with respect to God's knowledge of the future. Four types of material assist us in gaining perspective on God's relationship to the future.

## THE DIVINE PERHAPS

The use of *'ûlay,* "perhaps," in *divine* speech. This term is used in human speech to indicate uncertainty regarding the future, often tinged with a note of hope.[2] Especially common are those passages which express uncertainty about what God might do in the future (Amos 5:15; Exod. 32:30).[3]

There are five instances where *'ûlay* is used in divine speech. Two of the more striking read as follows:

> The word of the Lord came to me: "Son of man, . . . prepare for yourself an exile's baggage, and go into exile by day in their sight. . . . Perhaps [*'ûlay*] they will understand, though they are a rebellious house."
> (Ezek. 12:1–3)

> Thus says the Lord: Stand in the court of the Lord's house, and speak. . . . It may be [*'ûlay*] they will listen, and every one turn from his evil way, that I may repent of the evil.
> (Jer. 26:2–3; cf. 36:3, 7; 51:8; Isa. 47:12; cf. Luke 20:13)

It seems clear from such passages that God is quite uncertain as to how the people will respond to the prophetic word.[4] God is certainly aware of the various possibilities regarding Israel's response. One might even say that God, given a thoroughgoing knowledge of Israel, knows what its response is likely to be (cf., e.g., Pss. 11:4; 33:13; 94:9–11). There will be no surprises for God in the sense of not anticipating what might happen. Yet, in God's own words, God does not finally know. Every indication in these texts would suggest that God, knowing the depths of Israel's sin, should have been able to declare unequivocally that judgment was inevitable. This God does not do; it is possible that some spontaneous response to the preaching of the prophets will pull them out of the fire at the last moment. Thus, we can say generally that even if God knows every causal factor involved in shaping Israel's future, God still recognizes all this knowledge as being an insufficient basis for predicting that future in detail. For the future is not entirely shaped by such causes; there is room for spontaneity. And God in essence is hoping that an unpredictable event might, in fact, occur.

That God was actually uncertain as to how the people would respond also seems clear from passages such as Jer. 3:7 and 3:19:

> And I thought, "After she has done all this she will return to me"; but she did not return.

> I thought
> how I would set you among my sons,
> and give you a pleasant land,
>     a heritage most beauteous of all nations.
> And I thought you would call me, My Father,
>     and would not turn from following me.
> Surely, as a faithless wife leaves her husband,
>     so have you been faithless to me, O house of Israel.

Here, God is depicted as actually thinking that the people would respond positively to the initial election, or that they would return after a time of straying. But events proved that God's outlook on the future was too optimistic. The people did not respond as God thought they would. God's knowledge of future human action is thus clearly represented as limited.

This is an especially important matter when it comes to speaking of the *integrity* of God's command to these prophets. If God knew all along what Israel's response would be, then these commands were a sham, for they were predicated on the possibility that Israel might respond positively. If God knew in fact what would happen—namely, that Israel would not so respond—then the "perhaps" was an outright deception of the prophet. It might be suggested, I suppose, that God really did know, but that it was necessary, for reasons unknown, for God to put the matter this way. But, aside from this being a strained reading, with no justification in the text itself, one then buys an absolute form of omniscience at the price of placing the *integrity* and coherence of all of God's words in jeopardy: does God really mean what is said or not? These texts show that Israel's future is genuinely open and not predetermined. The future for Israel does not only not exist, it has not even been finally decided upon. Hence, it is not something that even exists to be known, even if the knower is God.

It may be said that God knows God's ultimate salvific goals for the people and world will be achieved one way or another, and that God's purposes in moving toward those goals will be constant. But there are innumerable paths for the people to take along the way; these are known to God as probabilities or possibilities. A limited analogy may help: when I play chess with my young daughter, I know the possibilities for play which she has, how I will respond to many of them, and that I will finally win the game. (It won't be long, however, before I can no longer say that!) The way in which the game will progress and finally be won, and the amount of time it will take, however, will be determined only in light of the various moves she will make.

All of this means, of course, that God's future is somewhat—as we will see, God knows what God will do—open-ended as well; what God will do at least in part depends upon what Israel does. God's actions are not predetermined. Thus, Israel's response will contribute in a genuine way to the shaping not only of its own future, but to the future of God.

THE DIVINE IF

The "perhaps" passages are paralleled by a number of conditional sentences found in *divine* speech.[5] While conditional sentences are written in a variety of ways in Hebrew,[6] our concern here is with those constructions using the particle *'im* ("if"), with the imperfect form of the verb in the prodasis: "If you truly amend your ways . . . then I will let you dwell in this place" (Jer. 7:5; see the negative formulation in 26:4–6).

The people's opportunity to "dwell in this place" is a future possibility, dependent on their amendment of their ways. In order for God's promise to have integrity, God's future action must be a possibility and only a possibility, too. For God, or anyone, to speak in terms of a possibility (or probability), suggests an awareness of at least one other possibility, but uncertainty as to which, in fact, will occur. If God knew, at the moment God delivered this word to Jeremiah to give to the people, what, in fact, did occur later—the people did not amend their ways and they were not allowed to dwell in that place—then the word to the people is both pointless and a deception. In fact, God would be holding out a false hope; for dwelling in this place would not have been a possibility from God's perspective. Thus, even though Jer. 7:13—8:3, with the oracle of judgment, indicates that future which is more probable, the future for God in this case consists of two possibilities, not a certainty.

Both negative and positive options are presented in Jer. 22:4–5:

> If you will obey this word, then there shall enter the gates of this house kings who sit on the throne of David . . . but if you will not heed these words . . . this house shall become a desolation.

Two specific future possibilities are open to the king (and the people, 8:2), depending upon the fulfillment of justice according to the command of the Lord (8:3). For each of these options to have integrity, it is necessary for God not to know what will in fact happen—namely, that the negative judgment will be exacted. If the positive future of v. 4b is a genuine possibility for the king, then it must be a possibility, and only a possibility, for God as well.[7]

Once again we see how deeply God has entered into the human situation. God is faced with possibilities as Israel is, with all that a dilemma means in terms of reflection, planning, and openness to alternative courses of action, depending upon the course of events. Where the divine perspective exceeds the human may be said to lie in the ability to delineate all of the possibilities of the future, and the likelihood of their occurrence, in view of a thoroughgoing knowledge of the past and present. Thus, an Old Testament view of omniscience must somehow take into account these more limited perspectives.[8] In fact, in more general terms, such a definition may be necessary for God in order for there to be a truly personal relationship: God, too, faces possibilities. For God the future is not something which is closed. God, too, moves into a future which is to some extent unknown.

## THE DIVINE CONSULTATION

It is clear from the foregoing that God will take into consideration human thought and action in determining what God's own action will be. In other words, human response can contribute in a genuine way to the shaping of the future of both God and Israel—indeed, the world as well. There are other passages which may serve to fill out this picture, specifically those which speak of God's consultation with prophetic leaders.

   (a) Gen. 18:7–22:

> The Lord said, "Shall I hide from Abraham what I am about to do . . . ? No, for I have chosen [or known] him. . . . Because the outcry against Sodom and Gomorrah is great and their sin is very grave, I will go down to see whether they have done altogether according to the outcry which has come to me; and if not, I will know." . . . And the Lord stood before Abraham.[9]

Before God does what he is "about to do," Abraham is made privy to the divine intention.[10] In fact, the "Shall I hide from Abraham?" suggests that, given the relationship, it would be unnatural to do anything of the sort. Such a sharing of matters seems to be viewed as integral to the relationship. Verse 21 makes it clear that God has not *finally* determined that Sodom shall suffer doom, as he "goes down to see whether."[11] This divine if (*'im*) relates not to God's actual knowledge of the situation in Sodom, but to whether its inhabitants' behavior is commensurate with "the outcry against"[12] and what it no doubt called for—namely, destruction. This names the issue for God: justice for the city.[13] Thus, Abraham's question in v. 23: "Wilt thou indeed destroy the righteous with the wicked?" identifies the very issue that God's advent is intended to address. But it is God's agenda before it is Abraham's. Even more, if God has come "to see whether" (v. 21), and then proceeds to "stand before Abraham," this certainly means an intent to invite consideration from Abraham regarding the matter of v. 21. The conversation with Abraham follows smoothly. Abraham is drawn into the divine deliberation regarding proper justice for the city.[14] Abraham's questioning and intercession thus lead to both God and Abraham being clear that God's decision is just.[15]

For this conversation to have any integrity, it thus seems necessary for the destruction of Sodom to be only a probability or a possibility, waiting upon the God/Abraham discussion before the final "go ahead" in the execution of the decision is given. Thus, human thought is taken into consideration by God in the shaping of the future.

(b) Exod. 32:7–14 (cf. Deut. 9:13–29). This text reveals a comparable relationship between God and Moses with respect to the future of the people of Israel. As Childs points out,[16] a key phrase for understanding this passage is God's unusual charge to Moses: "Now therefore let me alone, that my wrath may burn hot against them" (v. 10). For such a word to make sense, one must assume that, while God had decided to execute wrath (v. 14, "the evil which he thought to do"), the decision had not yet reached an irretrievable point; Moses could conceivably contribute something to the divine deliberation that might occasion a future for Israel other than wrath. The devastation of Israel by the divine wrath is thus conditional upon Moses' leaving God alone. While one might wonder about the strange language used—we cannot hear the tone of the remark, "leave me alone," but it may well relate to the isolation desired to suffer grief— God thereby does leave the door of Israel's future open. Remarkably, Moses does not heed the divine request; his boldness matches that of Abraham. He then proceeds to give God a number of reasons why consuming wrath should not be executed (vv. 11–13), and thereby convinces God to reverse the decision (v. 14).

The nature of Moses' argument is striking. It bears certain similarities with the lament, particularly those statements designed to motivate God to act (see Pss. 13:3–4; 79:9–10; 89:3–4, 19–37; cf. Ps. 106:8; Ezek. 20:8b–22, 42–44; 36:22–23). The three points of the argument are as follows: (a) if the people have only just been delivered, what sense does it make to turn immediately and reverse that action (v. 11); (b) a concern for God's reputation among the Egyptians (v. 12; see Exod. 9:13–16, 29–30); (c) a reminder of God's promises to the fathers.

While these ought not be considered arguments that God had not thought of before, to have them articulated in a forceful way by one who has been invited into deliberation regarding Israel's future gives them a new status. That is, God takes Moses' contribution with utmost seriousness; God's acquiescence to the arguments indicates that God treats the conversation with Moses with integrity and honors the human insight as an important ingredient for the shaping of the future. If Moses thinks these things, they take on a significance that they do not carry when treated in isolation by the divine mind. Hence, Moses' arguments include a concern not only for the future of Israel but also for the future of God.[17]

A virtual parallel to this passage is Num. 14:11–20, except that the divine lament accompanying the announcement of judgment is made more explicit (v. 11, cf. v. 27).[18] Moreover, the argument relative to God's reputation is fuller (vv. 13–16) and, in addition, God's gracious nature is appealed to (vv. 17–19). In this connection, one should also note Num. 16:20–27. This passage contains a direct appeal from Moses and Aaron, with a remarkable resemblance to Gen. 18:23–25: "O God, the God of the spirits of all flesh, shall one man sin, and wilt thou be angry with all the congregation?" (Num. 20:22). The issue raised is one of justice. To this argumentation God acquiesces; God will be just. God has Moses separate the congregation from the guilty party so that only the guilty experience judgment (vv. 23–27). Thus, God not only invites the considerations of prophetic leaders, he accepts the argumentation and honors it as an important ingredient for the consideration of the shape the congregation's future should take. When God makes a decision, God is open to changing it in light of the ongoing conversation with the leadership of the community of faith.

Turning from the Pentateuch to the Deuteronomic History, one ought to take note of 1 Samuel 15. Upon hearing of God's decision to repent that he had made Saul king, "Samuel was angry; and he cried to the Lord all night" (v. 11). The only plausible explanation for Samuel's behavior (cf. v. 35; 16:1) is that he was thereby seeking to persuade God to take another course regarding the future of Saul. Thus, at least in Samuel's thinking, the announcement of God's decision to repent that he had made Saul king (v. 11) was not irrevocable. While Samuel was not successful in his intercession on Saul's behalf, the point is still made that God, through the announcement of his decision, had given Samuel the opportunity to respond to that decision before it became irrevocable.

From the preceding texts a pattern begins to appear with respect to God's approach to matters of judgment. Having made a decision or devised a plan, God consults with the prophetic leadership regarding possible insight they might having regarding the situation before God proceeds to carry that decision forth into action.

Upon turning to the prophets we find ample evidence to show a continuance in the usage of this pattern. For example, God's decision for judgment is twice revealed to Amos in visions (Amos 7:1, 4). In both instances, however, it is apparent from Amos's response (vv. 2, 5), and God's response to Amos (vv. 3, 6), that God's decision with respect to Israel's future is not irrevocable. Amos is given an opportunity to state a contrary case, and he is twice successful in turning back the divine decision (vv. 3, 6). The initial announcement of God's decision of judgment means that that is a probable future for Israel, but the openness to Amos's response entailed in the announcement means that there is also another possibility for the future which is just as real for God as for Israel.[19]

Consider also Amos 3:7: "Surely the Lord God does nothing, without revealing his secret to his servants the prophets" (cf. Jer. 23:18, 22).[20] While this passage may sound as if God announces a series of *faits accomplis* to the prophets, the examples cited above suggest another interpretation. Namely, God reveals his secret to the prophets precisely in order to draw them into the sphere of decision making with respect to the future of the people.[21] God does nothing without consultation! Though J. L. Mays[22] is not particularly fond of the implications of this verse, he is right in saying that "the prophet becomes a *sine qua non* of divine action." But even more, *consultation* with the prophet becomes the *sine qua non*. This *does* "bind Yahweh's sovereign freedom," precisely because God has chosen to give the prophet such an important role to play in the decision-making process. The future thus remains open-ended to some extent even for God, depending on the results of the prophetic conversation. The announcement of God to the prophets does not have the status of an immutable decree, but of a possibility to be explored together, as we have just seen in connection with Amos 7:1–9.[23]

Finally, consider the oft-debated commands of God to Jeremiah that he not intercede on Israel's behalf: "As for you, do not pray for this people, or lift up cry or prayer for them, and do not intercede with me, for I do not hear you" (Jer. 7:16; cf. 11:14; 14:11; 15:1). If only from a negative perspective, these passages indicate that the role of the prophet entailed such mediatorial activity, and that such activity would affect God's actions toward his people. Jer. 18:20 (cf. 15:11) speaks positively of Jeremiah's effectiveness in turning aside the wrath of God, and in a way that parallels Moses' (cf. Ps. 106:23). Moreover, these prohibitions parallel God's word to Moses in Exod. 32:10, "let me alone," though they are somewhat more sharply reinforced by the uselessness of such an effort. But why should God be so insistent on this point? Certainly not to save Jeremiah some time on his knees! It may reflect a God/prophet dispute as to whether the divine decision should proceed to action.

The redaction of these passages suggests that Jeremiah, like Moses, went on interceding in spite of—after each, except the last of—the divine commands (cf. 8:18–22; 14:1–9, 19–22, where the prophet serves as representative for the people in their lament).[24] Even in the face of the prohibition, Jeremiah believed that his prayers might be effective, that God's decision might be revoked. But only for a time, as 18:20–23 and 20:11–12 (cf. 11:20) make clear. Jeremiah turns from his role as intercessor (cf. 15:5), though not out of personal pique or crankiness (cf. 17:16), to what Mauser calls conformity with the wrath of God.[25] Thus, the repeated prohibition is finally recognized by Jeremiah as, in effect, an announcement that the divine patience on this matter is at an end (see 15:6), that the onslaught of judgment is now inevitable (cf. Amos 7:7–9 and Genesis 18).[26] But the repetition is also important *for God*; the prophet now stands with God with respect to his decision regarding the future, for the future has now been reduced to only one possibility: judgment. Jeremiah does.

## THE DIVINE QUESTION

Finally, we turn to the questions present in divine speech. What kinds of questions does God ask? The normally unexamined assumption is that all such divine questions are rhetorical, asked by God for effect in one situation or another, and not "real" questions seeking to elicit an answer. Yet there is considerably more variety here than one might at first suppose. It is not our purpose here to examine closely the various types of questions God asks.[27] Here we consider two types.

First of all, certain passages seem to talk about the divine decision-making process with respect to Israel's future:

> What shall I do with you, O Ephraim?
> What shall I do with you, O Judah?
>                 (Hos. 6:4; cf. 11:8a)

> How can I pardon you? . . .
> Shall I not punish them for these things?
>                 (Jer. 5:7, 9; cf. v. 29; 9:7, 9)

With respect to the Hosea passage, Wolff states that God is "struggling with himself,"and is engaged in "self-questioning";[28] Mays uses the word "perplexed"; [29] Janzen speaks of God being "baffled";[30] and Freedman and Andersen use the following language: "God searches in his mind what to do"; his is an "agony (turbulence) of indecision"; God is "vacillating."[31]

It is striking that these scholars can use such language in the first place, given the general status of God-talk in OT theological work. In addition, with the exception of Janzen, there is little reflection here on what the use of such language might entail regarding the nature of the God of these prophets. One wonders whether they have carefully considered the use of such language, or whether their analyses are off-hand, perhaps experimental. Perhaps they would insist that such language is "only" analogical, and must not be literally pressed.[32] Yet, as we have seen,[33] metaphoric language must have some reasonable relationship to reality; such language says something about God just as much as words like "constant" or "wise" or "decisive" do. At the least, it needs to be admitted that this scholarly language is elusive in what it intends to say about the God of the text. One could conclude from such comments that God's wisdom is not sufficient for the task at hand. Or, that God simply does not have the resources to know rightly what to do. Or, that indecisiveness and vacillation are generally characteristic of God's relationship to people and world; and, if in this case, why not whenever God is faced with difficult decisions? Another direction of thought seems preferable.

I suggest that these questions are reflective of the divine council deliberations between God and prophet (see chap. 10). But, whereas in most prophets this deliberation is not so directly conveyed to the people, in Hosea (cf. 6:4) and Jeremiah in particular a more direct reflection of that conversation is set forth. For what purpose?

One, to elicit repentance.[34] The announcements of judgment are "interrupted" with such divine questions in order to move Israel to repentance. But, how might that be expected to happen? When God shares such questions with Israel about its own future, God's questions then become questions for Israel, and they are drawn into the process of moving toward an answer.[35] The people now have a role to play in determining what the answer to the question will be, not unlike that given a rebellious child when asked by the parent: "What am I going to do with you?" A dialogue should ensue regarding the question, and by the responses God and people share with one another regarding the question, a resolution may begin to emerge. But, what is crucial for the discussion is the kind of God who is revealed in the sharing of the question. The very fact that God shares such questions reveals something about God; God opens himself up to risk; God becomes vulnerable. For the more one shares of oneself, the greater the possibility of being hurt. Finally, it is such a portrait of God, a suffering God, that, it is hoped, will prompt repentance. If the people do repent, then the question for God and people is resolved. If the people do not repent, then the answer for God and people would seem to be resolved in the direction of judgment. Yet, Hos. 11:8–9 reveals that, in spite of the lack of repentance, God has moved toward an intermediate response: judgment without annihilation.

Two, it relates to the perception the people would have, should such judgment be forthcoming. In sharing such questions, the people can see very clearly the divine agony that has preceded and would accompany any judgment. Thus they could have no uncertainty regarding the highly personal—nonlegal, nonhasty, nonvindictive, and noncapricious—way in which God has deliberated over the matter. Indeed, God has shared the decision-making process with those whose future is at stake.

This latter point needs to be underscored. Whereas God has shared the decision-making process with prophetic leaders, here God extends that process to include the people as a whole. A decision has been announced (e.g., Hos. 5:14), but God "return[s] to [his] place" (5:15) to see if repentance might yet be forthcoming. In this context, the questions of 6:4 are addressed, to function as we have noted. The future remains open-ended; the decision for judgment is not irrevocable. Thus, by the questions, God indicates that the divine moves into a future which is as yet unknown; there can be no certainty with respect to what will happen as God pursues this new direction. The clear implication is that the future will bring new knowledge for God, as well as for the people; this will affect what God says and does.

What does this direction in the text say about the use of words such as "indecisive" and "vacillating"? While the lament character of these materials needs to be explored further, it would appear that such language is not true to the mark. The questions are addressed by God to the people between the decision and the execution of the judgment, for the purposes noted. Preliminarily, God has decided what to do; it is the execution of the decision that remains in question. This time-lag does not reveal indecisiveness in God, but the sharing of the decision-making process with the people, and an openness to their response. God holds back on a final decision, not because God is indecisive, but because God wants the decision to be shared. And yet, it is a genuine question for God, and one from which God will learn, as God and people move toward an answer together.

Then there are the questions which speak more of the present as related to the past than to the future. These questions also seem to go beyond the common rhetorical question or counterquestion characteristic of "disputation-speeches" (e.g., Isa. 40:21–31).[36]

> Have I been a wilderness to Israel,
>     or a land of thick darkness?
> Why then do my people say, "We are free,
>     we will no more come to thee"?
>                           (Jer. 2:31)

> Why then has this people turned away
>     in perpetual backsliding?
>                           (Jer. 8:5)

> Why have they provoked me to anger with their graven images,
>     and with their foreign idols?
>                           (Jer. 8:19c; cf. 2:14b; 30:6; Isa. 5:4; 50:2)

These questions seem to imply a genuine loss on God's part as to what might explain the faithlessness of the people. The use of "why?"

(*maddûaʻ*) elsewhere in Jeremiah by people (14:19; 32:3; 26:9; 13:22; cf. 14:8–9) and prophet (8:23; 12:1; 22:28) suggests a genuine questioning with regard to the explanation of events. "Why" can certainly be used in divine speech in an accusatory fashion, without any implications regarding divine knowledge (e.g., 36:29), but that does not seem to be the case here.[37] The lament character of the passages suggests that pain and frustration are primarily in view. The "why" would thus be a poignant cry, with no specific answer being sought. Yet there might be another note here. God knows all there is to know about what has prompted the people to take this direction with their lives; it still makes no sense. Thus, it would appear that there simply is no explanation available, nor will there ever be, even for God.

A contrary claim regarding divine foreknowledge seems to be made in other OT passages such as Ps. 139:1–6 or Isaiah 40—55.[38] Yet it is doubtful that such texts can be called upon to support complete divine knowledge of the future. Psalm 139 makes only limited claims in this regard.[39] God has so "searched and known" (v. 1, cf. vv. 23–24) the psalmist that there is a thorough acquaintance with him and his ways (vv. 2–3), even to such an extent that his thoughts are known before they issue in speech (v. 4). Such divine knowledge is indeed wonderful, unattainable by the human (v. 6), but not necessarily limitless with respect to the future. Second Isaiah testifies to the unsearchability of God's knowledge (40:28), and speaks of God's predictions of things which are to come (e.g., 42:9; 46:10–11), a point at which Israel's God is differentiated from other gods (e.g., 41:21–23; 44:7–8). Yet, such passages only claim that God knows what *God* will do in the future, and that God will accomplish God's purposes. Thus, from a Christian perspective, God will send God's Son; God will pour out God's Spirit; God will raise the dead from their graves. Most future-oriented prophetic texts are open-ended, dependent in some way on human response, and hence indeterminate.

From these considerations regarding divine foreknowledge one may conclude that any talk about divine omniscience in the OT must be limited when it comes to talk about the future. It is limited in such a way as to include a genuine divine openness to the future—an openness which, however, is constantly informed by the divine will to save.[40]

One might also say that the OT does not limit divine omniscience at all, if properly defined. Traditional formulations of omniscience have always recognized that God cannot know contradictions, and the point made here is simply an extension of that—namely, God cannot know that which is only possible, that which does not yet exist to be known. God knows everything there is to be known. As new things happen and come to be knowable for the first time, God knows them as actualities, not only as possibilities. This, of course, implies that God's knowledge is thereby increased, which entails change for God; new knowledge means real change. Again, we see that God's relationship to others in time and history is real and affects the very life of God.

We now need to indicate what are the implications of the God-world discussion to this point; they will often inform subsequent considerations. It is clear that the finite is capable of the infinite, that the created is capable of being a vehicle for divine immanence; this is a perspective which will inform our considerations of theophany and of the prophet's relationship to God. Moreover, given God's immersion in and commitment to the world, God can never again act in complete independence from the world; all that God is and does will be for the sake of the relationship. It is also evident that divine self-limitation is an integral aspect of the God-world relationship. This free act of self-limitation, taken entirely at the divine initiative for the sake of the relationship, might be described as a divine *kenosis,* a self-emptying, an act of self-sacrifice. The very act of creation thus might be called the beginning of the passion of God. God has so entered into the world that God cannot but be affected by its life, including its sinful life. Because this condescending God fully relates to sinful creatures with integrity, and with the deepest possible love, God cannot but suffer, and in manifold ways.

This understanding of the God-world relationship also has implications for the world side of the relationship. It means that there is no experience of the world without a concomitant experience of God, for where there is world there is God; there will be differences in the degree and kind of experience, and these will not always be realized. Moreover, this means that a relationship with God does not entail an escape from the world, for it is precisely in the world that one meets God and lives with God. Life with God will always also mean life in the world, and not in a specific slice of the world or in the gaps of the world, but wherever one is in the world.

Yet, there are distinctions that need to be made with respect to the *way* God is in the world. And to that issue we now turn, using the category of presence.

# CHAPTER 5

# God and World:
# Presence and Power

One could conceivably use "presence" in a univocal way: presence equals thereness. To be present is to be here or there, period! Yet we do speak of people having a certain "presence," whose "thereness" is such that it has the effect of being more felt and effective than that of others. Differences in energy level, focus, direction, or attention also determine degrees in our understanding of the presence of someone (e.g., "she really wasn't with us today"). Also to be considered is the competing presence of others. The presence of some persons can make others "back off" or be less forceful for a variety of reasons. Thus, I will speak of differing intensifications of the divine presence.

I do not intend to speak of issues relating to the divine presence in any full way.[1] Rather, I am interested in those issues which will fill out our understanding of the God-world relationship, and set the stage for subsequent considerations, particularly regarding theophany. Four such matters need to be discussed at this point.

## INTENSIFICATIONS OF THE
## DIVINE PRESENCE

Presence does not necessarily mean the same thing wherever it is encountered in the pages of the OT.[2] Thus, the God who appears promises to be with the recipients beyond the time and place of appearing (e.g., Gen. 26:24; 28:15). Though Jonah flees "from the presence of the Lord" (Jon. 1:3), he still professes belief in a Creator God (1:9). The departure of the tabernacling God from the Temple (Ezek. 10:1–22; 11:22–25) does not mean that God's accompanying presence can no longer be spoken of (11:16). Though the psalmist prays to a God who has forsaken him (22:1), the very existence of the prayer indicates that "forsakenness" has reference to the loss of a certain intensification of presence, and not to the loss of presence altogether (cf. also Exod. 33:1–3).

Undergirding all forms of presence[3] is God's presence in the created order, what might be termed "structural" or general presence (see 1 Kings 8:27; Job 38—41; Psalm 139; Jer. 23:23–24;[4] Amos 9:2–6).There is no reason to doubt that this understanding was present from earliest times in Israel.[5] It was drawn at least in part from Israel's Babylonian/Egyptian heritage, and provided important conceptual materials for the articulation of, among other matters, the meaning of God's redemptive activity (cf. Exodus 15; 1 Samuel 2).[6] More specific modes of God's presence are thus handled well theologically only in the context of this all-pervading presence of God in the creation. It is this presence which provides for the actual possibility of those more specific forms of presence in the community of faith, because it is this which places God within and related to the creation in the first place. Without this as the given, or being neglectful of this as the given, the idea of a God who is present can be perceived only as an interruption of the natural order, or as radically discontinuous from life in creation generally. Unless this underlying principle is carefully guarded, havoc can develop in any community of faith—as it perhaps did for Israel during the exile, and hence the special emphasis on creation in the literature of that time. For when the specific forms of presence are no longer evident, the community might perceive there is no real divine presence left to fall back on. Thus, God's structural presence provides the necessary context for developing and understanding more specific and concrete ways of divine presence in the community of faith.

With this principle as a base, one can perhaps think in terms of a continuum to describe the more specific modes of divine presence. God's accompanying presence could be placed on one end, God's theophanic presence (appearance) on the other, with God's tabernacling presence (and perhaps others) at intermediate points. One might speak of a greater intensification of presence as one moves across the continuum toward that which is more and more specific, articulate, tangible, and formful. God's presence in the created orders of time and space is concurrent with these intensifications. Thus, God is believed to be continuously present, yet God will also be especially present at certain times; God is believed to be everywhere present, yet God will also be especially present in certain places.

What is it that occasions this variety in intensifications of presence? Such variety is not to be laid at the feet of some notion of divine incoherence or inconstancy. It is, rather, to be closely correlated with the specific needs and experiences of people in particular times and places. As human beings, God's people are inextricably bound up in space and time, and have differing needs and experiences associated with both, depending upon the life situation. Thus, for example, people experience different intensifications of both time and space. There are those times which are especially filled or concentrated, and which consequently inform all of life in a way that few other times do (e.g., a conversion experience). Moreover, contemporary discussions of "rootedness" have recognized that certain spaces are more filled with meaning than are others (e.g., a home town). And so God, knowing the need of people for God's presence in the *totality* of their existence, has chosen to enter both time and space, to be with them there in the varying intensities of their experience, and to meet their need for the specific, the tangible, the personal, and the articulate. These varying intensities of the divine presence are thus related to the varying intensities of human need and experience.

Among other things, this means that, while God is always present, God's presence is significantly affected by human experience.

First, we note that this correlation of human and divine times and places had an immeasurable effect upon Israel's practice of the presence of God. Israel's life of worship could not afford to be careless of times and places. Thus, provisions were made, not only in cognizance of the needs of people for those moments and those spaces, but also in view of God, who acknowledged those structures of human existence in determining the nature of the way in which God could be present among the people. Thus, one of the functions of a regularized worship was to set aside times and places, not only for the people, but also for God. In providing vehicles for the divine presence, God acts not only for the sake of the people but also for the sake of God's name (Exod. 20:24; Lev. 21:6; 22:2) and glory (Lev. 10:3), so that God could be as intimately and effectively present as possible with the people whom God loved.

It is not in order for us to pursue in detail the various intensifications of presence, but a few remarks are important in order to provide some context for our later discussion of theophany. God's *accompanying presence* refers to God's presence with his people in all their journeyings. Rooted in the time of the patriarchs,[7] God binds himself to families in all of their wanderings (cf. Gen. 28:15). This is especially prominent during the wilderness wanderings, in connection with which the language of name (Exod. 23:22), cloud and fire (13:21–22), messenger (23:20–21), and face/presence (33:14) is used. This mode of divine presence continues to pervade Israel's experience (e.g., Josh. 1:5–9; 2 Sam. 7:5–7; Psalm 23), and becomes important especially during exilic times (e.g., Jer. 29:12–14).

God's *tabernacling presence* refers to the divine choice of a specific place to dwell among the people (e.g., ark; temple).[8] This more intensified form of presence is different from the foregoing in that the community can with assurance say not only that God is among them, but that God's presence is focused in a particular place. This represents a gracious condescension to the need of the human for that which is concrete and focused. God chooses a place because God has entered into history with a people for whom place is important. If place is important for people, it is important for God. To speak of presence in connection with place also helps preserve the personal character of the divine presence, for persons are always associated with places.

God is determined to provide the people with regular access to God's more intensified forms of presence; such is the will of God to be as forcefully present with the people as possible. Thus, we find an emphasis on God's "desire" to be so present (cf. Pss. 132:13–14; 78:68; 87:2; cf. Hos. 6:6). This move from the side of God, however, seems to be as much for God's sake as for the people's. God desires a place for himself! This shows what more intensified forms of presence mean to God; such a closeness of presence will enhance the intimacy of the relationship with the people whom God loves. It makes a difference to both God and people.

To speak of place can lead to difficulties, however. It might suggest that God's abode is fixed and merely local, leading to notions that God might be controlled, with the place used as a talisman in the interests of "eternal security." This is particularly the case when the place no longer moves with the community (2 Sam. 7:5–7), but is anchored on Mt. Zion. Such dangers are especially present at those points where the contact between God and people is the most intimate (cf., e.g., the Lord's Supper in the Christian tradition). Those in relationship become more vulnerable the more they collapse the distance between them, the more they share of themselves. God's "homing" in Israel means for God a greater vulnerability; God can be more easily hurt by advantages assumed and presumptions advanced. Yet that is a risk which God is willing to take for closeness.

The prophets do speak out when such abuses arise (see, e.g., Jer. 7:3–12). Yet it is important to remember that it is not primarily the temple theology per se which proved to be the "culprit" (cf. Ezekiel 40—48). Idolatrous practices incorporated into Israel's worship, largely under continuing Canaanite influence (see 2 Kings 21), were seen to be the real problem in the various reforms which were carried out, not only in Jerusalem but in all sanctuaries (cf. 2 Kings 23).[9]

Deuteronomy 12, however, suggests that some new understandings of the nature of the divine presence in the temple were fostered in the seventh century, particularly in the so-called "name theology" (cf. vv. 5, 11).[10] This would seem to be a reduction in intensification of presence. Yet, even with all of Deuteronomy's tendencies toward individualization and spiritualization, the presence of God is still associated with a particular place. The divine presence is thus not reduced to spirituality, as if the human personality were somehow the only fit place on earth for God's presence, or even the community apart from times and places. Place remains important for God because it is important for people and their relationships with one another.

Continuing alongside of the name theology, however, is an older tradition which speaks of the glory of the Lord. This language for a particularly intensified divine presence is present in a variety of traditions (e.g., 1 Kings 8:11; Ezek. 9:3; Exod. 24:15–17), and is used both for tabernacling presence and with theophanies.[11] "Glory" may have been used for just such a concentrated presence so as to distinguish it from other types of presence which we have considered. Thus, through the use of such language, there would be less conceptual difficulty in continuing to think, say, of God's presence in Jerusalem after the glory of the Lord departs with the fall of the city (Ezek. 10:1–22; 11:22–25). Once the glory has been driven out by the wickedness of the people (Ezek. 8:6), one can no longer speak of the tabernacling presence of God in Jerusalem. Yet it is still possible to affirm God's presence in exile (Jer. 29:12–15) and after (Isa. 57:15), although the return of the glory of the Lord remains an expectation for the future (e.g., Mal. 3:1). Thus, a fluidity in the understanding of divine presence enables the community to be assured of God's presence in their midst, although the more intensified forms await a future moment. But the community knows that God desires to be as intimately present as possible, so its hope is a certain one (cf. John 1:14, for the NT shape of the fulfillment).

Finally, regarding tabernacling presence, it needs to be said that God's dwelling among the people is an act of grace, based on promise. From earliest days (e.g., Gen. 17:8), Israel believed itself to be the recipient of such a promise, with all that that meant for fullness of presence in relationship. It is God's gracious act of condescension to be near and accessible, to provide for the people's need for that which is concrete, and to be assured in such a tangible way that God is always with them and for them. And, because God loves them, God would like nothing better for himself.

## DIVINE PRESENCE AND DIVINE ABSENCE

Issues relating to divine absence are best understood within the context of varying intensifications of presence. Corresponding to intensifications of presence would be types of divine absence. The absence of God would appear never to mean more than the loss of one intensification of presence or another. The structural absence of God, however, never seems to be considered as a possibility in the Old Testament. The Old Testament language of absence (e.g., "hide," "withdraw," "forsake," etc.) always entails presence at some level of intensification, albeit diminished. This language cannot be considered in detail here, but certain general trends might be charted.

It is clear that human experience, especially human receptiveness or sin, can affect the intensity of the divine presence. Thus, because the people "have made their deeds evil," God "will hide his face from them at that time" (Mic. 3:4; cf. Deut. 32:19–20). Similarly, "your iniquities have made a separation between you and your God, and your sins have hid his face from you so that he does not hear" (Isa. 59:2; cf. 54:6–8; 57:17). Second Chron. 15:2 (cf. 12:5; 24:20) indicates that the divine forsaking is a reflex of human forsaking. Ezekiel 8:6 goes so far as to state that God has been "driven" far from the sanctuary by Israel's abominations. God's presence is not a "forced entry"; indeed, the human response can push God back along the continuum of presence so that it becomes less intense, and hence less felt and less positively effective.

This increasing distance would appear to make for an intensification of divine presence of another sort, namely wrath (see Jer. 33:5). Yet the images seem to function differently. The movement away *is* a movement of wrath (Isa. 54:8); wrath is a distancing. The result is that Israel's enemies flow into the "spaces" left by the divine withdrawal, and Israel is delivered into their hands (Isa. 64:7; Jer. 12:7; Ezek. 39:23). On the far side of hiddenness, in eschatological vision, the intensity of the divine presence pours into Israel's life again (Ezek. 39:29).

All of the prophetic references to this phenomenon of presence (except Isa. 45:15)[12] are apparently to be interpreted in these terms. The basic issue at stake is not one of knowing God; it is one of having God, having God present in especially intense ways, which will affect knowing, but that is a distinguishable issue.[13]

The Psalms in particular speak of an anguish over the divine absence because of sin (Pss. 44:23; 74:1, 10; 89:46; cf. Lam. 5:20), and wonder about the length of the absence and the seeming finality of it. A few texts (e.g., Job 13:24; Ps. 22:1) question the divine absence in the face of causes unknown, while 2 Chron. 32:31 speaks of a divine withdrawal from Hezekiah "in order to try him and to know all that was in his heart" (cf. Job). This last passage (and others, e.g., Hos. 5:15) speaks of a divine purposefulness which is at work in withdrawal from a certain intensity of presence. Even in such action, God's will for the salvation of his people remains intact. Thus, while God's presence *to* Israel is diminished in intensity, God's presence *for* Israel remains alive and well in the world, though that may remain hidden from their eyes.

One other matter needs to be dealt with here, namely, the question of structural or epistemic distance, perhaps best evidenced in the OT statement, "You cannot see God and live." The specific OT language of "hiddenness" seems never to have reference to epistemic distance. This is a distance which is structured into the created order of things for the purpose of preserving human freedom. For God to be fully present would be coercive; faith would be turned into sight and humankind could not but believe. For God to be loved by people for God's own sake, without being forced into it, requires a measure of human autonomy. Too direct a divine presence would annul human existence as a flame kills a butterfly. God must set people at a certain distance from God; whatever the intensification of presence, there must be an element of ambiguity. God's presence cannot be obvious. But it is important to remember that this is a given of creation, within which the divine will for intimate presence is at work.

All of this says something further about God. While God's saving will for his people is clear and God's desire for intimate presence is constant, God honors human decisions and structures of creation; sometimes, God cannot or will not be present in ways that God would like to be. This is not to say that God's presence does not "break through" in special intensifications from time to time, even when all the red lights seem to be on. Yet, even this is due to what becomes possible for God in view of what is happening in the world, most particularly the openness of the situation itself and the readiness and responsiveness of the people. But God is unsurpassed in watching for openings; God can discern a "fullness of time" when the whole world seems to be sleeping.

DIVINE FREEDOM AND ACCESSIBILITY[14]

This twin issue is often said to constitute a polarity: While God has promised to be accessible to the people, God's presence cannot be made into a possession; God is available and his presence is real, but there is an elusiveness which escapes any grasping. While an important principle regarding presence is being enunciated here, some discussions have so weighted the polarity on the side of divine freedom that the polarity itself is threatened.[15]

It seems to me that a rather general principle should guide our discussions of this matter: God *desires* to be as effectively present as possible, in all times and places. "For the Lord has chosen Zion; he has desired it for his habitation; 'This is my resting place for ever; here I will dwell, for I have desired it' " (Ps. 132:13–14; see also

1 Sam. 6:10–12).[16] God does not want to be elusive or be absent from his people. God is eager to be present. It may be, as we have seen, that in view of the human situation, God cannot or will not be present among them in a way that God would like. But this is not because of some desire on God's part to be elusive or inaccessible, but because of, and ultimately for the sake of, the people.

At the same time, God's (forced) withdrawal from one situation or another ought not to be interpreted in terms of divine freedom. Thus, for example, when in Exod. 33:3 God states that God will not go up with the people, the reason given is "lest I consume you." It is the well-being of the people that provides the motivation for the divine "pulling back" from a more intensified presence. Or, Ezek. 43:7–9 makes it clear that the departure of the glory of God from Jerusalem occurred because God's name had been profaned and defiled. God's actions for the sake of his name involve, at least in part, issues of credibility and apologetic, a concern for what might happen to God in relationship to the world, not just Israel, if certain actions are not taken. Ultimately, this sort of action on God's part is not motivated out of a selfish concern, but for the sake of God's relationship with the world. And the fact that God's glory does return to Jerusalem in this eschatological vision is a sign that the departure is for the sake of a larger, salvific purpose. Thus, far from being a display of divine freedom, God's forced departure is decisively informed by God's promises and saving purposes—the only way in which God's will for closeness and intimacy might eventually be realized.

God's constant will for presence can also be seen in other eschatological passages which speak of a future when distance shall no longer be characteristic of the God-people relationship. Thus, Isa. 52:8 (cf. Jer. 32:4 for a human situation): "Hark, your watchmen lift up their voice, together they sing for joy; for eye to eye they see the return of the Lord to Zion" (cf. Isa. 40:5). Thus, the OT stands in fundamental continuity with 1 Cor. 13:12: "For now we see in a mirror dimly, but then face to face."

On the whole, the desire of God for accessibility and closeness needs to be more decisively related to promise. As Hag. 2:4–5 puts it: "I am with you, says the Lord of hosts, according to the promise that I made you." At least three of the intensifications of presence are associated with a promise (accompanying, tabernacling, and theophany):

> I am with you and will keep you wherever you go.
> (Gen. 28:15; cf. Josh. 1:1–9)

> And I will dwell among the people of Israel, and will be their God.
> (Exod. 29:45)

> In every place where I cause my name to be remembered I will come to you and bless you.
> (Exod. 20:24)

God's promise, indeed God's election of Israel in the first place, places a decisive limitation on any talk about divine freedom. God has exercised freedom in making such promises; but having freely made the promise, thereafter God's freedom is truly limited by that promise. God will do what God says God will do; God will be faithful to God's own promises. In some sense, then, divine presence moving toward its fullest possible intensification is a *divine necessity;* it is that for which the God of promise will always strive, if it ever comes short of realization.[17]

Moreover, the fact that the entire system of worship is understood to be a gift of God to the people, means that God has graciously provided for just such promised closeness. As Lev. 9:4 puts it so boldly: "Today the Lord will appear to you." God wills to be present with and for God's people, and has provided the vehicles for it. It is true that God's promise can be misused, and God's presence taken for granted or viewed as an inalienable right (see Mic. 3:11; Jer. 7:4). This is an important point that must not be forgotten. Yet it does not detract from God's will for presence. As a result of such presumption, God may indeed be forced out of the temple, or out of one situation in life or another, so that God cannot or will not be present, or has to act for the sake of God's name. But such developments are not in order to demonstrate some freedom God has, as if God's freedom were what was really at stake in such situations—as if God were saying, "I will show this people that I am really free!" What is at stake, finally, is the profanation of the name of God, with all that that means for God's salvific purposes.

It would then appear that the freedom/accessibility language might be too problematic to be helpful; it does not capture what is really at stake here. It does not clearly delineate God's will for presence; neither does it sufficiently recognize the extent to which God has given up freedom for the sake of the promise. Hence, I suggest that it would serve our purposes better if we spoke of divine presence as gift, to be possessed though not presumed upon, and as promise, reliable though not irresistible.

## IMMANENCE AND TRANSCENDENCE[18]

A few words here on transcendence seem important. It is not uncommon to reflect on this matter by equating immanence and presence, with transcendence finding its place in talk about distance, "wholly otherness," or nonpresence. However, immanence should be more broadly understood in terms of "relatedness," of which presence is a significant component, while transcendence should be stripped of its narrow spatial associations and used to speak of the way in which the Godness of God manifests itself in this "relatedness"—for God, a permanent state of affairs.

Perhaps the phrase, "in your midst is the Holy One" (Isa. 12:6; Hos. 11:9; cf. Ezek. 20:41; 28:22) can assist us here.[19] This phrase indicates that holiness, one important biblical word for speaking of transcendence, and presence do not stand opposed to one another.[20] It is probably also true to say that the language of polarity does not capture the sense either, as if holiness and presence stood in some tension with each other. Rather, it is *as* the Holy One that God is present. As Isa. 12:6 puts it, "for great in your midst is the Holy One of Israel." The transcendence of God is thus manifested by the *way in which* God is present among his people.[21] It is not just that any God or God in some attentuated form is present among the people, it is the Holy God, a God who does great things and, in terms of Hos. 11:9, is compassionate and merciful in every way with Israel.[22] While holiness often speaks to the categorical difference between God and humankind, as Hos. 11:9 reflects (Godness and humanness are distinct categories), it is concerned with the fact that it is *this kind of* God who is present in a certain way. God's holiness is demonstrated not by the revelation of some categorical difference, but by the way in which God is present. And this God *is* present—not some emanation of God, nor some bits and pieces of God, but God in all of God's

Godness is present. All of this fits in well with common statements to the effect that "the personal nature of God" is "the focus of statements about holiness."[23]

Sometimes it is suggested that the holiness of God is used to stress God's unapproachableness.[24] But care must be used here. While it might be said that the "regulation of holiness in the cult" was in part done out of "concern not to be harmed by this unpredictable power,"[25] this was not because of the holiness of God per se, except perhaps in these cases where it has reference to epistemic distance, but because of the sinful lot of the people. The precautions in such passages as Exod. 19:21, 24, or Num. 1:51–53 are God-given for the sake of the sinful people. The fact that Moses and many elders (cf. Exod. 24:9–11), as well as the priesthood, *could* approach the special nearness of God seems to belie any notion that holiness in and of itself entails unapproachableness. At the same time, there is concern expressed here for God as well. Lev. 10:3 indicates that such regulations, and resultant effects upon transgression, were so that God "could show himself holy" and "be glorified" before all the people. But, while this is a concern for the future of God, it is not for God in isolation, but for the sake of the future relationship with God's people.

I suggest, therefore, that the immanence/transcendence polarity is not adequate for talk about divine presence. The God who is present is *both* immanent and transcendent; both are appropriate words for a constant divine state of affairs. God is "transcendent in relationship."[26] "God remains transcendent in His immanence, and related in His transcendence."[27]

## PRESENCE, RELATIONSHIP, AND POWER

While issues of the OT understanding of divine power—the strength to exert an influence—are indeed complex, a few comments here are in order.[28]

Two extreme possibilities can be eliminated immediately: deism, the image of God as clockmaker, whose influence in the present is only to be seen in the laws built into the clock in the first place, and determinism, God as the sufficient cause of all things.[29] The difficulty lies in determining where, between these two poles, Israel's understanding of the matter is to be found.

W. Brueggemann has assessed those OT and NT passages which stand in the "trajectory" of Gen. 18:14, "Is anything too hard for the Lord?" (cf. Judg. 13:18–20; Jer. 32:17, 27).[30] He notes that such passages reject "those regnant definitions of what is possible given by the culture." The power of God is not "contained in the best assessment of worldly possibility."[31] While Brueggemann makes the important observation that "only that is possible which is consistent with this God,"[32] he does not explore what this might entail. This is the key issue in the contemporary discussion of divine power. The OT does give certain directions for our thinking on this matter, and, at the same time, enables further directions for our thinking on the relationship between God and world.

1. Divine self-limitations with respect to power are implicit in the promises which God has made. Whenever God makes a promise, God limits the options available for action on any related matters. God cannot use power in such a way as to violate a promise God has made; that would mean unfaithfulness.

In addition to the above-cited promises, another one needs attention.[33] At the end of the flood story in Genesis 8—9, God promises that God will never respond to evil in floodlike ways again (9:11). This is a self-limitation with respect to divine freedom and power. God's use of power in dealing with evil in the world is eternally self-limited.[34]

2. Issues of power are closely related to intensifications of divine presence. We have noted that the intensity of the divine presence can be affected by human sinfulness or receptiveness. God can be driven away or forced into hiding as a result of what people do, with the result that God cannot or will not be present in ways that God would like to be. Thus, God's possibilities are closely related to the responsiveness of the people and the openness of the situation. Because it is not possible for God to be present at every occasion with the same intensity, the divine power that can be brought to bear on each occasion will vary. At the same time, because God's presence is not as contested in the created order as it is in history, God's influence in the former will be more pronounced than in the latter.[35]

3. Any relationship of integrity will entail a sharing of power. God gives up a monopoly on power for the sake of God's relationship with the world—individuals, Israel, and creation. This means that such

common images as master-slave or king-subject cannot be construed in a way to suggest that only the superior has power.

We now need to raise the question how the ever-present God exercises power in the world and what effects divine influence might have. The language of power-sharing would seem to be one especially helpful avenue of approach. At least two types of material seem distinguishable: where God and world are in a power-sharing situation; where a clash of power develops.

(a) The sharing of power can lead to cooperation in attaining those shared goals intended for God's creation. This is true in both the natural and historical orders.

With regard to the created order, the following representative examples will suffice.[36] The creative activity in Genesis 1 is often depicted only in terms of a sovereign unilateral divine act; it is a command performance.[37] For example, the verb *bārā'*, "create," used only for the creative activity of God in the Old Testament, is so stressed that any connection between divine and human creativity is denigrated, or even denied. As a result, creatureliness tends to be viewed solely in terms of dependence and humility, even impotence.

But Genesis 1 ought not be so interpreted. The common use of *'āsāh*, "make," with its many uses in the human sphere, makes it clear that God's creative work is not without analogy. Moreover, Genesis 1 speaks of creation as both mediate and immediate, indirect and direct. In v. 11, the earth is commanded to bring forth vegetation, and it does; in v. 24 it is commanded to bring forth living creatures, and it does so. While v. 25 states that God made the beasts, the nondivine involvement cannot be explained away. The separation sometimes made between divine word and "mother earth" is not appropriate. Although the emphasis throughout is on the divine initiative, the creative capacities of the created are clearly attested.

This *dual agency* is evident also in the ongoing activity of creation, witnessed elsewhere in the OT. Thus, while Ps. 104:14 testifies to God's making the grass and plants grow, Hag. 1:10–11 speaks of the ground itself bringing forth such vegetation, and of the earth withholding its produce. The latter passage also speaks of the *heavens* withholding the rains, while Job 37:6 makes it clear that God is responsible for *every* shower or snowfall. Other passages (e.g., Deut. 28:4 and Ps. 65:9–11, 12–13) also make clear that blessings are due not solely to divine activity, but to a sharing of that creative power with the created order itself.

In the natural order, then, there is neither a "letting go" of the creation on God's part, nor a retention of all such powers unto God. The texts reveal that creative powers are shared; the context determines where the emphasis ought to be placed.[38] *Both* God and the creation are involved in every such ongoing creative act, though God always relates to this order in ways that are appropriate to its nature. Thus it is clear that while God's ongoing creative activity is efficacious, there is a significant element of indeterminacy. If the creative powers of the earth are affected adversely, fundamentally through human sin (see Gen. 3:17–19; Deut. 20:19–20; Hos. 4:1–3), God's possibilities for the earth are thereby affected, and indeed limited.

This relationship between God and the nonhuman is intensified in God's relationship to the human. The command to be fruitful and multiply (Gen. 1:28; cf. 1:22) indicates a decisive sharing of creative powers with the human; Gen. 9:1, 7 indicates that this is an ongoing address from within the created order. Other passages (e.g., Ps. 139:13–16; Job 10:8–12) indicate that this ongoing creative process is not without continued divine involvement, even in the intricacies of the gestation process. Every birth, every appearance of life, testifies to God's participation in the continuing creative process; and this from *within* the created order.

Again, we meet with an understanding of dual agency in creation. Both God and the human are effectively involved in the process, and God's involvement is appropriate to the nature of the human and is not all-determinative. Human decisions and actions contribute to antecedent causes and can wreak havoc in the process.

These various texts witness to a continuity between God and creature, to a mutual sharing of creative powers that must occur if there is to be a creation as God intends. God is certainly present with the creative power; but it is within the causal nexus; thereby it is power which enables more than power which controls. God's Word and action are certainly indispensable, but the future of the created order is made dependent in significant ways upon the creaturely use of power. This, of course, entails a self-limitation with respect to divine sovereignty, because the future of the creation, and, indeed, the future of God is made dependent in important ways upon how the creatures respond with the power they have. Therefore, one must speak of divine risk *and* vulnerability, beginning with creation.

Comparable understandings of divine power-sharing are evident in the historical order. M. Noth has correctly perceived this to be the case: "History is not merely a constant repetition of complicated concatenations of cause and effect, if we believe that God is really active in history, not simply as first cause, but as the ever present Lord working *within* the superficial interplay of cause and effect."[39] Having so entered into history, God is present at every occasion and has a hand in every event, working along with other causes, rather than through interferences or interventions. Thus God's influence is effective to some degree in every event, though it is more significant in some events. Even in the worst situations (e.g., the Hitler era) God will have some impact. At the same time, in no historical event is God's influence completely determinative. In addition to the variety of antecedent causes for every event,[40] within the context of divine power-sharing there is a divine empowerment or enablement that leaves the creature freedom to maneuver.

Texts concerning the settlement of the land by Israel are representative:

> Curse Meroz, says the angel of the Lord,
> > curse bitterly its inhabitants,
> because they came not to the help of the Lord,
> > to the help of the Lord against the mighty.
> > > (Judg. 5:23)

It is clear here, as well as in Judg. 1—3, that God was not able to accomplish everything desired in the settlement of the land because of the failure of those who did not properly use the power they had received. While God's power seems all-determinate in certain of these texts (cf. Joshua 6), the role of the human is not completely discounted, and in fact has a more important place than is commonly recognized.[41] This power-sharing can also be observed in a positive sense in the Davidic traditions (see Ps. 132:1–5).[42]

In these texts it is made especially clear how God, though always aiming for the best in every situation, must often settle for that which is less than good. What is possible for God in certain situations is in significant part determined by the nature of the situation, with its antecedent causes and the sharing of powers. God has chosen to be dependent upon human beings in the carrying out of God's work in the world, and what God has to work with is often not the best, to say the least. God often has to accept what people do with the power they have. Thus, the results of God's efficacy in and through such instruments always has mixed results, and less than what would have happened if God had chosen to use power alone. Hence, as an example, force and violence are associated with God's work in the world, because, to a greater or lesser degree, they are characteristic of the means of those in and through whom the work is carried out.[43] In order to achieve God's purposes, God will in effect "get his hands dirty." It is necessary for God to enter into compromising situations, and work with whatever potential there is, in order to move toward God's salvific goals. But God, too, will suffer violence in such situations. God will not only absorb the effects of the human misuse of power, but will "look bad" in the eyes of all those who think that God's possibilities should not be so limited (see 1 Cor. 1:26–31).

(b) Implicit in what has been said, the sharing of powers opens the God-world relationship up to the possibility of a clash of powers. The creature is given power to reject God, power to make the world other than what God desires for it. Thus, human power can have an adverse effect on God's influence in the world. While God always works to overcome the effect of such wrongful uses of power, God has given up absolute power to this end so as not to violate the integrity of the established relationship.

There is a certain divine helplessness to which the OT bears witness, particularly in some of the divine questions we have observed in Hosea and Jeremiah. God tries everything possible to turn Israel around (see 2 Kings 17:13–16), but God, like a human parent, can finally only stand by as Israel goes to ruin: "What more can I do for you!?" God does all God can, but Israel cannot be forced to repent. Israel's no to God cannot be overpowered in the face of continued rejection without violating the God-human relationship.

God is not finally helpless, however, for the OT witnesses to God's involvement in the very context of Israel's sin,[44] as well as in any judgment which follows. Thus, while Israel itself is stubborn (Hos. 4:16), God's sending of the prophets can also be said to occasion Israel's stubbornness (2 Kings 17:13–20). God's work in the lives of those who sin can lead to repentance, but it can also lead to a hardening of the people in their sinful ways (cf. Exod. 8:15 with 9:12). God intensifies the sinful behavior of people, involved as God is in every sinful event. Yet, God's gracious purposes remain the same, though life may only be possible through death. God's power can then become effective to this end "when he sees that their power is gone" (Deut. 32:36).

In matters of judgment, Israel's own iniquity causes the ensuing judgment—in a snowballing, act-consequence schema (Hos. 8:7; 10:13–15); yet God is seen to be the one who quite directly exacts the judgment (Hos. 13:7–9), and Assyria wields the sword (13:16). An efficacious force is thus ascribed both to God and to the sinful actions of the people, and indeed to those who exact a judgment in specific ways (from the ground, Gen. 4:12, to the Assyrians). God is active in the interplay between human actions and their consequences. Both worldly and divine causative factors are interwoven, within a single complex of cause and effect, to produce the one judgmental result. Our own sin, as well as the sins of our forebears, presses in upon us, but no less the hand of God. For history is our judgment and God enables history, carrying the world along, not in mechanistic ways but with a personal attentiveness. God's salvific will remains intact in everything, and God's gracious concern is always for the best; but in a given situation "the best that God may be able to offer is burning the chaff to fertilize the field for a new crop."[45]

It now seems clear that the OT understands God's power as limited, in some ways, in order for God to be consistent with the way in which God has chosen to relate to the world. While such understandings cannot be refined in such a way as to speak with precision as to what is possible for God, they do set certain limits regarding divine possibilities. It seems to me that this does not mean that the language of omnipotence is no longer usable for OT God-talk. Traditional understandings of omnipotence have never meant that God could do contradictory things (e.g., make a stone so big he could not lift it), or could use power in a way that would be inconsistent with the kind of God God is (e.g., act in an unloving way). These suggestions simply allow us to define what is possible for God while being consistent with the way in which God has chosen to relate to the world.[46]

From a variety of perspectives, to which others could be added,[47] this examination suggests that the OT reveals a fundamental continuity between God and world. God is graciously present, in, with, and under all the particulars of the creation, with which God is in a relationship of reciprocity. The immanent and transcendent God of Israel is immersed in the space and time of this world; this God is available to all, is effective along with them at every occasion, and moves with them into an uncertain future. Such a perspective reveals a divine vulnerability, as God takes on all the risks that authentic relatedness entails. Because of what happens to that relationship with those whom God loves, God suffers.

# CHAPTER 6

# God in Human Form

## THEOPHANY

We have explored the relationship between God and world. Now we will pay attention to the most intense way in which God is present in the world: the theophany.

In W. Eichrodt's opinion, it is in the theophany that "God's connection with the world can be most clearly observed."[1] Here God is manifested within the life of the world in a way that is highly specific, articulate, tangible, formful, and revealing of a divine vulnerability.[2] We will seek to show that all theophanies were in human form, and that the empirical element of the theophany was very important indeed for the accomplishment of God's intentions. God's Word is thereby embodied, made visible; enabling a knowing, a becoming, a convincing, and a living that would not otherwise be possible. There are also important implications here for ethics, a theology of creation, and for the roots of NT theological perspectives, not least those associated with Incarnation and Sacrament.

The analogy of the laser beam might be used with profit to help explain the theophanic presence: sharply focused, highly intense moments of divine appearance. These are moments when God is supremely present to individuals or the community of faith. They are commonly "face to face" encounters, and though not always recognized for what they in fact are by those encountered, at least at the moment of the encounter, they are so recognized by those who have preserved the traditions and handed them down. Such appearances of God are to be found throughout the OT and during most periods of

Israel's history; there are both continuities and development as one moves from the patriarchal period to the prophets.

Theophanies are commonly associated with watershed moments in the lives of individuals or the community; they provide significant directions for the future of the relationship between God and people. In fact, many theophanies constitute highly directive moments in Israel's history (for example, the appearance of God to Moses in Exodus 3).

The word "theophany" means an appearance of God.[3] Although some scholars would collapse all theophanies into one basic type,[4] most would now make a distinction between two or more types of theophanies:[5] those where God appears as the divine warrior to help in time of need, and those where God appears as a bearer of a word. I have divided the latter category into various types.

"Theophanies of God as Warrior" are less important for our purposes, and will be only briefly noted. Some representative texts are Judges 5; Habakkuk 3; Psalms 18, 29, 77, 97. In these theophanies God appears in order to help the people in time of need. The time and place of the appearance is the historical context of the distress of the people, for example, in a battle. The imagery used is primarily associated with that of the divine warrior and meteorological agitations, particularly those associated with the thunderstorm (see Ps. 18:7–15). The reaction is terror. No form of God is seen, however, and no word is heard. While the language of "appearance" is problematical, it is apparent that the poets involved consider God to have been present in an especially intense way, so that only the language of appearance affords the proper degree of intensification.

The ultimate origins of the imagery are to be found in the theophanies of the Canaanite Baal in particular,[6] though there are Israelite adaptations.[7] Peculiarly Israelite roots are often evident, particularly the Exodus event (e.g., Habakkuk 3) or the Holy War tradition (cf. Judges 5). The prophets pick up this theophanic tradition to speak of God's judgment (Micah 1) or the salvation (Habakkuk 3) of Israel. It is used in a universal sense in apocalyptic (cf. Isa. 26:21), and much of the "second coming" language of the NT has its roots in this tradition (e.g., the Book of Revelation). Finally, it has an important place in the Psalms, usually in hymns or songs of thanksgiving (Psalms 18, 29, 77, 97, 114). While there is no indication that these psalms were used in a cultic reenactment of these battles, the grandeur of the description of God's advent certainly must have mediated something of the reality of the divine presence so effective in the actual deliverance being celebrated. In Psalm 97 (particularly when associated with Psalms 96 and 98) the past, present, and future merge, with the result that the materials are given an eschatological thrust, and assure the community of God's continuing involvement in their life in such ways.

While it is helpful to separate these types of materials from those which follow, the interconnections should not be forgotten. The comparability in language must have meant for similar responses on the part of those who used and heard these materials. Because no word was heard nor sight seen, the way in which these materials were received must have been dependent in some way upon the theophanies bearing the Word of God. One moment of intense presence gives the clue to the interpretation of subsequent moments where no word is heard and no sight seen.

In "Theophanies of God as Bearer of the Word" the divine appears in order to speak and embody a word, usually favorable.[8] Little scholarly consensus has emerged regarding distinctions among the various theophanies that fall under this rubric.[9] We will examine differences and similarities.

The reports of the divine appearances range from the simple announcement (e.g., Gen. 12:7) to the complex narrative (e.g., Exodus 19). The report of the appearance is sometimes heavily couched in liturgical language (e.g., Exodus 19; cf. Ps. 50:1–7), thus probably reflecting cultic practice, while at other times no such language is evident (e.g., Genesis 18).[10] God appears to individuals (e.g., Genesis 17), to small groups of two or more (e.g., Num. 12:4–5), and to the community as a whole (e.g., Exodus 19; Num. 16:19; cf. Judg. 2:4).[11] The phenomena accompanying God's appearance vary from a pillar of cloud/smoke (e.g., Exod. 33:7–11; Num. 11:25; 12:5; cf. Lev. 16; Isa. 6:4), a flame of fire (Exod. 3:2; cf. Gen. 15:17), the glory (Num. 14:10), a complex of meteorological and other phenomena (cf. Exodus 19; Isa. 6) to none at all (e.g., Gen. 12:7).

Appearances are said to occur "in person" (e.g., Gen. 35:9; 1 Sam. 3:10), in a vision (Gen. 15:1); in a dream (Gen. 28:12; 1 Kings 3:5), in a "man" (Gen. 32:24; Judg. 13:6; Josh. 5:13) or a messenger (e.g.,

Judg. 6:11). At times it is immediately recognized that God has appeared (e.g., Gen. 35:9), while at other times it is not clear that God has appeared until during or after the encounter (Judges 13). While the appearance is often spontaneous (e.g., Gen. 26:24–25), it is sometimes also reported as expected and regularized (e.g., Lev. 9:4–6; Exod. 33:7–11). God may appear in any place (e.g., Gen. 12:7) or in certain special places (e.g., Exod. 33:7–11), yet always giving the place of appearance a special status as a place where appearance may be expected, if not regularized (Exod. 20:24). While God's advent may occasion fear or dread in the recipients either at the time of the appearance (e.g., Exod. 3:6; 19:16) or after (e.g., Gen. 28:16–17; cf. Judg. 13:22), as well as a worshipful response (e.g., Exod. 33:10; Gen. 26:25), the human response may also be more matter-of-fact (e.g., Genesis 18).

This vast array of variables is sufficient to show why it has been difficult for scholars to bring much order to the discussion. While source criticism may be helpful in explaining some of the diverse data, the latter is probably due most to the complexity of the phenomenon of God's appearance and difficulties in grasping what actually happens. Yet, while confusion may seem to abound, the available amplification may also make for a certain clarity not otherwise possible. While efforts to approach the subject from a historical perspective are certainly in order, this discussion will be more synchronic.

To begin, certain *similarities* in the various theophanic appearances may be discerned, besides the fact that in them God always speaks a word. For one thing, the appearances are always *temporary*. Some appearances are momentary (e.g., Gen. 26:24–25), while others entail a stay of at least mealtime length (e.g., Gen. 18:9, 16; Exod. 24:11; cf. 34:28!). Such limitations, however, ought not be viewed in terms of limits of God's desire to be so intimately present, but rather in terms of honoring the structures of existence.

Second, the divine appearances are always, at one stage or another, *initiated* by God. This occurs either in individual cases, or through the (initially) free gift of a promise in which God commits himself to appear, as in Exod. 20:24, "In every place where I cause my name to be remembered I will come to you and bless you" (see Exod. 29:42–43). God's coming may also be occasioned by the prayers of the people in time of need (see Isa. 64:1–4). God has provided for structures of worship and prayer in the context of which God has promised to come to God's people. The situation may be such, or the wickedness of the people may be of such magnitude, however, that God is not able to come, or will not come for the sake of God's name, and ultimately for the sake of God's salvific purposes, or will come in judgment (see Ps. 50:1–7; Amos 4:4–12). Whatever the circumstances, God will not be manipulated into coming. God's advent will always be a gracious act based on promise; God *will* be gracious—of this the people can be assured. Thus God's coming to the people is never capricious.

Third, God's appearances are always *effective*. God's comings are of no little moment for the individuals and communities involved; they make a difference. While one could point to the fear or worshipful response associated with God's coming, the divine aim is to produce other effects. Where there is fear, God seeks to quell it (cf. Gen. 21:17; 26:24). The desired effect is focused in the word spoken, usually a word of promise. Thus God will give the land (Gen. 12:7) or a child/descendents (Gen. 16:10–11; 18:10), or wisdom (1 Kings 3:10–11), or greatness (Gen. 21:18), or redemption (Exod. 3:7–10), or presence and blessing (Gen. 26:2, 24; 28:15). These latter passages in particular show that the assurance of non-theophanic presence is an effect of appearance. God may also use the occasion to lament (Num. 14:10–11) or announce a judgment (Num. 14:12; 16:19–20; cf. Ps. 50:1–7). Or God may actually give the spirit (Num. 11:25) or the law (Exodus 19—20) or a name, either for others (Gen. 16:11; 17:5; 32:28; 35:20) or God's own self (Gen. 35:11; Exod. 3:14–15). Or, God may call to a task (1 Sam. 3; 1 Kings 19; Isa. 6) or to obedience (Gen. 17:1; 1 Kings 9:2), or even clarify a difficult matter (Num. 12:1–8). Thus, God uses an appearance to carry out a wide spectrum of activities among the people; words and deeds are forthcoming which make a difference in life.

One can speak even more specifically with respect to the effectiveness of the divine appearances. One key effect is certainly a *new level of knowing,* a knowing that is needed for true life. Promises are stated which were not known before, responsibilities delineated, matters clarified and judged. This entails new knowledge of God and God's purposes. The emphasis on knowledge in Exod. 33:12–17 (cf. 3:7) shows that such knowing has effects on the very nature of the relationship between the knower and the known.[12]

This means that theophanies also enable a *new level of being,* of becoming in at least some respects what one was not heretofore. Perhaps this is why new children and new names are such common subjects of theophanies; they reflect new status and newly shaped relationships, a becoming of people and world. This is true not only for the individuals involved, but also for God. God's gift of names means a new level of knowing for God as well (see Exod. 33:12c), which in turn entails new commitments (see Exod. 33:17c; 3:16–17; Gen. 17:5–8), so that it is difficult not to speak of God's becoming in at least some sense of that word. This would also entail God's gift of his own name (Gen. 35:11; Exod. 3:14–15). It should be noted here that God's offering of God's own names allows for a new level in the relationship with those who now know and can call on those names, and will as a result forever effect change in the very life of God.

Concomitant with the effect that theophanies have on relationships, God's coming brings redemption (Exod. 3:7–10) and effects reconciliation between individuals (cf. Gen. 32:30 with 33:10–11) as well as between God and people (cf. Lev. 16:2, 12–13, 21); it calls the participants to a task within the relationship (e.g., 1 Sam. 3; Isa. 6). We will see that God's coming not only brings knowing and enables becoming, but that it also elicits a convincing.

## VISIBLE WORDS

How does the theophany work such great things? Through both the word *and* the associated empirical phenomena. It is often said that the word spoken is the focus of the theophany. But the fact that there is always some empirical reference to God's appearances, something concrete and tangible associated with them, has not been sufficiently appreciated.[13] While the word that is heard (or deed done) is more at the center of the appearance than the sight that is seen, the empirical reference is of no little moment. There is a kind of sacramentalism evident in the combination of the word and the visible vehicles in and through which the word is always "enfleshed" and conveyed.

What is, in fact, the importance of theophanies at all for Israel's faith? Why would it not have been enough for God just to speak words as God commonly does throughout the whole OT period (e.g.,

Gen. 12:1–3; Exod. 17:5; Judg. 7:2)? Why is it necessary for God to appear to speak some of them? Those who say that the word is the only important thing about the theophany really collapse the distinction between theophany and other divine speech. It seems clear that the OT does give to theophanies a significance which is different from that given to an "unclothed word," as in 1 Kings 11:9–10, for example:

> And the Lord was angry with Solomon, because his heart had turned away from the Lord, the God of Israel, who had appeared to him twice [3:5; 9:2], and had commanded him concerning this thing.

Why bother with the underlined phrase at all, unless God's appearance carried with it a special import? God had not only commanded Solomon, but God had actually appeared to command him; thus Solomon's turning away was even more extraordinary than if he had only been spoken to. Hence, even in a dream the command associated with an appearance was expected to carry more weight than one without an appearance. Not that the word in itself was of any greater import, but the appearance would have impressed the word upon Solomon in a way that just words would not have. God does speak to Solomon at other times (e.g., 1 Kings 6:11), with a word not much different from that given during the appearances (vv. 12–13); but it is the theophanic word that is recalled in 11:9 and is the occasion for the marvel at Solomon's disobedience. Thus, the theophanic word must have been understood as a more convincing word.

Although God spoke to Jacob at times other than appearances (e.g., Gen. 31:11–13), it is the appearances that are recalled later (Gen. 35:1, 9; 48:3) and considered of special import. It is recalled not simply that God extended promises to him, but that God appeared to him. The appearance itself must have been intended to carry special weight with Jacob that a bare word would not have. One might also note the importance given to the appearance in Exod. 3·16. When Moses reports to the elders of Israel, it is deemed important to say not only that God has spoken, but that God has appeared.

These instances strongly suggest that the appearances accompanying the word are not to be viewed merely as "accessories."[14] The considerable amount of textual material devoted to such descriptions ought not to be ignored.

Perhaps we need to broaden our understanding of the theology of the Word of God in Israel. The biblical understanding of the Word has both oral and visible components. From the symbolic acts of the prophets to the liturgical acts of worship, the Word of God is not simply spoken, it is in some sense made visible or enacted; it takes on flesh and blood, both literally and symbolically. The God who appears in order to speak stands in fundamental continuity with these other broad understandings of the Word of God in Israel's life and worship. "Visible words" have a kind of import that merely spoken words do not.

These phenomena affirm that the Word of God is not intended solely for minds or spirits, but for the whole person. Bodies are as much involved in relationships as are minds. They therefore render the personal element in the divine address more apparent. Because the whole person is caught up in the encounter, the word that is spoken may also prove to be more convincing. Moreover, the intensity of the relationship between speaker and addressee is heightened when bodily presence is involved. Greater intensity of presence on the part of the speaker makes for greater directness in the word spoken and sharper focus in the attention of the addressee. Spoken words can thus be more persuasive. Further, issues of continuity and identifiability are sharpened: it is made clearer whose word it always is, and provides for more stability over time regarding the origin and fundamental shape of that word. Finally, it provides incisiveness to both the immanence and transcendence of God. Transcendence, because it is made clear that the source of the word is not "of their own minds" (Jer. 23:16) but is outside of oneself; God *appears* in order to speak. Immanence, because the God who speaks, speaks from within the world, directly, "face to face."

We assume throughout this discussion that not only is the encounter with God believed to be real, whether by the recipients named in the text or by those who transmitted the tradition or both, but that the reality of God is experienced in a way involving more than internal sight.

(a) In one type of appearance, it is not immediately apparent that it is God with whom individuals are dealing; it is recognized only upon reflection (e.g., Judg. 13:21–23; Gen. 16:13; 32:30; cf. Judg. 6:22). Nevertheless, such recognition scenes are regularly accompanied by notices that God has in fact been seen. Thus, the reflection is not simply centered on the word spoken, but also on the sight seen; in fact, in these three passages the sight occasions more reflection than the word spoken. In Genesis 16 and 32, the sight is memorialized in the naming of the places of the encounter: Beerlahairoi and Peniel. Those who remember the theophanic encounter, as well as those who experience it, consider what has been seen to be of paramount import. That God has appeared, and not just that he has spoken, is considered significant for Israel's memory, and hence for Israel's faith and understanding of God.

(b) In a second type, the divine nature of the appearance is not immediately recognized, yet recognition comes before the conclusion of the encounter (e.g., Exod. 3:1–6; Josh. 5:13–15; cf. 1 Samuel 3). Here the effect of the appearance, as over against an "unclothed word," is recognized since the place is made holy ground (cf. Exod. 20:24). The particular intensity of presence has effects in the world that the spoken word does not, not only upon the individual recipient, but on the created order at that particular place. Appearance makes a difference; it is a more efficacious presence. 1 Samuel 3 is particularly striking because the transition from voice to appearance (3:10) seems to be occasioned by the openness and faith Eli expresses in 3:8–9. It is as if Eli's openness creates an opening for God; human response does have an effect upon the way in which God can be present in the world (cf. Ezek. 8:6). Moreover, it is noteworthy that Samuel's positive response is occasioned not only by Eli's suggestion but also by the fact that God "came and stood forth."

(c) In a third type, signs are given to theophanic recipients who question some aspect of the appearance (Judg. 6:15–24; Exod. 3:11–12; Jer. 1:11–19). In these instances, it is noteworthy that no spiritual or mental insight is given, but further empirical data. There is explicit concern here for convincing, persuading, engaging in a kind of apologetic. Nowhere are the recipients chided for a lack of faith.[15]

In each of the preceding cases, the appearance is not obviously theophanic. There is a certain impressionism in the sight that is seen. At the same time, the word spoken is not obviously divine either. Thus, even after the messenger speaks words to Gideon, words that any good Israelite would have recognized as divine speech both formally and materially (Judg. 6:12, 14, 16), he is still not certain that it is the Word of God (v. 17). In the case of either word spoken or sight seen, the ambiguity is not removed; it may not be from God. Yet, in all these cases, nothing experienced is so disjunctive with what one might expect from the divine, that doubts *finally* remain regarding the nature of what in fact has happened. That God speaks and that God appears is not anywhere viewed as extraordinary or "miraculous"; the only marvel expressed is that the people who have seen God have lived to tell about it. This effect is especially clear in those cases where the divine appearance is apparently obvious (Gen. 12:7; 17:1; 26:2, 24; 35:9). At least a few individuals seem to expect such a possibility; yet the traces of a human form suggest that the appearances were not absolutely unambiguous to the recipients.

(d) The appearances that occur in a dream or vision may be viewed as a fourth variation on the theme (Gen. 28:12–13; 1 Kings 3:5; 9:2; cf. Gen. 3:11–13; 15:1). It is striking that these appearances are referred to later in the respective narratives without any reference to the fact that they occurred in dreams (see Gen. 35:1, 9; 48:3; 1 Kings 11:9). They are apparently recognized as no different in kind from those which occur during wakefulness. Yet, Num. 12:6–8 (cf. Jer. 23:25–29) suggests some difference:

> And he said, "Here my words: If there is a prophet among you, I the Lord make myself known to him in a vision, I speak with him in a dream. Not so with my servant Moses; he is entrusted with all my house. With him I speak mouth to mouth, clearly, and not in dark speech; and he beholds the form of the Lord."

It is important to recognize that the issue in this passage pertains not only to what is seen ("the form of the Lord") but also to what is heard ("clearly, and not in dark speech"). The difference would thus appear to be in clarity, not in kind. And that may be the issue because in a dream the whole person, with all senses functioning, is not engaged in the experience, particularly from a physical point of view. Thus, the full engagement of the person, not just the eyes, is seen to make for some difference in the experience. An actual appearance creates the supreme effect. Nevertheless, J. Barr is certainly correct[16] in observing that there is no elimination of the *form* of God in dream appearances (cf. Gen. 28:13; 15:5). They are no less anthropomorphic because of the dream context.[17]

## METEOROLOGICAL PHENOMENA

Two distinct types of empirical phenomena associated with such appearances deserve a closer look: the human form and the meteorological activity. First, the latter. These include the cloud, flame of fire (lightning), the glory, and a variety of meteorological displays.[18] It is difficult to determine the extent to which this material reflects a literal happening or poetic imagery. Certainly much of the present textual tradition has been shaped in part by liturgical practice, which included simulation of meteorological phenomena (e.g., smoke/cloud; fire/lightning; trumpets/thunder), as a comparison of Lev. 16:2 with 16:12–13 shows. Such phenomena served primarily to reveal rather than conceal God. The language used in and of itself, as well as any experience of such phenomena, would be disclosive of a highly focused divine presence. It would also serve to place God's appearance to Israel within the context of God's pervasive presence within the structures of creation. Israel knows that God's manifestation is not to be interpreted as an "intervention" (a much misused term), or as an interruption of God's normal nonpresence within the creation, but as a special intensification, just as storms would be within the regular weather structures of the created order.

Such phenomena—glory, the pillar of cloud, fire[19]—were also used in association with accompanying presence (Exod. 13:21–22; 14:19–20, 24; Num. 14:14),[20] as well as the tabernacling presence (1 Kings 8:10–12; cf. Exod. 40:34–38). That these are different from theophanic presence is clear from the fact that the pillars "did not depart" (Exod. 13:22; 40:38) from Israel (cf. Exod. 33:9). Moreover, given the absence of the spoken word, the empirical dimension becomes the significant, indeed the only, point of contact with the reality of the divine presence.

It is clear that the empirical phenomena were not absolutely necessary to accomplish the tasks of guidance and protection. The Lord "in" the pillar did that (Exod. 13:21; 14:24), and God could have accomplished the same end without the pillar (cf. Gen. 28:15).

These empirical phenomena are primarily important as a tangible assurance for the people that God is indeed present and active among them. They elicit a convincing. To the eyes of faith, they bring home the reality of God's presence among the people. They impress that fact upon all the people's senses, not just their minds or their spirits. Thus, the *whole person* experiences the presence of God. It is characteristic of storm phenomena that those involved know and experience the weather in ways different from those times when weather conditions are normal. God desires that the people realize his presence in an intensified way, both for God's own sake, because God loves them, and for their sake, because of their need and experience.

Nevertheless, while the primary function of the empirical phenomena may be said to reveal and not to conceal God, they also suggest that about God's presence which cannot be controlled or contained. God's coming is not something which can be grasped in its fullness, either by the mind or the eye. No final clarity of vision, in both senses of the term, is achievable. Such phenomena, particularly the cloud, have the capacity to conceal God literally. Yet the fire (light) in the cloud means that the participants apprehend neither transparence nor opaqueness, but translucence. There is a "seeing through," but as in a mirror dimly.

Given the diversity of empirical phenomena, there seem to be degrees of intensification within theophanies as well.[21] Not all clouds are storms; messengers are more articulate. It would appear that the empirical aspects of a theophany are related in some important way to the needs and circumstances of the situation. Thus, the appearance in *direct* human form always occurs to individuals, and normally to leaders of the community. The appearance in more veiled forms (cloud, fire, glory) usually occurs in communal or institutionalized contexts.[22] Thus, there is something about the communal context as such that occasions the appearance of God in a less direct way.

It has been suggested, particularly in view of the discussions in Exod. 33:1–3, following upon the golden calf debacle in Exodus 32, that this muted directness has to do with the sinfulness of the people.[23] There may be an element of truth in this, but comparable phenomena are present already in Exodus 13, 14, and 19 (cf. 16:10). And, of course, individuals are sinful as well. It may also be due in part to later cultic simulations which have been read back into these earlier texts. But, the fact that the individuals are leaders who enjoy a special relationship with God may be a more basic factor, as implied in Num. 12:6–8. Moreover, when God does appear to the entire community (e.g., Num. 14:10; 16:19; Exod. 33:7–11), the people see the cloud, but only Moses and Aaron hear God speak directly, "face to face." This discrepancy suggests that the basic reason for the individual/communal distinction is structural in nature, relating to issues of interpretive control and human freedom.

Regarding the first of these, God relies upon key individuals to hear the word with understanding and to convey it to others in appropriate ways. God's concern for clarity with respect to both hearing and seeing is emphasized in Num. 12:6–8. Inherently, individuals enjoy a communicative capacity which cannot be shared equally by all members of a crowd. Theologically, as well as experientially, the special role of leaders in God's relationship to the world remains evident.

Regarding human freedom, the divine appearance in the cloud preserves both human choice and perspective: apprehension as well as distance, is involved. The individual viewer, in this case, is free to an extent not allowed a leader such as Moses, who carries God's words to the community. Nevertheless, an essential ambiguity in the theophany (see, for example, Exod. 33:18–23) preserves in the witness a sense of God's mystery. Disbelief always remains a possibility.

In this connection we need to return to the oft-repeated concern that "man shall not see me [i.e., my face] and live" (Exod. 33:20; Judg. 13:22).[24] We begin by noting that worldly reality is capable of experiencing theophanies, though not of producing them; the God-world relationship is of such a nature that God can appear without disruption. The intensity associated with certain theophanies does not happen because God stands in some fundamental disjunction with the world, requiring much "sound and fury" to occur in God's wake. Some of the most "face to face" comings of God are very quiet, it should be remembered, even childlike. There is a certain "nexus" here that cannot be denied. Although God and world are categorically different, they are not as irreconcilable as repelling magnets or oil in water.

Statements about not seeing God and living seem to contradict such basic understandings, however, or at least qualify them in an important way. It has often been pointed out that Scripture does not say God cannot be seen; rather, it assumes God can be seen, but one cannot live if this happens. The issue is always a matter of life, not visibility. Even then, it seems that God is capable of allowing God to be seen by certain individuals who live to tell about the experience (see Judg. 6:22–23; 13:22–23; Gen. 16:13; 32:30; Exod. 24:10–11; 34:29; Num. 12:8; cf. Exod. 33:11; Deut. 34:10). The partial allowance of Exod. 33:20–23 would seem to stand in some contradiction with these other passages, but they do not necessarily suggest that God was seen in all of God's fullness. In any case, sufficient sight was allowed so that the manifestation could be recognized and reported.

It is sometimes suggested that the reason for this common formula is human sinfulness when faced with divine holiness, but the exceptions suggest otherwise. There is no direct word in these narratives that concern is necessary for God, as if sovereignty would be unduly compromised by sight.[25] Nowhere is it suggested that *God* is being protected or shielded. Not even in a text like Exod. 33:12–23 does it say that Moses is presumptuous or that God is displeased with him; in fact, God constantly moves with Moses in conversation.[26] As in all the other texts, concern is expressed only for human life (v. 20). God allows a partial vision, not as a rebuke to Moses, but as a demonstration of God's mercy; that is the only reason the text gives for the partial vision. God's freedom is thus a freedom *for* Moses. In this context, we also need to remember the ideas of epistemic distance and human freedom, which in this case are specifically identified with the preservation of human life. True human life is possible only if the vision of God is of such a nature that disbelief remains possible. The concern is not to keep people ignorant, but to preserve them.

To summarize, the empirical phenomena, particularly the human form, show that God appears in the world without disruption. They reveal that the finite is capable of the infinite. God can come and be present in the pillar of fire/cloud. God can appear in the human form of the messenger. The world can serve the task of clothing God; in these theophanies God assumes chosen aspects of the created order and "wears" them in order to be as concretely and persuasively and intensely present with the people as possible. Theophanies demonstrate that God is not identical with the world, but they also reveal that God takes on creaturely forms so that humankind may discover God embodied within the world itself.

IN HUMAN FORM

It is probable that all theophanies were in human form, though it is perhaps more true to the evidence to say that there are no theophanies which are incompatible with an appearance in human form. Many appearances are very explicit in this regard (e.g., Genesis 18); others are more allusive (e.g., Exod. 24:10–11), while still others contain only an appearance and a speaking anthropomorphic reference (e.g., Num. 14:10–11). The latter text contains no explicit references to a human form, but it is not possible to draw contrary conclusions on the basis of such texts either. We are concerned here with the textual evidence for the human form of God, to seek to determine what it might mean, and what continuing significance it might have.

1. The most explicit theophanies in this regard are those where *God appears in anonymous human form*, as a "man" *('îsh)* or "angel/ messenger" *(mal'āk)*.[27] They are brief, direct, and personal, as well as usually occurring to individuals; Judg. 2:1–5 is an exception. God comes not in some extraordinary way, but in and through the commonplace events of life, within the framework of everyday life and experience.[28]

One of the more common observations relative to these passages is the oscillation evident between the man/messenger and God or the Lord. A common pattern is that a messenger appears, and then at some subsequent point in the story, God is suddenly present or speaking. In Gen. 16:7, for example, the messenger finds Hagar by the spring and carries on a conversation with her in vv. 8–12; then v. 13 abruptly reports, "So she called the name of the Lord who spoke to her, 'Thou art a God of seeing'; for she said, 'Have I really seen God and remained alive after seeing him?'" It is apparent that God himself appeared in the form of a human being, as recognized both by the narrator and by Hagar herself. In Judges 6, the messenger encounters Gideon (vv. 11–12, note that he "came and sat" before he "appeared") and starts the conversation with him (vv. 12–13); then abruptly it is stated that the Lord turned and spoke to Gideon (vv. 14, 16). Thereafter, Gideon requests a sign as proof of God's identity (v. 17). While the Lord promises to stay until Gideon returns with a gift (v. 18), it is the messenger who responds when Gideon returns

(vv. 20–21), only to disappear (v. 21). Gideon is now convinced that he has seen the messenger "face to face" (v. 22), and God assures him that he will not die (v. 23). This last conversation assumes that to look at the messenger "face to face" is the same as looking at God, for the idea of seeing God and dying is certainly the operative principle at issue (Exod. 33:20; Judg. 13:22).[29]

That the form God assumes is a human form is made especially clear by the oscillation between 'îsh ("man") and mal'āk ("messenger") in some passages. Genesis 18—19 is the most complex of these passages, as it moves from "men" (18:2), to the use of both singular and plural pronouns (vv. 3–8), to "the Lord" (vv. 10, 13), back to "men" (vv. 16, 22), to the "two messengers" (19:1), and finally to "lords" (19:2; cf. 18:3). Here it would appear that God not only appears in human form, but in all three figures, which prompts von Rad to speak of "God's singular, yet personally differentiated activity."[30] In Judges 13 the entire chapter moves back and forth among "man," "messenger," "man of God," and God. In two passages, however, "man" appears without reference to "messenger" (Gen. 32:24;[31] Josh. 5:13).

There are also certain texts which do not explicitly mention the "man" or the "messenger," but are probably to be understood in the same terms. Gen. 35:9, for example, simply states that God "appeared," yet 35:13 reports that God "went up" ('ālāh) from the place. A human figure seems to be the only possible reference, especially given the natural way in which the description is given; exactly the same language is found also in Gen. 17:1, 22. What might be called supernatural elements are missing. Still other passages contain only the language of "appearance," but just that word, without any other reference to the contrary, suggests a human reference (Gen. 12:7; 26:24; 1 Kings 3:5; 9:2).[32]

Certain contexts in which the messenger is mentioned do not speak of an actual appearance, but only of speech to human beings from heaven or in a dream. They are germane here for what they reveal about the relationship between the messenger and God. Gen. 31:11–13 states, "Then the angel of God said to me in the dream, 'Jacob . . . I am the God of Bethel' " (cf. v. 16).[33] In Genesis 22 the messenger intervenes to stop Abraham from killing his son (vv. 11–12); his language does not differentiate the messenger from God: "You have not withheld your son . . . from *me*." In vv. 15–16, the angel is said to call and speak, but the speech of v. 16 contains the phrase, "says the Lord" (cf. also Gen. 21:17–20 and the use of "I" in v. 18). Even when speaking from heaven (Genesis 22), God and the messenger are interchangeable. In the theophany, there is a continuity between heaven and earth.[34]

Other passages dealing with the messenger assist us on one point we are seeking to develop, but not the other. These view the messenger in terms of human form (e.g., Dan. 8:13; 10:16–18; cf. 7:13), but they commonly assume an increased distinction between the messenger's and God's own speech and appearance. Thus, for example, Exod. 33:2–3 (cf. 32:34; Num. 20:16) seems to make the point that the messenger is at some remove from the full presence of God. Other passages seem to move in the direction of subordinate beings or intermediaries of God.[35] There seems to be little doubt that this range of passages speaks of a specific form of divine self-manifestation—namely, the human form.[36]

2. A second kind of theophany of this basic type might be described as follows: *God appears in human form, but veiled by fire, cloud/smoke, or light.* Such theophanies commonly have a communal context, though individuals or small groups may be the only ones who hear God speak.

First of all, it should be noted that there are certain theophanies which may be said to be transitional from the first type to this one. Thus, Exod. 3:2 speaks of the "messenger of the Lord" appearing "in" a flame of fire.[37] The text goes on to speak of God calling from the bush, identifying the speaker in terms of the God of the fathers. Moses then hides his face, "for he was afraid to look at God." The use of messenger language here makes it clear that the flame of fire is not to be identified as the form of the divine self-manifestation, but only as a veil or envelope for the human form of the divine appearance (see also Exod. 19:18; Deut. 4:12, 15). Ezek. 1:26–28 speaks in comparable ways about the relationship between the fire "round about" and "the likeness as it were of a human form."

Just as we have seen continuities between theophanic and accompanying presence in the pillar of cloud/fire, so we also see continuities in the use of messenger language. Thus, Exod. 14:19 testifies to the proper relationship between the pillar and the messenger. When combined with Exod. 14:24 (see also Exod. 13:21; Num. 14:14; Deut. 1:33), where the Lord is said to be "in" the pillar, the messenger also should be understood to be "in" the pillar. Thus, like the theophanic presence, the pillar itself is not a form of the divine manifestation,[38] but envelops a form of God.

These passages point the way toward an appropriate interpretation of God's veiled appearance when messenger language is not used. Consequently, it is not the pillar of fire or smoke/cloud which is thought to be a speaking form of God; rather, God in human form speaks from within such surroundings.

Passages from a variety of traditions speak of the Lord appearing "in" the (pillar of) cloud (Exod. 19:9; 34:5; Lev. 16:2; Num. 11:25; 12:5; Deut. 31:15; cf. Exod. 20:21; Isa. 6:4) or fire (Exod. 19:18; Deut. 4:12, 15). The cloud/fire thus serves to envelop the God who speaks. Given the virtual identification of glory and fire in some Priestly texts (cf. Exod. 40:34–35 with 40:38), with the glory understood to be "in" the cloud (see Exod. 16:10; cf. 1 Kings 8:10–11), those passages which refer only to the appearance of the glory (e.g., Num. 14:10; 16:19; 20:6) are probably to be understood in terms of a translucent cloud with fire/light being visible within it (cf. Lev. 16:13). Thus, this complex envelope for God's manifestation (see Lev. 16:2) is finally very similar to what we have seen to be God's relationship to the accompanying pillar of cloud/fire of Exodus 13—14.[39]

The people are commonly said to see the cloud, though only in Exod. 19:9 are the people said to hear God. Elsewhere (e.g., Exod. 33:7–11; Num. 14:10; 16:19), it is only Moses and Aaron who are said to hear. Moses probably regularly entered the cloud in the tent for such a purpose (cf. Exod. 24:18; 33:9; Deut. 31:14–15).

Some of these passages strongly suggest that the God who appears in the cloud/fire appears in human form. Most specific is Exod. 24:9–11, where Moses and others are twice said to have seen God, a God whose feet and hands are both mentioned (vv. 10–11). Num. 12:8 speaks of Moses beholding "the form of the Lord," which, given the context, can hardly admit of any other form but human. Deut. 4:15— "you saw no form" at Sinai—does not contradict this conclusion. It speaks not of Moses but of the people *not seeing* any form; in particular, it says nothing about the possible absence of form altogether. As we have seen, a description of God as standing occurs in some of these contexts (e.g., Exod. 34:5–6; Num. 12:5). While the phrase "face to face" is capable of a nonliteral interpretation, and must be considered in the light of "face" serving as the regular word for "presence" (e.g., Exod. 33:14), the reference to a human form cannot be dismissed as "mere" metaphor.[40] The seemingly "super-fluous"[41] explanation of Exod. 33:11, "as a man speaks to his friend," underscores the many OT references to God's veiled and yet clearly human appearances.

It is reasonable to conclude that all such veiled appearances of God are finally, when the veils are removed, in human form. In fact, it may be misleading to use the language of veiling to set this type of theophany over against the first type. Even in the obviously human form of the messenger, there is a veiling; only occasionally is God seen to be immediately evident in the appearance. Yet the second type of theophany is at least more obviously veiled; or one might say that there are additional veils, at least for communal sight. For our purposes, it is not necessary to determine the precise lineaments of what was seen, or how much of the fullness of God was sensorily available or grasped, only that God deigned to allow himself to be seen and what was seen had at least the likeness of a human form.[42]

It should also be noted in this context that certain prophetic passages bear important continuities with those we have discussed heretofore. Barr states that "the older tradition of direct and an-thropomorphic theophany lives on in the prophetic movement."[43] Amos 7:7 and 9:1 speak of God "standing." Isa. 6:1 informs us that Isaiah "saw" God "sitting."[44] Jer. 1:9 says that "the Lord put forth his hand and touched my mouth," while Ezek. 1:26 sees "seated above the likeness of a throne . . . a likeness as it were of a human form." Even in late eschatological visions (Dan. 7:9; Zech. 14:4) the descrip-tion of God in human terms persists. Thus, from earliest traditions to latest, there is a consistency in the way in which the human form is used to speak of God.

We now turn to a discussion of some of the components present in these various theophanic passages; the theme of vulnerability emerges in a special way.

## DIVINE VULNERABILITY

Form-critical studies of the theophanic passages have isolated cer-tain elements common to many of them.[45] Gen. 26:24–25 is some-times cited as a convenient reference point.

> And the Lord appeared to him the same night and said, "I am the God of Abraham your father; fear not, for I am with you and will bless you and multiply your descendants for my servant Abraham's sake." So he built an altar there and called upon the name of the Lord, and pitched his tent there. And there Isaac's servants dug a well.

After an introductory description of God's appearance, there is commonly an introductory formula of self-identification such as "I am Yahweh, the god of your fathers," or "I am the God of Abraham your father" (Exod. 3:6; Gen. 26:24).[46] Less common is some statement designed to quell fear (e.g., Gen. 21:17; 26:24). The assurance of continuing presence is again more common (e.g., Gen. 26:24; 28:15; Exod. 3:12; Jer. 1:8), implying a distinction between theophanic and accompanying presence.[47] Then follows the word which provides the focus for the particular appearance (e.g., Gen. 16:9–12; 35:11–12). A descriptive statement concludes the unit.

Components common to the material content of many theophanies thus serve to name, to reassure, to promise presence, and to tell. The focus is on the telling, but the other words serve the focal point in crucial ways. Before the telling can have the desired effect, words are spoken which serve to make the telling as forceful, as personal, and as trustworthy as possible.

The reassurance may be said to be the most momentary. It relates specifically to the identification, so that any fear of who is speaking does not prevent the right hearing of the specific word. The promise of presence also contributes to the reassurance, but moves on to specify continuing divine presence in the context of the working out of the word spoken. The God who appears deems appearance to be insufficient for the divine purpose, however important that may be. Continuing divine presence in the world of those involved is necessary not only for their sake, but also for the sake of the word. The God who gives the word does not, as it were, leave the word to do its own work, however forceful that may be.[48] Word of God and presence of God must always remain together. Word depends finally on presence. If the word is to accomplish God's intended aim, God must continually be at work in the world to see it through. God cannot leave a word and go.

But, while God continues to work on behalf of the word, it is now not only in God's hands. The word is now in the world. It has been received by those who can misuse the word, can twist it toward ends not consonant with God's purposes for it, and prevent it from having its intended effect. In being given to the world, the word is made vulnerable. Thus, for example, Exodus 32 witnesses to what happened to the word given at Sinai. Further divine appearances, beyond continuing presence, were deemed necessary in order to seek to correct the course that the recipients of the word had taken with it, or even to propose more drastic measures (see Exod. 34:1–7; Num. 14:10; 16:19).

Moreover, what happened to the word in turn affected presence, as Exodus 33 shows. Not only is God's Word vulnerable upon being spoken in the world, God's promise of presence is as well. The response of the recipients of the word can effectively push God back into less intensified and less desired forms of presence. God is thus not able to be present with his people and to see to God's Word (see 1 Sam. 3:1), in ways that God would like. God is not given ample opening into the life of the world by the way the world responds to God. This, then, brings us back to our earlier remarks about the vulnerability of the divine presence.

This vulnerability, seen to be so much a part of theophany to this point, is intensified when we consider the naming component.[49] It is striking that there is a commandment specifically designed to protect the name of God: "You shall not take the name of the Lord your God in vain, for the Lord will not hold him guiltless who takes his name in vain" (Exod. 20:7; Deut. 5:11). The concern here is expressed somewhat more fully in Lev. 19:12, "And you shall not swear by my name falsely, and so profane the name of your God: I am the Lord."[50] What is of special interest here is that in this commandment God is concerned about God, about God's own future. This says something very important about what it means for God to name God's name.

What does naming involve, that it should carry such implications even for God?[51] Naming entails life. Names are given to those who are living, and the importance of the perpetuation of the name in one's descendants is understood to be related to some continuing form of life. Naming entails distinctiveness, setting one off from others who have names. God gives God's name and thereby is set off from other gods who have names. It may often, but not always,[52] be reflective of some factor of the life of the one who is named, whether origins (Gen. 4:1) or some experience in life (Gen. 32:26) or char-acter (1 Sam. 25:25). There is at least some concentration of the self in some names. To reveal the name to others commonly entails *some* insight regarding the one whose name is known. It can be an act of self-disclosure, a revelatory act. For God to say "I am the God of Abraham your father" (Gen. 26:24) immediately ties the name to a certain history and reveals something about the God who gives this name. This is seen, too, in the fact that God's name is a gift; God is not named by others; the name comes from God and thus reveals transcendence.

Moreover, naming entails a certain kind of relationship. Giving the name opens up the possibility of, indeed admits a desire for, a certain intimacy in relationship. A relationship without a name inevitably means some distance. Naming the name is necessary for closeness. It makes for a greater intensity of presence, a certain concreteness that would not otherwise be there for God. Naming makes true encounter and communication possible. God and people can now meet and address one another, and at a level that makes for intimacy and depth. Naming entails availability. By giving the name, God becomes ac-cessible to people. God can be addressed by name, and the God one may address means that this God makes certain self-commitments regarding accessibility. Naming entails historicality. Anyone whose name is known is a part of that community which has names. God's own history is thus intimately integrated with the world of God's people in particular. God becomes a participant in that story, sharing in its life, making for a greater depth in identification.

Finally, naming entails vulnerability. In giving the name, God becomes available to the world and is at the disposal of those who can name the name.[53] This is a self-giving act of no little risk, for it means not only that God's name can be honored, but also that it can be misused and abused. And thus, name-giving always carries with it the possibility of pain, with adverse effects upon the very life of God. The more intimate the relationship, which comes with name-giving, the greater the possibility of hurt. For God to have a name entails the possibility of suffering; indeed, given what God knows about people and world and what is apt to happen to the name, God thereby chooses to assume suffering.

When God's name is given, this means life, distinctiveness, con-

creteness, intimacy, accessibility, communication, historicality, identification and vulnerability. One can easily see how speaking the name
of God became for Israel a speaking of God's self (see Pss. 20:1; 54:1;
124:8). The gift of the name of God entailed the gift of God's self.
Thus, "to put the name upon" the people (Num. 6:27) meant that
they were God's people in the most intimate sense of that phrase; they
were now known as the people of God's name, the people among
whom God was truly present, and vulnerably so.

THE HUMAN FORM OF GOD

It is important to place this discussion within the above-noted
context regarding the inevitable empirical element in theophanies.
Concerns for the concrete and tangible are evident, and the personalistic element is sharpened as the divine address to the whole person
is made more apparent. There is greater intensity of presence, with
greater directionality and potential effectiveness for the word spoken.
We sometimes speak of individuals having a certain "presence." They
command attention, respect, and so forth, not simply by the words
which they speak, but also by the words they embody. As a result,
their words will commonly have a greater impact than if they had just
written or recorded them. A word spoken "in person" has a certain
potential power and life which words on pages or on recording
instruments do not have. Appearance makes a difference to words.
To say "a God who appears" is to say something more about God and
the God-people relationship than saying, "a God who speaks." Moreover, to speak of a God who appears in the flesh, in the form of a
human being like ourselves, says even more about God and God's
relationship to the world. Further, it has more explicit implications for
human life as well; the human response can never be simply to believe
or speak, it must also mean to do, to reembody the Word in the
world. Seeing adds something to hearing.[54]

Moreover, the fact that the human form is constant throughout the
literature gives it a level of significance beyond that of the other
empirical phenomena. It may be said that the human form says
something not only about God, but also about the relationship between God and world/people.

With respect to God, it can be said unequivocally that the human
form is not somehow foreign to God's Godness. However one views

the relationship between God and the human form, the finite form is capable of the infinite. Providing one does not incorporate NT understandings, it is possible, with Eichrodt,[55] to speak of God as one who "can temporarily incarnate himself." God can take the form of the human in his appearances, without thereby compromising God's transcendence.[56] The almost matter-of-fact way in which these texts speak of the matter, makes clear that the narrators perceived no difficulties in this regard; there is a naturalness or propriety about the reference that is inescapable.[57] No compromise of God's Godness or "unworthy familiarity" was thought to be implied by such language.[58] At the same time, it is clear that the texts are devoid of speculation in this regard. That there was a form and that the form was human are clear, but there is no interest displayed in the lineaments of the form (the late Dan. 7:9 is a somewhat surprising partial exception to this stance). Particularly in the more veiled appearances, the partialness of the reference (hand or foot) suggests not only a disinterest in such speculation, but a concern to create a somewhat impressionistic picture.

The next question to ask is somewhat more difficult. Is the human form one which God *assumes* only for the sake of the appearance; or is there an essential continuity between the form and God as God is, or both? It would be a mistake to move to a consideration of God as spirit in this connection. It is remarkable how seldom the OT, and even the NT, uses such language to speak of God. Isa. 31:3 is sometimes cited in this connection:

> The Egyptians are men, and not God;
>    and their horses are flesh, and not spirit.

Yet, as Eichrodt indicates,[59] this passage does not serve to set spirit over against matter, but the "inexhaustible power of the divine life" over against "the essentially transitory." The spiritual and the physical/material are not mutually exclusive categories. To speak of God as spirit does not necessarily entail formlessness.

One perspective on this issue uses language which shies away from speaking of an appearance of God's self, though there is no consensus with respect to the proper language. Thus, for example, Koehler eliminates words such as "hypostasis," "emanation," and "substitute," before settling on "representation."[60] Jacob is attracted to notions of "outward soul," or Yahweh having a "double."[61] The language of "alter ego" is regularly encountered, while A. R. Johnson speaks in terms of a personality "extension."[62] Such qualifying attempts seem to be prompted by a concern that speaking of the actual presence of God in a given appearance would preclude God's presence elsewhere.[63] But the matter should be stated without qualification: *God* appears. Those who use the language of *self*-manifestation are correct.[64]

It might be claimed, however, that the use of "messenger" language is an attempt to introduce some such qualification. It is a qualification of sorts, but of a different order than that commonly claimed for use of such language.

A few texts do speak of God's appearance in an apparently direct way (Gen. 12:7; 17:1; 26:2, 24; 35:9), though there may have been the ambiguity of the human form of which only traces remain. There is, however, no specialness about these appearances that sets them off from others where the appearance of God is more veiled or more obviously ambiguous. The appearance of God more directly, or the messenger/God oscillation, is so irregular that a certain arbitrariness of usage seems evident, though there may be ultimate origins which are different. Although our argument does not depend on this, these ways of speaking are possibly intended to be interpreted in the light of one another.[65] It is God who appears, yet not directly or unambiguously. Both sides of this statement are to be affirmed. It seems clear that the messenger language is not used to avoid anthropomorphic talk; if anything, this is intensified with the human form reference. As in the dreams, the issue is indirect appearance—an ambiguity of reference. But this does not mean that it is not actually God who appears and speaks: *It is God himself who assumes human form to appear and to speak.* The human form is the form of divine self-manifestation. This in no way implies that God is not being God elsewhere in the world; it only speaks to a special intensification of God's presence at the moment of appearance.

At the same time, to "identify" God and messenger would be misleading, but not because there is less than God present, but because there is *more than God* present. In the form which God assumes there is that which is other than God; the infinite takes on the finite for the sake of the appearance. Thus, rather than the language of separation or identity, one might use the language of distinction, distinction between God and God enfleshed in human form. This discussion thus suggests that the effort to find some qualifying or intermediate word to speak of "who" has appeared is not helpful. It is *God* who appears, enfleshed in human form.[66]

To this point, however, we have pursued only one part of our question. Is it sufficient to speak of anthropomorphic language solely in functional terms, that is, as a vehicle for divine self-manifestation, or can one also speak of essential continuities with the very form of God's self? Fewer scholars have tread into this territory, not least because the evidence is so elusive. One direction taken, perhaps more often by scholars of an earlier generation, has been that of progressive revelation. Early Israel may well have conceived of God as essentially in human form, but it eventually outgrew such a notion in the increasingly spiritualistic directions of its thought.[67] Yet the constancy of the anthropomorphic references throughout the literature, even if ambiguous at times, undercuts such a conclusion.[68] Thus, it is more common today to ascribe the use of anthropomorphic language to issues of human need, communication, or theological emphasis, rather than to any specific relationship to some form God may be presumed to have. Thus, for example, Eichrodt states, "The immediate proximity and reality of God, which for us are all too easily obscured by spiritualizing concepts, are outstanding features of the divine revelation, and *compel* men to clothe the divine presence in human form" (italics mine).[69]

A few scholars are bolder in this regard, and seek to draw tentative conclusions, not only on the basis of material such as we have discussed above, but also Gen. 1:26, "Let us make man in our image, after our likeness." Thus, for example, without qualifying language, von Rad boldly states, "Actually, Israel conceived even Yahweh himself as having human form."[70] As he notes, however, the Genesis passage reverses the usual question by considering the human to be "theomorphic," rather than God being anthropomorphic. The Priestly writer "insists on the fact that the pattern on which man was fashioned is to be sought outside the sphere of the created."[71] While von Rad proceeds to make clear that there was a vast—inconsistently, von Rad says "infinite"—difference seen between God and the human, particularly as regards sexuality, the basic claim that he makes is indeed a striking one; this is not some naive conception of early Israel, but a relatively late formulation, and in material which is highly reflective in character. It has also been suggested that at least some roots of the aniconic nature of Israel's religion is to be found here, namely, that God can be "imaged" only in terms of a living, human likeness.[72] While final clarity cannot be achieved at this point on the basis of the evidence we have, it is probable that Israel did not conceive of God in terms of formlessness, but rather that *the human form of the divine appearances constituted an enfleshment which bore essential continuities with the form which God was believed to have.*

What are the implications of such an idea for Israel's understanding of the relationship between God and world/people? W. Vischer, for instance, says that God "empties himself, and lays by the form of divinity; he humbles himself and assumes the form of man. He appears to men not as distant conception or lofty idea, not as the Absolute, the Incomprehensible, the Infinite, but as the one who is truly closest to all, as supremely the personal friend or foe of that humanity in which he reveals himself."[73] While this quotation may bear a facile continuity with NT realities (see Phil. 2:6–7), it lifts up a divine decision for the world which cannot so easily be set aside. The theophanies in human form bear witness to a God who has determined to be present in the world and to God's people in such an intensified way. This God has done in order to encounter the people and communicate with them in as personal a way as possible.

Even more, God in this fashion chooses to demonstrate how God identifies himself with the people. However transient the appearances might be, herein is exemplified how God has made the human situation God's own. Here, in some real sense, God shows that God chooses to share in the human condition; God participates in human history. In fact, the promise of presence commonly associated with the theophany indicates that God's intimate involvement in human history is not confined to the moment of theophany. That is to say the theophany provides the clue to the interpretation of God's ongoing relationship to the world. It provides a concentrated moment of vision into God's ways beyond the times of intensity; wherever there is world, there God has chosen to be as fully a participant as possible. The theophany thus provides an especially effective way for that word to get through to the recipients. They now know not only that God has promised to be present among them but that God is sharing the life of their world in a most intense and personal way.

This may well be the point at which it is best to cross-reference the theophanies of God as Warrior with those of God as Bearer of the Word. At those points in Israel's history when it confessed God's especially intense and personal activity on its behalf in time of need, then God was believed to be present in the same intensified ways as in the personally focused theophanies. Though no sight was seen nor word heard, Israel could believe that God was present and involved in especially intense ways. But without the personal theophanies, such faith, assurance, and understanding of divine immanence would not have been possible to the same degree.

Finally, God's appearance in human form reveals God's vulnerability. Appearance only associated with storm phenomena could give a quite different impression. It could suggest that God is totally in control of the situation; the only possible responses before God would be fear and dread. But appearance in human form, even in the midst of such phenomena, reveals another perspective. It suggests an entering into the life of the world that is more vulnerable, where the response can be derision (see Gen. 18:12–13) or incredulity (Judg. 6:13–17). It is to put oneself concretely into the hands of the world to do with as it will. It is revealing of the ways of God that the word is enfleshed in bodies of weakness within the framework of commonplace, everyday affairs, and not in overwhelming power. For, even in those instances where the vestments of God's appearance are threaded with lineaments of power, they clothe a vulnerable form. There is no such thing for Israel as a nonincarnate God.[74]

# CHAPTER 7

# God Suffers Because

We have broached the subject of God's suffering in a variety of ways. It is striking how frequently the matter has arisen in connection with the variety of subjects associated with the relationship between God and world. Here I will examine the specific language of suffering, as well as reflect on what is involved, indeed what is at stake, in speaking of a suffering God. I focus on the reasons for the divine suffering, because the various texts seem to evoke such issues.

These passages have rarely been examined by OT scholars; even commentaries and other studies of the contexts in which these texts are found explore the issues infrequently and briefly. A. Heschel and U. Mauser have offered the most complete look at the subject in their major works on the prophets,[1] while C. Westermann has touched on the matter in a number of studies.[2] Westermann's list of the passages he deems important to be studied on this topic is imposing indeed.[3] His list will provide the nucleus for these chapters, though it will need to be expanded in a number of ways. Among older works, those of H. W. Robinson should be noted; it appears that they emerged as a part of the more general discussion of the impassibility of God in Britain, especially in the years following World War I.[4] While the issues of human and divine suffering are integrated in his work, this has not generally been true of studies of human suffering in the OT. A few other books and articles have appeared along the way.[5]

Most of the passages to be examined here occur in divine speech, and mostly in laments or "lament-like" material; some of the vocabulary of suffering occurs in more isolated contexts. It is difficult at times to identify divine speech in the prophets. The messenger formula, and other means of determining divine speech, are not always present. Moreover, the prophet's words are often integrated into divine speech, so closely related are the prophet and God; they will need to be interpreted in the light of one another.

The form and language of the human lament materials are used as a basic guideline for determining the presence of divine lament. There is, however, an interesting variety of human lament language which is *not* used in divine laments. While one does need to be wary of conclusions drawn from such observations—if we had more divine speech literature, such language might appear—they can help us understand the nature of the divine suffering. Thus, for example, the rather common form or outline which the human laments take is not to be found in the divine laments.[6] The laments are also not occasioned by sickness or other physical ailments. On the other hand, language peculiar to the divine laments is comparatively rare (e.g., Isa. 42:14), but this is almost certainly due to the fact that the words are *hapax legomena* or very rare in the Hebrew Bible. Had we the full complement of Israel's lament language available to us, it is probable that no such language would appear to be peculiarly God's. The human cry becomes God's cry. God takes up the human cry and makes it God's own.

The variety of texts and the language associated with the divine suffering may be ordered according to a threefold schema in conjunction with the reasons for the suffering of God.

1. God suffers *because* of the people's rejection of God as Lord (cf. chap. 7).
2. God suffers *with* the people who are suffering (cf. chap. 8).
3. God suffers *for* the people (cf. chap. 9).

Such a synchronic approach cuts across the various traditions, seeking to determine commonalities more than differences among them. At the same time, at least the outlines of a diachronic view are not difficult to discern. Although all three categories may be said to have their roots in early material, it is the fall of the northern kingdom which first brings this material into prominence; this event, in turn, provides the most basic raw materials for the flourish of thought in this area during the events associated with the fall of Jerusalem and its aftermath. The history of the material tends to parallel the character of Israel's relationship with God. Thus, the three categories noted become more prominent as, respectively, the rejection of God by Israel becomes more and more pervasive, the people experience more and more suffering, and the future of Israel becomes more and more problematic.

It will become clear that the preponderance of the divine lament materials are to be found in the prophets. This source may be due in part to their special role in reflecting upon historical events that relate closely to issues of divine suffering. A more important factor, however, is that divine speech is much more prevalent in the prophetic literature than in any other, and it is upon such divine speech that we are most dependent for insight into the character of the divine life. Closely related to this phenomenon is the fact that the prophet had a relationship with God that no other individual in Israel enjoyed; it was of such a character that the prophet's life was increasingly reflective of the divine life. This relationship means that no separation can be made between the suffering of the prophet and the suffering of God. While a distinction between prophet and God must be maintained, the prophet's suffering mirrors the suffering of God before the people. God is present not only in the word which the prophet speaks, but also in the word as embodied in the prophet's life. In a real sense, those who hear *and see* the prophet, hear and see God. We will return to this issue (cf. chap. 10), but we will need to be attentive all along the way to those passages where the sufferings of prophet and God are so interwoven that they cannot be meaningfully separated.

## A BROKEN RELATIONSHIP

God suffers because the people have rejected him, have broken the relationship, and, as a result, tensions are experienced regarding what to do.

Using human lament materials as the basic guideline for determining divine laments, the most striking correlation at this point is with those laments where the psalmist complains of being falsely accused by enemies (e.g., Psalms 4, 17, 109). Here the psalmist not only laments his own situation, but brings accusations against his accusers while affirming his own innocence. He commonly asks that God visit upon them the same penalty that he would suffer if he were guilty (cf. Deut. 19:16–21, where the law provides for just that in the case of those who bear false witness). It is precisely this combination of lament and accusation that is characteristic of much of the divine lament material in this category. God is accused by the people, though innocent of the charge, and uses the language of these human lament materials in response. At the same time, two differences should be pointed out. While for the psalmist no special relationship with the accusers is regularly assumed, with God it is a close relationship which has been ruptured. Thus, the lament of God is focused on the broken state of the relationship in a way that is not the case for the psalmist. Moreover, while the concern for future justice and wellbeing which characterizes the psalmist's lament may also be said to be true for God—we have seen this to be the case in other contexts—God's concern includes the future of the relationship with the people involved, without a narrow focus on God's own self.

It has been common for scholars to make note of the combination of lament and accusation in divine speech in the prophets, though without noting the striking parallels to these particular lament psalms. Westermann, for instance, exclaims "how near the judicial complaint and the utterly personal lament can come to each other!" in passages such as Isa. 1:2–9.[7] Raitt notes this same combination in connection with his study of the accusatory questions the people direct to God (seen particularly in Jeremiah and the exilic Psalms [44, 74, 79, 89] as well as Lamentations) and God's response in the form of counterquestions.[8] We should be attentive to the effect that the ideas of lament and accusation have on each other. It might be noted here that this combination characterizes the wrath of God in a most basic way. Lament is always an integral aspect of the wrath of God.

We need to take note of this motif in nonprophetic texts. Although not always of certain date, they would seem to root the idea of divine suffering in the preprophetic period. At least from the redactors' perspective, this understanding of God is rooted in the constitutive era of Israel's life.

Two early texts which speak of the suffering of God use the language of "grieving" (*'āṣab*). One is Ps. 78:40–41: "How often they rebelled against him in the wilderness and grieved him in the desert! They tested him again and again, and provoked[9] the Holy One of Israel." These verses contain themes of rebellion and trial which are repeated often in the psalm (cf. vv. 8, 17–18, 56), and constitute a summary statement of the variety of ways in which Israel has been faithless to its God.[10] "How often . . . again and again!" Just as Israel's rebellion continually reoccurred (cf. Num. 14:22), so God's grieving was not a one-time matter; it was something that occurred as often as the rebellion. How often they grieved and pained God! As for the content of the grieving, the associated ideas in passages which speak of human grieving are striking: forsakenness (Isa. 54:6); mourning (2 Sam. 19:3); distress and anger (Gen. 45:5); injury (Ps. 56:5). The verb points to a considerable range in the divine response to the rejection by the people. And all of this at the very birth of Israel as a people of God! And if then, certainly ever since then. The grief of God is as current as the people's sin. This divine grief manifests itself in a variety of ways in the life of the people, as God in many and various ways seeks to bring the wayward sons and daughters back home again. It accompanies both anger (vv. 21, 31) and compassion/restraint of anger (v. 38), the working of death (vv. 31, 34) and life (vv. 23–29).

It is striking that Isa. 63:7–10 recalls these events in similar terms: a God who grieves because the people have rebelled (the same verbs are used in Isa. 63:10) against a holy God (again in both texts), who acts both in terms of anger and compassion. Perhaps especially to be noted is the fact that it is the *holy* God who is said to be grieved in both instances. It is not considered in the least incongruous to juxtapose grieving and holiness; it is God in all his Godness who grieves. The use of comparable language in Eph. 4:30—"Do not grieve the Holy Spirit of God"—points to continuity between the testaments at this point, and indicates that the history of God in this respect has not changed. God's grieving continues.

The context of both passages indicates that God will seek every conceivable means to keep the relationship intact; throughout history the salvific will of God for the people remains constant. Thus, while indicating that God is indeed a vulnerable God, touched and affected in the deepest possible way by what the people have done to the relationship, God's grief does not entail being emotionally overwhelmed or embittered by the barrage of rejection. Through it all, God's faithfulness and gracious purposes remain constant and undiminished.

The other preprophetic reference to divine grief is Gen. 6:5–6:

"The Lord saw that the wickedness of man was great in the earth, and that every imagination of the thoughts of his heart was only evil continually. And the Lord was sorry that he had made man on the earth, and it grieved him to his heart."

I have previously examined this passage.[11] Here it is to be noted that the grieving divine response to a rebellious people is not simply characteristic of the relationship with Israel; God's grieving goes back to the morning of the world. Grief has been characteristic of the history of God almost from the beginning of things. I have noted (cf. chap. 5) that the flood story witnesses finally to God's promise to allow the creation to endure in spite of continuing human sinfulness. Yet such a decision entailed a new direction for the world. God promises: I will not respond to evil again with such devastation. This is a self-limitation with respect to the exercise of divine power.

This decision now needs to be related to divine grief. Here, God is revealed as one who, from creation on, is open to and affected by the world. The sinful response of humankind has indeed touched God; God is not apathetic. Even more, it indicates that God's judgment is not a detached decision. God is shown to be one who does not, indeed cannot, remove self and feelings from such a momentous judgment regarding the future of the creation; such a decision is not like flicking a switch or sending an impersonal command through a subordinate. God is caught up in the matter; and in some respects God will never be the same again. And so the judgment is a very personal decision, with all the mixed sorrow and anger that go into the making of decisions that affect the people whom one loves. Grief is always what the Godward side of judgment looks like. But, given God's decision to bear with the creation in all of its wickedness, this means for God a continuing grieving of the heart. Thus the promise to Noah and all flesh in Gen. 9:8–17 *necessitates* divine suffering. By deciding to endure a wicked world, while continuing to open up the heart to that world, means that God has decided to take personal suffering upon God's own self. Thus, to return to Psalm 78, it may be said that this psalm witnesses to the "How often!" of God's grief as it relates, not to the creation as a whole, but to the life of Israel.

The ongoing significance for Israel of this aspect of the flood story may be seen in Isa. 54:9–10 (cf. also Jer. 31:35–37):

> For this is like the days of Noah to me:
>     as I swore that the waters of Noah
>     should no more go over the earth,
> so I have sworn that I will not be angry with you
>     and will not rebuke you.
> For the mountains may depart
>     and the hills be removed,
> but my steadfast love shall not depart from you,
>     and my covenant of peace shall not be removed.

The flood story was finally shaped at about the same time as this passage was written. Thus the word to the exiles in the flood story is at least, in part, a word about divine self-limitation and the grief necessary in order to maintain the "covenant of peace" in the face of human rejection. The juxtaposition of the Noachic promise in Isaiah 54 and the "Suffering Servant Song" of Isaiah 53 is certainly not fortuitous. Here, God's grief is not simply a reference to the internal life of God; it becomes embodied in the world in the life of the servant. It is no longer simply a response to the rejection of the people; it now becomes a vehicle for their salvation.

Previously (cf. chap. 4) I have differentiated between those questions which have a past/present reference from those which have a present/future reference. A closer look at some of these questions in this context reveals the breadth and depth of divine suffering. The above-noted elements of lament and accusation are regularly interwoven in these questions and their contexts.

These questions with a past/present reference regularly make some reference to the past history of God with this people. Here I will also look at a number of related passages which, while not focused in a question, recall the past in a form that contains elements of lament. Two of the grieving passages already discussed, Psalm 78 and Isa. 63:7–14, also have this element of memory, although they are not in the form of divine speech.

THE MEMORY OF GOD

In these texts we confront the memory of God, wherein the past of God stands in disjunction with the present of God. It is this collision of past and present in God which occasions suffering. God remembers how good things used to be, and sees how that has now all changed. Memory functions for God in ways not unlike the way it functions for human beings, except that for God there is "total recall," and that must make the hurt in the present even more severe. What might have been! Thus, God's present has been significantly affected by God's memories, by God's experiences with the world in the past, and by their present recollection. God does not keep those memories to himself; God shares them with the people.

The prophecy of Isaiah (1:2–3) begins in a startling manner:

> Sons have I reared and brought up,
>> but they have rebelled against me.
> The ox knows its owner,
>> and the ass its master's crib;
> but Israel does not know,
>> my people does not understand.

The entire first chapter of Isaiah, which is commonly considered to be a summary of all that is to follow, is largely an admixture of lament and accusation.[12] Regarding Isa. 1:2–3, Heschel's comments suffice: "The speech that opens the book of Isaiah, and which sets the tone for all the utterances of the prophet, deals not with the anger of God, but with the sorrow of God. The prophet pleads with us to understand the plight of a father whom his children have abandoned."[13] It is important to note, in addition, that the focus is not on Israel's disobedience to an external legal code, but on the broken state of a relationship between parent and child. Jesus' parable of the prodigal son cannot help but be recalled here. The rebellion occurs even though God has lavishly bestowed love and care. The people had not been deserted, nor had they been mistreated. In the face of the best parenting possible, they had left home. They did not see that God the parent had been concerned with their welfare: "Sons . . . have forsaken the Lord" (v. 4).

This lament element is pervasive in the verses which follow, particularly in Isa. 1:4–9 and 1:21–23. It is returned to with special force in the song of the vineyard in 5:1–7 (cf. Jer. 2:21; contrast with the delight of God in Isa. 27:2–5). Two of these lament questions, expressing divine wonderment over what has happened, occur in Isa. 5:4: "What more was there to do for my vineyard, that I have not done in it? . . . Why did it yield wild grapes?" And this in the face of the inordinate care that the beloved has showered on those whom he loves!

The prophecy of Jeremiah (2:2) begins in a manner remarkably like that of Isaiah, though using marital rather than parental imagery:

> I remember the devotion of your youth,
>     your love as a bride,
> how you followed me in the wilderness,
>     in a land not sown.

Once again a prophetic work begins, not with hellfire and damnation, but with a picture of the pain and anguish of God. The memories of how good the marriage used to be makes the present, with its absence of devotion and love on the part of the bride, all the more painful. All the subsequent accusations and announcements of judgment can only be understood properly if seen as spoken out of the deeply pained heart of God. God's memory-filled grief informs all that follows, making it clear that these developments are the last thing in the world God wanted.

In the verses which follow in Jeremiah 2, one encounters a series of questions in which at times lament seems to predominate, at other times accusation. These in turn are interwoven with quotations of the people, which give the whole a dialogical character.[14] That is to say, God's words are not simply imposed on the people, but interact with what they have in fact said. The rhetorical questions in particular (vv. 5, 14, 17, 31–32; 3:1–2) are designed to respond to accusations of the people that God has not cared for them as God ought to have; like the questions in the lament psalms, they demonstrate God's faithfulness in the face of such accusations. At the same time, they show the reasonableness of both the divine lamentation and accusation. Basically, however, they serve the divine intention to elicit a change of heart in the people (see 3:12–14, 22; 4:1–2). Quickly Jeremiah enunciates the anguish of God in 2:29–32:

> Why do you complain against me?
>     You have all rebelled against me, says the Lord. . . .
> Have I been a wilderness to Israel,
>     or a land of thick darkness?
> Why then do my people say, "We are free,
>     we will come no more to thee?"

> Can a maiden forget her ornaments,
>     or a bride her attire?
> Yet my people have forgotten me
>     days without number.

The second and fourth questions are rhetorical, with the answer no understood. These questions eliminate one possible answer to the first (cf. Job 10:2) and third questions: the responsibility for the present situation does not lie with God. Yet, the lament-accusation cries of "Why?!" have no answer. His abandonment makes no sense, even to God, and never will. The "Why!" is thus reflective of the continuing anguish of a God who must live with such questions. And thus this unit ends with only the reality of the situation poignantly expressed by God: "My people have forgotten me!"

This painful cry is repeated, usually in the first person, throughout the opening chapters of Jeremiah (see 2:13; 3:21; 5:7; 13:25; 16:1; 17:13; 18:15; 19:4). The use of the intimate phrase "my people" or "my dear people" (the daughter of my people) rings with hurt and disappointment wherever it appears.

Jer. 3:19–20 (cf. 3:7) again focuses on the memory of God and the suffering occasioned by its encounter with the present:

> I thought
>     how I would set you among my sons,
> and give you a pleasant land,
>     a heritage most beauteous of all nations.
> And I thought you would call me, My Father,
>     and would not turn from following me.
> Surely, as a faithless wife leaves her husband,
>     so have you been faithless to me, O house of Israel.

What intimacy God desired in his relationship with the people, and what disappointment is expressed here! While literary purists might deplore the mixing of the parental and marital metaphors here, the effect is almost overwhelming in its pathos. God has been rejected both as parent and as husband! God is like a person who has been rejected not only by his spouse but by his children as well. God suffers the effects of the broken relationship at multiple levels of intimacy. The wounds of God are manifold.

In Jeremiah 8—20 we find a concentration of prophetic and divine laments interwoven.[15] The lament-filled situation is voiced by both

God and prophet in such a way that they seem to be echoing one another. Two of the divine laments may be noted here. The first is Jer. 8:4–7:

> When men fall, do they not rise again?
>> If one turns away, does he not return?
> Why then has this people turned away
>> in perpetual backsliding? . . .
> I have given heed and listened,
>> but . . . no man repents of his wickedness. . . .
> Even the stork in the heavens
>> knows her times;
> and the turtledove, swallow and crane
>> keep the time of their coming:
> but my people know not
>> the ordinance of the Lord.

Here again we find the admixture of lament and accusation. The combination of rhetorical question (v. 4) and bewildered question (v. 5) is repeated. Ordinarily, if a person goes away, that person will return. Even the animals have instincts that bring them back (v. 7). Not so with Israel; they refuse to return. Why?! There seems to be no explanation whatsoever for such behavior, even for God. Thus God, in laying out the accusation against a people who refuse to repent, does so with a bewilderment that does not mask an inner anguish.

In a similar vein Jer. 18:13–15 continues:

> Ask among the nations,
>> who has heard the like of this?
> The virgin Israel
>> has done a very horrible thing.
> Does the snow of Lebanon leave
>> the crags of Sirion?
> Do the mountain waters run dry,
>> the cold flowing streams?
> But my people have forgotten me, . . .

Not only are there no analogies in the animal world to what Israel has done, but nothing comparable can be found among all the nations of the world. Here the series of rhetorical questions contain only an implicit "Why?!" They move immediately to a repetition of the oft-voiced cry: "My people have forgotten me!"

At this point we take note of those desiderative particles characteristic of lament, which express that combination of the intimacy which God desires so much and the disappointment of nonrealization:

> O Israel, if you would but listen to me!
> (Ps. 81:8; cf. v. 13)

> O that you had hearkened to my commandments!
> (Isa. 48:18)

> Oh that they had such a mind as this always.
> (Deut. 5:29)

Psalm 81, commonly referred to as an example of prophetic speech within the context of Israel's worship (cf. Psalms 50, 95),[16] again focuses on matters of divine memory. God points up the disjunction between what the people have experienced at the hands of God (in distress they called and God answered, v. 7), and what God has experienced from the people: "My people did not listen to my voice; Israel would have none of me" (v. 11). Here we see how, within the life of worship, the suffering of God was brought home to the people in striking ways. What anguish it must have meant for God to say: "Israel would have none of me!"

Psalm 81 makes reference to a dominant motif in the lament psalms, namely, calling and answering. Usually, the laments testify to the fact that God does or will answer when called by those in distress (e.g., Pss. 4:3; 17:6; 138:3), or God is confidently requested to respond (Pss. 27:7; 141:1). Yet there are a few instances where the complaint is that God does not seem to answer (Pss. 22:2; 69:3; 88:9). It is primarily in Isaiah 40—66 that the calling and answering motif appears in divine lament. It is now God who calls, and the people who are not answering. Especially striking in the way it pictures the divine invitation is Isa. 65:1-2:

> I was ready to be sought by those who did not ask for me;
>> I was ready to be found by those who did not seek me.
> I said, "Here am I, here am I,"
>> to a nation that did not call on my name.
> I spread out my hands all the day
>> to a rebellious people.

Here God recalls how the divine eagerness for intimacy has been ignored. God stands and offers himself in a cry that, in view of the invitation having been rejected, is almost heart-rending: "Here am I, here am I." God's hands are extended all day long in invitation, even to a rebellious people; but they would have none of God. Judgment must fall, but again it is accompanied by a heart full of grief.

This motif occurs elsewhere in Isa. 42:18, 23; 48:12, 18; 65:12; 66:4 (cf. Jer. 7:25–26). The familiar question form occurs again in Isa. 50:2: "Why, when I came, was there no man? When I called, was there no one to answer? Is my hand shortened, that it cannot redeem?" As we have seen above, here again is the rhetorical question which responds to the "Why?!" question, making it clear that God is not the one who is guilty of the implicit accusatory questions of the people (see Isa. 49:14; 40:27; cf. Ezek. 9:9). But God's "Why?!" remains without answer, voicing that incomprehensible divine hurt that, in spite of all God had done for the people, they have ignored the call.

Mic. 6:3 should also be noted in this context: "O my people, what have I done to you? In what have I wearied you? Answer me!" While the accusatory element may well be much stronger than the lament element here, connections with the latter cannot be denied. We meet the memory of God associated with a questioning which assumes accusatory questions from the people. The calling and no answering motif reappears, as well as the implicit "Why?!" in the face of what has happened. The questions suggest that we ought not interpret this context in terms of the coldness and objectivity of a typical courtroom scene. While it may be proper to say that God is engaged in self-defense, it is not with an "it's not my fault, I'm clean" approach; God is not so concerned about self. The image perhaps best approximates that of a divorce proceeding where the two parties are asked to relive what it is that has brought them to this point. It is a time of pain and anguish for both the faithful God and the unfaithful spouse.[17]

The memory of God is expressed in its most poignant form in Hosea 11, one text in a series of divine recollections in Hosea (cf. 9:10–13; 10:11; 13:4–6; cf. 2:14–15):

> When Israel was a child, I loved him,
>   and out of Egypt I called my son.
> The more I called them,
>   the more they went from me;

> they kept sacrificing to the Baals,
>     and burning incense to idols.
> Yet it was I who taught Ephraim to walk,
>     I took them up in my arms;
>     but they did not know that I healed them.
> I led them with cords of compassion,
>     with the bands of love,
> and I became to them as one
>     who eases the yoke on their jaws,
>     and I bent down to them and fed them.

The image here, obviously, is not that of some heavenly General Patton having difficulty tolerating acts of insubordination. Rather, it is the image of the long-suffering parent and, given the roles in child-rearing in Israel, it is probably more the image of mother than father. God is pictured as one in great anguish over what the children have done, but her love is such that she cannot let go. Any parent with a prodigal child should know something of what God must feel. Those memories of how good things used to be. The images simply flow: growing in relationship; holding them by the hand when they took their first steps; gathering them up in the arms when they were sick or tired or anxiously caring for their daily needs. But now other images are interwoven with these: the anguish over the rejection; the yearning for a restoration of relationship; the repeated efforts made to get them to see the light and return home; the heartache that is felt all the more deeply as they seem to stray farther, and yet the reluctance to give them up; the inner turmoil as decisions are contemplated.

The striking note of Hosea is that, whereas the common human reaction in such a situation would be give up, God's love is such that she cannot let go. The parental pathos in the heart of God! The complaint against the children has been spoken; the word of complete abandonment is expected. But then, in Hos. 11:8 in particular, there is that pouring out of mingled sorrow and love which prevents the final ruin of the children. Thus, God's Godness is revealed in the way in which, amid all the sorrow and anger, God's salvific purposes remain unclouded and the steadfastness of divine love endures forever. Heschel once again grasps the essential point: "Over and above the immediate and contingent emotional reaction of the Lord we are informed of an eternal and basic disposition" revealed at the beginning of the passage: "I loved him" (11:1).[18]

THE FUTURE OF GOD

The questions God asks in the larger context of this passage have a future rather than a past orientation, and it is to this dimension of the divine suffering we now turn. It should also be noted that v. 8 pushes the interpretation of God's suffering into "suffering-for" directions.

While the above-noted questions focus on the relationship of past to present, they are at times interwoven with lament-filled questions which have a present/future reference. Given the pervasive rejection of God by his own people, what does this mean for their future? Recall here our previous discussion (cf. chap. 4) regarding the use of future-oriented questions in God's sharing of the decision-making process. These are questions which are open-ended, in which the future response of the people is uncertain; both God and people are therefore faced with at least two possibilities.

First of all, there are the questions introduced by "How long?!" It is clear from the laments of the psalter (e.g., Pss. 6:3; 13:1–2) that this question cannot be interpreted as a straightforward request for information; it represents a cry that contains two key elements: complaint with respect to something that is believed to have gone on long enough, and anguish over the abandonment and its seeming finality. Thus, the combination of lament and accusation is present here as well, but an issue for the future is explicitly raised.

Three of these questions are found in the traditions associated with the wilderness wanderings. Thus once again an understanding of God is rooted in Israel's early life, at least from the perspective of the redactor: "How long will this people despise me? And how long will they not believe in me, in spite of all the signs which I have wrought among them?" (Num. 14:11); "How long shall this wicked congregation murmur against me?" (Num. 14:27; cf. Exod. 16:28; 10:3; 1 Sam. 16:1). It is interesting to note that these questions follow upon murmurings of the people against God, which also take the form of lament and accusation (Num. 14:2–3; cf. Exod. 16:3, 7–9). One is thus given to wonder why the lament-accusations of the psalter, which are directed not only to enemies but to God, do not receive a comparable response. This is most likely because they are uttered from within the context of faith—manifestly not the case in Num. 14:11 or in the complaints reported in the prophets.[19] It is also to be noted that the questions are directed in each case to Moses and Aaron, not to the people. As such, their function would seem to be similar to other instances of prophetic consultation we have seen before. Thus, in Num. 14:11, the question is followed by an announcement of judgment (v. 12). Yet that announcement is not irrevocable, as the subsequent discussion indicates (cf. also 14:39–40 following upon 14:27). Thus, the question is a genuine question, intended to draw forth a positive response in leaders and people, so that the announced judgment may be forestalled.

The prophets also report such "How long?!" questions of God: "O Jerusalem, wash your heart from wickedness, that you may be saved. How long shall your evil thoughts lodge within you?" (Jer. 4:14); "Woe to you, O Jerusalem! How long will it be before you are made clean?" (Jer. 13:27); "My anger burns against them. How long will it be till they are pure in Israel?" (Hos. 8:5). These questions are different from those in the pentateuchal texts because they are directed to the people as a whole, rather than just to the leadership.

Certain other divine questions in the prophets should also be noted. These types of questions appear to be unique to Hosea and Jeremiah: "What shall I do with you, O Ephraim? What shall I do with you, O Judah? Your love is like a morning cloud, like the dew that goes early away" (Hos. 6:4). The last line in particular makes it doubly clear how pained God is that the beloved of his soul has a love which is fickle, which does not return the love so lavishly extended to it. "How can I give you up, O Ephraim?! How can I hand you over, O Israel?!" (Hos. 11:8).

The pathos of God in these questions is a part of the larger context; it draws upon the intimacy of past experience. Memory intensifies the painfulness of the present as God struggles over what shape the people's future should take. "How can I pardon you? Your children have forsaken me. . . . Shall I not punish them for these things?" (Jer. 5:7–9). "Behold, I will refine them and test them, for what else can I do, because of my people? . . . Shall I not avenge myself on a nation such as this?" (Jer. 9:7, 9).

Some of these questions would seem to be merely rhetorical, with the divine answer to the people's unfaithfulness absolutely clear: judgment without further ado. Yet the lament-filled character of the questions indicates that God's final decision is not so clear. The actions of the people certainly indicate that divine judgment would be entirely justified. But the questions appear to mean that God holds back from executing what is expected. Again, as in the case of questions in Hosea, here we encounter the moment between the preliminary decision to "refine and test," and the final execution. Now is the time for sharing with the people the question of their own future. Now the people have a role to play in determining what God's final answer to his own questions will be. The questions may open up some dialogue between God and people, in light of which an alternative path into the future may become clear. The questions are thus designed to elicit the people's repentance, particularly as they glimpse the emotional involvement of their God in their life. The anguish-filled heart of God hopes against hope that they will respond positively so that God will not have to act on the preliminary decision.

SUMMARY

1. These texts just examined give us a glimpse into the heart of God. God is revealed not as one who remains coolly unaffected by the rejection of the people, but as one who is deeply wounded by the broken relationship. The interaction between God and people thus takes place not simply at the intellectual level as it were, nor in a law court; the exchange occurs also at the emotional level. God shares feelings, not just thoughts. The people know not only what God thinks, but what God feels. Thus, a holistic picture of God emerges. God relates at every level with the whole person of each individual.

2. In some respects, God is no longer seen to be the God prior to the brokenness. For God to make these responsive statements to what the people have done means that the world of the people has been internalized by God. God has absorbed the people's rejection, has reflected upon what it means, and through statements and questions seeks to find a way into the future that will transcend the breach. Thus, not only is God's present affected by what has happened, but God's future is at issue as well. For how the people respond to these divine efforts will determine the shape of the future that God and people have together. What happens will thus make a difference, not only to the people, but to God. In hearing these divine statements, the people should be able to get some sense of what a broken relationship means for God.

3. While God's suffering is in many respects analogous to the suffering of the people, there are a number of ways in which the divine suffering differs. This contrast is especially apparent in those human lament materials not used by God. Thus, God's suffering is not such that he is overwhelmed by the experience; his emotions do not get out of control or lead to incapacitation. Nor is God embittered in any way by what has occurred. God is able to "be angry and sin not." God is able to absorb all the arrows of outrageous fortune that pierce him through and, instead of becoming callous or removing himself from the line of fire, still seek to bring about a future which is good for those who inflict the wounds. In spite of the suffering God undergoes, God's salvific will does not waver; God's steadfast love endures forever. In this respect, God offers the supreme example of what to do with suffering.

4. The very fact that the divine suffering issues in efforts to repair the breach means that, in some sense, God's statements of suffering are in coordination with redemptive purposes and goals. While these statements do not yet imply a suffering on behalf of the people, they do indicate that God has chosen to allow the people to participate in a consideration of their future. To bear the suffering, while making continuing efforts to heal the relationship, means at least that God chooses to suffer for the sake of the future of that relationship. God does not choose to walk away; God enters fully into redemptive goals regardless of what it might mean for God's own life.

5. It is now clear that we need to make a distinction between two different dimensions of the divine life. While God is in some respects never the same again, in other respects God remains the same yesterday, today, and forever. While the divine life is indeed affected by what the people have done, God's nature is such that, in the face of whatever the world will dump on him, God will remain gracious and merciful and abounding in steadfast love. God will remain faithful to his promises. God will remain constant in working for the salvation of all.

6. God is revealed as one who accepts the human party in the relationship with complete seriousness, allowing them full opportunity to participate in shaping their own future. The questions reveal a God who is not capricious, whose lordship does not depend on summary executions or autocratic pronouncements. God gives the

people a chance to appeal and engage in interaction with God before any final decisions are made. There is thus an honoring of the human view of the matter at issue, and an openness to the responses that the people might make to the questions that are asked. By sharing in the determination of their own future, the future is seen not as something which is imposed by a God who acts on the world from without; it is generated from within by the ongoing interaction between the people and the God who stands close to them in every way.

7. Finally, God is revealed as one who is not vindictive, legalistic, or exacting as to matters of judgment. The disappointment evident in these responses of God indicates that judgment is not something God wants: "What else can I do?" (Jer. 9:7). God is genuinely in search of an alternative way into the future. The poignant calls for Israel to return (e.g., Jer. 3:12, 14, 22) indicate what God desires above all. God is willing to "forgive and forget." God wants life and not death (e.g., Ezek. 18:23–32). Moreover, God's extraordinary patience reveals the lengths to which God will go for the sake of the future of the relationship. In patience, God goes beyond justice again and again. Judgment is thus never simply a juristic matter, as if measured objectively in terms of an external ordinance. A relationship is at stake, not an agreement or a contract or a set of rules. The judgment that does fall may in fact entail an "eye for an eye" correspondence, but that comes only on the far side of a slowness to anger revealing a fundamental "lack of fairness" on God's part, if God's actions are measured in terms of a strict standard of justice. In terms of any straightforward legal thinking, God is much too lenient. But such corresponsive thought is important; for should judgment come, it will be seen to be absolutely fair in terms of any human canons of accountability.

Generally speaking, judgment is thus viewed basically in terms of a breakdown in a personal relationship with its associated effects—all the anger, pain, and suffering which would commonly accompany such a breakdown. Should judgment come, the people should be able to see that they have been visited "not with the strict and icy indifference of a judge, but with the pain and the anger of one whose suit for a personal surrender has been rejected."[20] The analogy of a marriage breaking up is one that could be profitably used in this connection. As the closeness of the relationship ebbs, as the partners remove themselves from intimacy with one another, they experience the effects of the break in all aspects of their lives. From the prophets' point of view, the effect(s) of the broken relationship between people and God in life is called judgment. It is striking how commonly the language of God's judgment consists of images involving withdrawal, forsaking, hiddenness, or giving the people up. As the people remove themselves from God, God engages in major efforts at healing the breach, but may finally be forced into a tearful withdrawal, reluctantly allowing all the forces that make for death and destruction to have their way with the people. But, while God may give them up, God does not finally give up on them. Into the midst of those suffering judgments God returns.

CHAPTER 8

| God Suffers With

The God who tearfully allows the judgment to fall does not leave those in the lurch who suffer as a result. God is immediately back on the scene, sharing in the suffering of the people, according to Isa. 54:7–8:

> For a brief moment I forsook you,
>     but with great compassion I will gather you.
> In the overflowing wrath for a moment
>     I hid my face from you,
> but with everlasting love I will have compasssion on you,
>     says the Lord, your Redeemer.

## ROOTED IN ISRAEL'S EXPERIENCE

It can reasonably be claimed that the idea of a God who suffered with his people had its roots in the Exodus and in the subsequent reflections on the significance of that event. Two passages may be cited here:

> In the course of those many days the king of Egypt died. And the people of Israel groaned under their bondage, and cried out for help, and their cry under bondage came up to God. And God heard their groaning, and God remembered his covenant with Abraham, with Isaac, and with Jacob. And God saw the people of Israel, and God knew their condition.
> (Exod. 2:23–25)

> Then the Lord said, "I have seen the affliction of my people who are in Egypt, and have heard their cry because of their taskmasters; I know their sufferings, and I have come down to deliver them out of the hand of the Egyptians."
>
> (Exod. 3:7–8)

The verbs with God as subject are striking: God "heard"; God "remembered"; God "saw"; God "knew." In both texts, God has not only heard their cries of suffering, but God has also *seen* the people (the verb "see" in 3:7 is an intensified form). As we have noted in our earlier discussions, "to see" entails a level of perception of greater depth and breadth than simple hearing. Moreover, memory entails not simply a mental act, but an activity associated with that which is "remembered." Thus God generates such activity in the present as is entailed by the promises made in the past to the fathers. God is actively faithful to the implications of the promises made. In addition, this faithfulness means knowledge of the sufferings of the people. The verb "know" carries with it more than a sense of "knowing about." God has already "heard" about their sufferings and has "seen" in depth what is involved, reflecting on both in relationship to past promises. "Know" here must have the broader sense of "experience," even "intimate experience," as it commonly does in the OT. In some real sense, God is depicted here as one who is intimately involved in the suffering of the people, having entered into their sufferings in such a way as to have experienced what they are having to endure, too.

God is thus portrayed not as a king dealing with an issue at some distance, nor even as one who sends a subordinate to cope with the problem, nor as one who issues an edict designed to alleviate the suffering. God sees the suffering from the inside; God does not look at it from the outside, as through a window. God is internally related to the suffering of the people. God enters fully into the hurtful situation and makes it his own. Yet, while God suffers with the people, God is not powerless to do anything about it; God moves in to deliver, working in and through leaders, even Pharaoh, and elements of the natural order. Thus, it seems clear that this early experience of Israel with its God has become constitutive for all its subsequent reflections upon God and God's relationship with the people (see e.g., Exod. 22:21–27).

This depiction of God is, however, not constant throughout the literature; Israel is not always presented in a suffering situation. For Israel as a whole, it is only with the classical prophets that we will encounter a situation like that in Egypt again. Two texts from the period of Judges may provide a transition, however.[1] Take for example, Judg. 2:18 (cf. Deut. 32:36; Ps. 135:14):

> And he saved them from the hand of their enemies all the days of the judge; for the Lord was moved to pity [*nhm*] by their groaning because of those who afflicted and oppressed them.

In some instances this language parallels that of Exodus 1—3. The context, however, is somewhat different in that their groaning is related specifically to the effects of their sinfulness. Yet God responds to their distress, and quite apart from any repentance on their part. God's response is due finally to being moved by the desperate straits of the people (cf. Judg. 2:15).

The same basic understanding is present in Judg. 10:16, where God does act because of the people's repentance (v.10), but finally because of their "misery." While the meaning of the Hebrew phrase, "his nephesh [soul] was shortened" (RSV, "became indignant"; KJV, "grieved"; JB, "he could bear their sufferings no longer"), is uncertain, the words imply that God's life was in some sense being expended. In Num. 21:4 and Judg. 16:16, the phrase is associated with death, and hence with some diminishment of life.[2] The JB translation captures this sense well; for God to bear the sufferings of the people means that the people's suffering had a negative effect on God. God's life was somehow expended because of the internalization of the sufferings of the people; God suffered because they were suffering (hence the KJV translation is appropriate as well).

In both of these Judges passages, then, God's response to the community is not determined by some retributionary schema. God is revealed as one who is caught up by the situation, who is genuinely anguished over what has occurred, and who is moved to take action.

Alongside the passages which speak of Israel's misery are those passages, particularly in the Psalms, which speak of the suffering of individuals. While the language used is quite varied, reference rather commonly occurs to God's presence with those who suffer. Consider Pss. 91:15, 23:4, and 16:8 (cf. also Pss. 34:6–7, 18; 73:21–28; 109:31):

> I will be with him in trouble.

> Even though I walk through the valley of the shadow of death,
>     I fear no evil;

for thou art with me;
>    thy rod and thy staff
>    they comfort me.

I keep the Lord always before me;
>    because he is at my right hand, I shall not be moved.

The Priestly oracle of salvation spoken to those who prayed the lament psalms may well be the origin for this material (cf. Ps. 12:5; Lam. 3:55–57).

Such a testimony to the nearness of God achieves clarity only if it is recognized what kind of God it must be who is near to those who are in trouble. Any human being who is present with those who are in distress of one kind or another knows that a true and helpful presence will entail some form of empathy, an entering into the situation of the troubled. If so with human beings, how much more with God! God's powers of commiseration, of shared suffering, must be considered unsurpassed. God's presence with the distressed and the oppressed must mean that God has so entered into their situation that it truly becomes his own.

## GOD AS MOURNER

We now turn to those prophetic passages which portray the God who suffers with the people. Generally speaking, the language is not that of lament and accusation; it is the language of mourning and compassion. At the same time, these two types of material involving suffering are commonly interwoven in the texts as we now have them. That is to say, only occasionally do we have the sequence: lament-accusation; judgment; empathy. The empathetic passages often appear in contexts which are prior to the judgment, both historically and redactionally. As such, they *anticipate* the judgment which is about to fall. God is thus represented as one who engages in speeches of lament-accusation, but at the same time, in anticipation of what is likely to happen, takes up lament for the fallen.

We first meet with such lamentation for Israel in Amos 5:1–2:

> Hear this word which I take up over you in lamentation, O house of Israel:
> "Fallen, no more to rise,
> >    is the virgin Israel;

forsaken on her land,
    with none to raise her up."

While vv. 1–2 are not divine speech, Amos intends that his own words be descriptive of God's Word which follows in v. 3. Here there is no reference to Israel's sin and guilt. Rather, it is a "funerary lament, singing in traditional mourning rhythms of the recently transpired death" of Israel (cf. 2 Sam. 1:19–27).[3] The fall of Israel, usually spoken of as a future event in Amos, is represented here as having already occurred, so inevitable does it seem. Its effect on those who heard Amos "would have been something like the shock of reading one's obituary in the newspapers."[4] That such an end is neither inevitable, nor what God wants, is made clear in the present redaction by the fact that this lamentation serves as a striking way of introducing the lines "Seek me and live" (v. 4; cf. vv. 6, 14).[5] The intent of the funerary lament in its present context is thus to startle the people into seeking the Lord, so that they will have life rather than a funeral. One ought not, however, view the lament as a threat. It is a genuine mourning song. It is thus not God's threat that is intended to move the people to repentance, but God's sorrow! (cf. Isa. 52:14–15 with Isaiah 53). At the same time, the use of the funerary lament is not a rhetorical ploy; the situation has in fact deteriorated so much that death is likely.

Thus, we are presented with the kind of response to be expected from God upon the death of Israel: God will undertake lamentation. Just as the people are described (5:16–17; 8:10) as "submerged in a single swell of funerary lamentation,"[6] so also will God be so submerged. God will join the people in taking up a lament over what has happened; God mourns as they do.

Ezekiel in particular makes further use of the divine funerary lament. The content of his message is to include "words of lamentation and mourning and woe" (2:10), words which reflect God's own response to the situation. While lamentation is voiced over the "princes of Israel" in Ezek. 19:1, 14, it is primarily used in the oracles against the foreign nations (27:2; 28:12; 32:2, 16; cf. 30:2; 32:18).[7] Because it is God who asks the prophet to take up the lamentation, this initiative must reflect God's own feeling concerning what has happened. Just as the princes of this world will mourn (26:17–18), so also will God.

Ezekiel 19 is especially striking in that it follows 18:32, "For I have no pleasure in the death of any one, says the Lord God; so turn, and live" (cf. 33:11). Given the parallels of the last phrase to Amos 5:4, 6, 14, this lamentation is intended to function as it does for Amos (the function of the oracles against the nations is problematic).[8] Yet from Ezekiel 19 it is clear that the reality of death has so entered into the house of David that no other end seems likely. While this lamentation has its origins in the context of a funeral ceremony, this source should not "be allowed to hide the fact that in it something of the hidden 'compassion' of God with the downfall of such a strong and youthful king is expressed."[9] Zimmerli comments further in this connection that, given the profanation of God's name by the people among the nations (cf. 36:20), "the judgment upon God's people is God's own suffering in that by it his own name enters into the twilight of dishonor."[10] This comment would suggest that God's suffering is rooted in two factors: suffering with the suffering Israel, and suffering in the face of other nations who have seen God's name dragged through the mire. Israel's failure reflects back upon God; God is disgraced because of what Israel has done to his name. But, even though Israel has besmirched God's honor, God does not hold a grudge against Israel. God endures that suffering, too, while entering compassionately into the suffering of Israel.

While these passages and others speak of the lamentation of God in more indirect ways, in a number of texts God speaks directly. A variety of mourning speech is used, language that is commonly found elsewhere on the lips of human beings.

One should note that the lamentations in Ezekiel's oracles against the nations are also present in Isaiah and Jeremiah, only in direct divine speech. Thus, Isaiah 15—16, an oracle against Moab, is explicitly identified as "the word which the Lord spoke concerning Moab in the past." These chapters, of uncertain origin, are filled with the language of mourning over the destruction of Moab by either Assyria or Babylonia. The most pervasive reference is to the weeping and wailing of the Moabites themselves (15:2–5, 8); others are also asked to take up lamentation (16:7). But God himself also mourns for Moab in Isa. 15:5, 16:9, and 16:11:

My heart cries out for Moab.

Therefore I weep with the weeping of Jazer . . .

I drench you with my tears.

My soul moans like a lyre for Moab
and my heart for Kir-heres.

Jer. 48:30–32, 35–36 contains another recension of this oracle
against Moab, and we find similar language used there in divine
speech:[11]

I know his insolence, says the Lord. . . .
Therefore I wail for Moab;
   I cry out for all Moab;
      for the men of Kir-heres I mourn.
More than for Jazer I weep for you.

I will bring to an end in Moab, says the Lord. . . . Therefore my heart
moans for Moab like a flute, and my heart moans like a flute for the men
of Kir-heres.

To hear such mourning on the part of God for a non-Israelite people
is striking indeed. Most of this language is also used to describe the
weeping and wailing of the Moabites, so that the impression created is
that of a God whose lamentation is as deep and broad as that of the
people themselves. As with Israel, God is the one who has occasioned the judgment in the first place (e.g., Jer. 48:38); but once the
judgment has occurred, God joins those who mourn.

Similar language is used of God in relationship to Israel in Jer. 9:10
and 12:7 (cf. 15:5–9):

Take up [Heb.: I will take up] weeping and wailing for the mountains,[12]
   and a lamentation for the pastures of the wilderness.

I have forsaken my house,
   I have abandoned my heritage;
I have given the beloved of my soul
   into the hands of her enemies.

What heart-rending distress God feels over what has happened to the
people! Even more, as both passages show in their larger contexts,
God mourns not only because "no flesh has peace" (12:12), but
because the *land* is devastated and mourns (cf. 23:10; Hos. 4:2–3).
While the people may be the focus for God's suffering, God is
anguished over the consequences for all aspects of the created order
affected by the devastation.

The depths of God's pain over the havoc wreaked on people and land is recognized in another striking way in Jeremiah 12. God's suffering is to some degree focused on God's own futue. Heschel captures this aspect of the passage well: "Israel's distress was more than a human tragedy. With Israel's distress came the affliction of God, His displacement, His homelessness in the land, in the world. . . . Should Israel cease to be home, then God, we might say, would be without a home in the world."[13] In addition, Heschel points out that this theme also appears in Jer. 9:17–18 (cf. 30:6):

> Thus says the Lord of hosts:
> "Consider, and call for the mourning women to come;
>     send for the skillful women to come;
> let them make haste and raise a wailing over us,
>     that our eyes may run down with tears,
>     and our eyelids gush with water.

The use of the first person plural in this text clearly includes God. The professional mourners are to come and weep not only for Israel, but for God as well! Once again we are confronted with the issue of the future of God. God's future is tied up in so many ways with the future of Israel. Because of what has now happened to Israel, the future for God is different from what it would otherwise have been. This, too, is an occasion for mourning, for God has not been able to accomplish what would have been possible with a faithful Israel. In terms of Jeremiah 45, we need to speak in some sense of a temporary failure in what God has attempted to do in the world. Because of this, the mourners should take up a lamentation for God as well.

On the far side of the judgment, a later passage in Jeremiah is even more poignant in its expression of the divine compassion (31:20; cf. v. 3):

> Is Ephraim my dear son?
>     Is he my darling child?
> For as often as I speak against him,
>     I do remember him still.
> Therefore my heart yearns [moans] for him;
>     I will surely have mercy on him, says the Lord.

The same combination of words is to be found in Isa. 63:15: "The yearning [moaning] of thy heart and thy compassion are withheld from me." Here the lament of the people presupposes that the action of God revealed in Jer. 31:20 is something that is normally extended to them in times of trouble, but now it seems to be withheld; there are no signs of it that can be discerned. It is clearly evident, however, in Jer. 31:20.[14] In context we find Rachel, the figurative mother of Israel, weeping for her children (v. 15). In v. 20, God takes up the role of mother in place of Rachel. As Rachel remembers her children, so now God remembers. As Rachel weeps for her children, so now God weeps. Yet, a difference is seen in that, while Rachel seems to be incapacitated by her mourning (v. 15), it is different with God. God will turn their mourning into joy, and give them gladness for sorrow (vv. 13, 21–22).

It is not only God who picks up the mourning of the people, but the prophet does so as well. An even fuller range of lamentation is ascribed to the prophet than to God, often at God's behest (e.g., Mic. 1:8; Isa. 21:3–4; 22:4; Ezek. 21:6, 12E; Jer. 4:19; 8:18—9:1; 10:19; 13:17; 14:17). At this point it is enough to say that the prophet in these texts mirrors the mourning of God. The people not only hear the prophet as spokesman of God but they also *see* the lamentation of God embodied in the person of the prophet.

Finally, we turn briefly to the so-called woe oracles of the prophets. While we can barely address the topic here,[15] these materials are commonly interpreted in terms of the human mourning cry (see Amos 5:16; Jer. 22:18; 34:5). The "Woe" or "Alas" is "a marker of pain," with "the power to express intensely the emotional content of reversal from a desirable to an undesirable state of existence."[16] For example, Jer. 30:5–7:

> Thus says the Lord:
> We have heard a cry of panic,
>     of terror, and no peace. . . .
>     Why has every face turned pale?
> Alas, that day is so great
>     there is none like it;
> it is a time of distress for Jacob.

Here God takes up the mourning cry which is on the lips of the people who are suffering; God mourns with those who mourn.

Mourning is also an integral part of a number of prejudgment contexts where woe occurs (e.g., Amos 5:16–20; 6:1–7; Mic. 2:1; Isa. 1:4; 10:1–4). The language of woe serves to anticipate the disaster which is to fall on people and land. Thus, for example, in Amos 5:16–

17, God makes the announcement that wailing shall be taken up in the streets; then, in 5:18 God begins to mourn over the anticipated desolation which Israel will experience. The personal character of these woes[17] indicates the way in which God relates to the anticipated mournful situation. Even before the judgment falls, God anticipates the response to the suffering of the people: God will mourn. At times the accusatory element in the woe oracles crowds out the mourning element (e.g., Isa. 5:8–23), though it is doubtful that the idea of pain is altogether absent. These passages might thus be profitably related to the lament-accusation combination of the first category, though here the lament is more future-oriented.

## SUMMARY

1. God's response to Israel's judgment is to take up the cry of a mourner, or, where suffering without judgment is in view, an empathetic presence. This serves to eliminate all other possible understandings of the God of this suffering people. God is not indifferent to what has happened to the people. God does not view Israel's fate with a kind of detached objectivity. God is not an executioner who can walk away from the judgment exacted, thinking: "I only did my duty." Nor is there any satisfaction, let alone celebration, that justice has now been done. Nor any sense of punitiveness: "They deserved what they got!" However much this may be so, God does not "rub it in" or try to make it doubly clear to all that Israel's fate is not only what it had coming, but that it deserves to continue to wallow in the ill effects of the judgment, to bear the judgment alone in perpetuity. For God to mourn with those who mourn is to enter into their situation; and where God is at work, mourning is not the end.

2. The God who in anguish visits judgment upon the people does not thereby sever the relationship. God immediately turns from the role of judge to that of fellow-sufferer; God even anticipates the latter role in the language used to consider the distressful future. Judgment is thus clearly not intended to be the end of the relationship as far as God is concerned. God will be present among those who are suffering. God does not wait until the suffering has had its full effect before God works in the situation to bring about good. God is at work *in* death to bring about life. And God works in that situation, not as someone who stands on the outside, working upon it externally like

some welfare administrator signing vouchers for food stamps. God enters into the mournful situation, working for good from within.

3. God's mourning, as well as that of others, means that judgment finally is indeed death for Israel and not discipline. God voices a funerary lament, not parental pain after a spanking. All forms of discipline have failed to result in correction (Jer. 2:30; 5:3; 7:28). The result is "a great wound, a very grievous blow" (Jer. 14:17–18). Israel has been brought to the depths of Sheol; the people no longer have any capacity to turn (Jer. 13:23). Because the situation is so deteriorated (Jer. 30:12–15), "therefore" only God can raise them up and restore them to wholeness. God's redemptive activity must precede any return on the part of the people (Isa. 44:22; cf. 52:3). God will lead those home who are not able to accomplish the task for themselves (Jer. 31:7–9). Judgment is not salvation, but it is the necessary prerequisite for the salvation of the people. Death is necessary for such a people before life is possible again. In the midst of judgment God works his salvific deed.

4. That God is represented as mourning over the fate of non-Israelite peoples as well as Israelites demonstrates the breadth of God's care and concern for the sufferers of the world, whoever they might be. Israel has no monopoly on God's empathy. All people everywhere have *experienced* the compassion (and judgment) of God, even though they may not realize that fact. There is a universal extension of the compassion of God in these passages that is matched by such texts as Jon. 4:10–11 and Jer. 12:14–15. What the people of Israel should be able to see is that not only have they experienced the compassion (and judgment) of God but they also *know* from whom the experience has come. How much more, then, should their experience mean to them! Such material should thus bring to Israel the realization of (1) the scope of God's suffering (and judging), (2) the consistency of that activity wherever in the world it is found, (3) the commonality of their experience of God, and (4) the special privilege it has received in knowing the one who has so entered into the suffering of the world and has absorbed it.

# CHAPTER 9

# God Suffers For

## GOD'S SELF-GIVING

Here one will encounter the most difficult of the divine suffering materials. There is no "doctrine" of the atonement entailing divine suffering which is presented or presupposed in the OT. Yet there are significant clues in this direction in various OT passages. That Israel needs forgiveness and salvation is clear throughout the OT. That God has so graciously provided vehicles through which the divine forgiveness is extended to Israel is also evident. The sacrificial system is the most visible of these, a tangible means in and through which God grants forgiveness to the believer. At the same time, sacrifices were not considered essential for the granting of forgiveness. A "broken and contrite heart" could also suffice (see Ps. 51:16–19; 2 Sam. 12:13).

The cost to God in the various expiation texts is not made clear. That commonly the life of animals is taken and their blood spilled is seen to be integral to expiation (though not necessary, see Lev. 5:11–13). Such practices point us in the direction of "cost," perhaps even cost to God. Thus, Lev. 17:11, "For the life of the flesh is in the blood; and *I have given it* for you upon the altar to make atonement for your souls; for it is the blood that makes atonement, by reason of the life." It is not the blood itself that is expiatory, but the fact that it was thought to bear life. But especially striking here is that the life in the blood has been given *by God*. It is God who provides the key element in the sacrifices, namely, the life. Human beings thus bring not only their repentant and trusting selves to the sacrificial act, but they are bearers of life from God. If all life belongs to God, then it may be said that God gives of himself to make forgiveness possible. In some sense God's life is expended for the sake of the life of the people.

This expending of the divine life, this giving of self for others, is a profitable direction to explore further. It may well contain the seeds for Israel's further reflection on the cost of atonement to God. Here we need to examine those passages which speak of God being burdened by the sins of the people.

The Hebrew word *nāsā'* (cf. also *sabāl*) is often used to denote "forgive" (e.g., Hos. 1:6; 14:2); in other texts it has reference to God's providential care (e.g., Isa. 40:11; 46:3–4; Deut. 1:31). Two other related usages are especially important for our considerations, however. Occasionally human beings are said to suffer for the iniquities of others (e.g., Num. 14:33; Pss. 69:7; 89:50; Lam. 5:7); elsewhere, representatives of Israel bear the sins of the people: the scapegoat (Lev. 16:22); the priest (Exod. 28:38; cf. Lev. 10:17);[1] the prophet (Ezek. 4:4–6);[2] and the suffering servant (Isa. 53:4, 11–12). In the latter two examples we anticipate our later discussion of how the prophet mirrors the life of God. The people not only hear that God bears their sins, but they *see* that he does so in the person of the prophet. See the passages with God as the subject of the verb used in this sense:

> The Lord could not longer bear your evil doings
> and . . . abominations.
>
> (Jer. 44:22)

> Your new moons and your appointed feasts
>     my soul hates;
> they have become a burden to me,
>     I am weary of bearing them.
>
> (Isa. 1:14)

The images in these passages is that of an eminently patient God who has again and again gone beyond what justice would require; God bears the sins of the people rather than exacting judgment. Yet, there comes a time when God's patience is at an end.

> But Joshua said to the people,
> "You cannot serve the Lord [and other gods];
> for he is a holy God; he is a jealous God;
> he will not forgive [bear] your transgressions or your sins.
>
> (Josh. 24:19)

While difficult, this passage makes the point that God will not bear the people's sins perpetually. One needs to reckon with an end to the divine patience. Their sins will not be carried forever. (For the use of the related noun "burden," see Job 7:20 and Jer. 23:33, where people are said to be a "burden" to God.)

An especially striking passage in this connection is Isa. 43:23–24:

> I have not burdened you with offerings,
>     or wearied you with frankincense.
>
> But you have burdened me with your sins,
>     you have wearied me with your iniquities.

The word for "burdened" here is *'ābad,* from which the word for "servant" is derived.[3] The same verbal form is used for the "burden" laid on the Israelites by Pharaoh (Exod. 1:13; 6:5) and Solomon (1 Chron. 2:18; cf. Ezek. 29:18). In the Isaianic passage (which refers back to preexilic times, cf. vv. 27–28), God is said not to have laid a heavy burden of expectations upon his people. The people, however, have laid a heavy burden upon God by their sins. God is said to be loaded down with their iniquities. One cannot help but be reminded of the "bearing sin" passages of Isa. 53:4, 11–12, as well as certain New Testament passages, where the Christ is said to have borne the sins of many (e.g., 1 Pet. 2:24). The servant of God thus assumes the role which God himself has played. Just as it entailed suffering for the servant, it must have entailed suffering for God. By bearing the sins of the people over a period of time, God suffers in some sense on their behalf. By holding back on the judgment they deserve, and carrying their sins on his own shoulders, God chooses the road of suffering-for.

A related notion, the weariness of God, also needs attention. Two of the above-noted passages speak of God being wearied by the sins of the people (Isa. 1:14; 43:24). Others reiterate this point:

> Hear then, O house of David! Is it too little for you to weary men, that you weary my God also?
>
> (Isa. 7:13)

> You have rejected me, says the Lord,
>     you keep going backward;
> so I have stretched out my hand against you and destroyed you;—
>     I am weary of relenting.
>
> (Jer. 15:6; cf. Ezek. 24:12)

You have wearied the Lord with your words.
(Mal. 2:17)

Finally, one might make note of Jer. 45:3. Baruch, Jeremiah's scribe, complains that he is "weary with my groaning, and I find no rest," as also does Jeremiah (6:11; 20:9; cf. Pss. 6:6; 69:3). The implication in Jeremiah 45 is that, while Baruch may be wearied, his distress is nothing compared to the weariness of God.[4]

How are we to understand such passages, especially in view of the fact that God is expressly said to be one who "does not faint or grow weary" (Isa. 40:28)? The latter context, with its reference to the weariness of human beings (vv. 30–31), suggests that the primary reference is to physical stamina. With God the Creator there is no limit in this regard. The idea of "tiredness," whether of the physical, mental, or emotional kind, does not seem to be the focus of these passages. I suggest that the references to divine weariness have a more general reference to the expending of the divine life (cf. Eccles. 1:8; Jer. 9:5); God's life is in some sense being spent. The vocabulary of weariness and the lament-accusation combination do tie these materials to the human laments and hence with the first category of divine suffering noted above. Yet something more seems to be implied in the divine weariness.

Perhaps an examination of the language of divine restraint in Isa. 48:9, Ezek. 20:21–22, Ps. 78:38, and Isa. 57:11 will help us with this dilemma:

> For my name's sake I defer my anger,
>     for the sake of my praise I restrain it for you.
>     that I may not cut you off.

> I thought I would pour out my wrath upon them. . . . But I withheld my hand.

> He, being compassionate . . .
> restrained his anger often.

> Have I not held my peace, even for a long time,
>     and so you do not fear me?

While the incredible patience of God with his people becomes evident in a special way here, further implications are present. It is clear from Ps. 39:2–3 that, when the psalmist held his peace, "my distress grew worse, my heart became hot within me" (cf. Ps. 32:3). For Jeremiah (20:9; cf. 6:11), such restraint has meant that "there is in my heart as it were a burning fire shut up in my bones," which in turn is associated with weariness. Once again we see here the prophet as the mirror of God. What is entailed in the divine restraint is also positively clear from Isa. 42:14 (cf. Isa. 63:15; 64:12E):

> For a long time I have held my peace
> > I have kept still and restrained myself,
> now I will cry out like a woman in travail,
> > I will gasp and pant.

This divine restraint implies something very much like what it did for Jeremiah and the psalmist, only in a positive sense. The divine restraint in the face of the suffering of the people stood for an intensification of God's suffering, a build-up of internal forces, finally bursting forth in the travail of creative activity.

The divine restraint at the people's unfaithfulness stood for something comparable in the divine life. We have seen how Israel's rejection occasioned God's suffering; continued divine restraint in the face of continued rejection must have meant for a greater and greater intensification of suffering, a build-up of internal forces in God, which finally (though not uncontrollably) burst forth in judgment. At the same time, this intensification of suffering is spoken of in terms of weariness. This must have something to do with a kind of exhaustion of life, a giving or expending of so much of the self for the sake of the relationship that, for the sake of the divine name (that is, the future of God), it must be brought to an end. To use other words, God experiences great intensity of suffering, but stops short of crucifixion.

Here we note that the good which happens in the world can contribute to God's enrichment. Thus God "takes pleasure in those who fear him, in those who hope in his steadfast love" (Ps. 147:11; cf. 149:4)—delighting and rejoicing with the people (e.g., 1 Kings 10:9; Isa. 62:4–5; 65:19; Zeph. 3:17). As J. G. Janzen puts it,[5] "one or another kind of human behavior toward another human being can and does bring joy or pain to the divine care for the world."

As God can be enriched, so we see in these weariness passages that blatant and pervasive unfaithfulness can impoverish God. "You have wearied me with your iniquities." Such human activity takes something away from what would otherwise have been possible for God. In some respects God is no longer the God who was before all this happened. God has internalized the people's rejection, and this process has created a profound weariness. It is just this weariness which makes it difficult to restrain the judgment any longer, for the sake of the future of God ("for my name's sake"), and hence for the future of the world.

Though the judgment does fall on Israel, the fact that it has been restrained for so long is a witness to the long-suffering God. God's bearing of the people's sins has occasioned divine suffering. Thus, there is an intimate relationship to be seen between the continued life of a sinful people and the suffering of God. It is only because of God's willingness to continue to suffer as long as he has that the people continue to live. God's suffering in these passages, while it does not yet mean redemption, does mean life. The connection is there to be developed further.

A further contribution to this development comes in Hos. 11:8–9, one of the most discussed prophetic texts.[6] We have seen how the questions in Hosea play a role in the decision-making process which God shares with the people concerning their common future. We have also noted how the memory of God, so evident in 11:1–8, occasions divine suffering. Here we focus on the divine suffering evident in these verses (v. 8, au. trans.):[7]

> My heart turns over within me,
>> My compassion is completely warm.

The unchanging salvific will of God for her people, rooted in love, needs to be at the center of any consideration of this passage. What God desires for their relationship is clear; there is no conflict or change whatsoever in God with respect to this goal. At the same time, Israel's unfaithfulness persists. The divine decision-sharing efforts with the people have not been responded to positively. Given the concern for the divine name, and hence the future of Israel and world, there appears to be nothing left to do but to take off the divine restraints and let the judgment burst forth upon the people. Yet, what happens is that Israel is to be visited, not with full destruction, but with an intermediate judgmental response (Hos. 11:10–11).[8]

Why this intermediate divine response? Verse 8 testifies that something has happened in God which prevents Israel from receiving the full brunt of the judgment. What has happened? God repents. God determines that she will not give the people up to total destruction, as was the case with Sodom and Gomorrah (v. 8a), and which vv. 5–7 announce. Israel will be taken captive, but it shall not experience the full force of God's anger;[9] Israel shall be removed from the yoke (contrary to v. 7) and return home (vv. 10–11). This event is comparable to other divine repentings that eventuate in partial judgments (e.g., 2 Sam. 24:16; Jer. 42:10),[10] decisions rooted in God's love without any human supplication or intercessory activity.

The report of God's repentant decision is unusual in its fullness. That the two lines of Hos. 11:8b are synonymously parallel is commonly recognized,[11] focusing on the two dimensions of repentance: the turning itself and the love which occasions the turning (cf. Ps. 106:45). At the same time, the language of warmth or heat suggests the build-up of internal forces, such as pent-up emotions (see also Gen. 43:30 and 1 Kings 3:26). God's suffering love boils up to such an extent that it occasions the repentant action. The divine suffering love, while not issuing in Israel's redemption, does alleviate the judgment. It is going too far to speak of conflict in God here, for judgment is never the will of God for the people; yet it is God's will to save that makes for an internal tension, and hence suffering, in God when confronted with the concomitant need for justice to be done. Here God resolves to continue taking that suffering upon herself in order to allow that will to be done.[12] This choice is another important ingredient for the development of Israel's thought about such matters.

DIVINE HUMILIATION

From a different perspective, a small group of isolated texts suggest the theme of divine humiliation, which in turn effects salvation for the community.

The ark narratives in 1 Samuel 4—6, as interpreted by Psalm 78, give some direction to this idea. At the very end of the period of the judges, the Philistine threat makes for a very troubled time for Israel. While there is no explicit language regarding the divine humiliation in the narratives reflective of this era, 1 Sam. 4:10—5:1 may speak indirectly to this matter. In this passage we have a sixfold repetition of the ark of God being captured. Because of the very close relationship perceived between the ark and the presence of God (cf. 1 Sam. 5:7, 11; cf. 4:7), one could speak of *the capture of God.* The reference to this capture occurs in counterpoint to the slaughter of the Israelites (vv. 10, 17), the trembling and pain of individuals (vv. 13, 19), and the departure of the glory from Israel (vv. 21–22). This pattern could well suggest that God himself is believed to be subjected to humiliation and suffering at the hands of the enemies also. The description of this event in Ps. 78:61 suggests this conclusion as well:

> [He] delivered his power to captivity,
>> his glory to the hand of the foe.

God has entered into the darkness of captivity! Terrien's[13] language here is striking: "The divine decision meant a divine humiliation. Yahweh surrendered his sovereignty to the shame of alien imprisonment. He voluntarily relinquished his royal magnificence to the power of the enemy." God thus works from within a situation of humiliation to bring about the deliverance of Israel. And the movement from humiliation to exaltation with respect to the ark of God meant a movement from trembling to life for Israel.

Another text sometimes mentioned in this connection is Ps. 18:35 (au. trans.):

> Thy right hand supported me,
> and thy humility[?] made me great.

The word "humility" (RSV, "help") translates a Hebrew term which, along with its cognates, is applied here uniquely to God in the OT (see its application to the suffering servant in Isa. 53:4, 7). Although the translation is not certain, Weiser is bold to suggest that "the king owes his rise to greatness to the 'condescension' of God."[14] Terrien places it in the context of the "descent" of God in the theophany of vv. 7–15, and speaks of "the self-imposed abasement of the omnipotent deity for the sake of man."[15] Given the theophanic context, this text might be considered support for our interpretation of theophanies (cf. chap. 6).

Isa. 63:9 should also be cited:

> In all their affliction he was afflicted[?],
>> and the angel of his presence saved them.

This RSV translation (cf. NEB, JB) of a difficult Hebrew text, "he was afflicted," suggests that God, by participating in the affliction of the people, enabled their salvation.[16] The context certainly indicates that God's loving and compassionate presence resulted in their redemption and care. The problematic character of the text, however, does not enable us to speak with confidence.

Another isolated reference that should be mentioned is Zech. 12:10, for no other reason than the role it has played in the NT (John 19:37) and subsequent Christian interpretation:

> And I will pour out on the house of David and the inhabitants of Jerusalem a spirit of compassion and supplication, so that, when they look on him [me?] whom they have pierced, they shall mourn for him, as one mourns for an only child.

While this text has traditionally been interpreted in terms of a crucified Messiah (e.g., Luther), most modern commentators tend to despair over what it might mean.[17] If it is metaphorically interpreted in terms of God being wounded by the sins of the people (so Calvin), it remains a testimony to divine suffering. Perhaps most common is an interpretation in the light of Zech. 13:3, where the parents of a prophet pierce him through. Thus, 12:10 could be a reference to a prophet who has been subjected to suffering by the people. Because of the close relationship of prophet and God, God suffers the effects of such an action. In any case, the reference is almost certainly to divine suffering in some sense.

One might also call attention to the use of the verb *ḥûs*, "pity," in Jonah 4:10–11: "You pity the plant, for which you did not labor. . . . Should not I pity Nineveh?" This verb is used in judicial contexts (cf. Deut. 19:13, 21), where the idea expressed is that of not allowing tears to flow from the eyes so as to deter the judgment required. And so "to have pity" would imply action with tears.[18] God, in being moved to spare Nineveh, engages in an act that entails suffering. God's tears flow in order to save Nineveh from just judgment; God takes their deserved judgment upon himself.

Finally, one passage which takes us about as far along this path as we can go in the OT is Isa. 42:14.[19] The text presupposes that judgment has fallen upon the people of Israel; they are languishing in exile. The context is one of chaos; one might even speak of a return to a precreation state of affairs; death characterizes their situation more than life. The experience of God for them has been that of a profound silence, a divine restraint with respect to any relief of their suffering (see Isa. 63:15; 64:12; Ps. 74:11). God's own experience of the self-imposed restraint is seen here in terms of a pregnancy, a necessary period of time between the death of the people and new birth.[20] The period of silence may also be reflective of the divine humiliation. That is, God's silence has been occasioned by the fact God has so deeply entered into the death of the people that she experiences what they are having to experience. Thus, this move on God's part is one that signals the move from "death" to resurrection in God. During this time, Israel is incapable of such a development; it is barren and cannot bring new life into being (49:21; cf. 66:7–14; Jer. 31:15–17). Whatever birthing will occur will be God's; she alone can bring a new creation into being. Just as God birthed Israel at the beginning of its life (Deut. 32:18), God will do so again. But, as we have seen, the period of restraint is a time of ever-intensifying labor pains for God, which finally burst forth in the travail of the emergence of a new creation. This birth-event, however, will entail not simply the emergence of a new people of God; the act of re-creation will affect the whole world (vv. 15–16). God, crying out, gasping, and panting, gives birth to a new order. The new creation *necessitates* the suffering of God.

Here suffering and new creation are intimately interconnected, and the image used suggests that new creation can come into being in no other way. Any birthing of a new order can come about only through what God does, and God can accomplish such a creative act only by way of a *via dolorosa*. But equally significant here is that what is happening in the life of God is not without its parallel on earth; Isa. 42:1–7 has just introduced us to the suffering servant, through whom God has chosen to accomplish the same divine purpose. Thus, we have in this chapter an earth/heaven correspondence, the suffering of the servant paralleled by the suffering of God (cf. parallels in Isa. 43:24 and 54:9–10). We should also note here that this earthly/heavenly correspondence is seen in the juxtaposition of the second servant song (49:1–7) and the compassion of God (49:13–16), as well as the third servant song (50:4–9) and the lament of 50:1–3. This pattern is in many ways similar to the interwoven laments of God and the prophet Jeremiah, though there are further developments here with respect to the efficacy of the suffering involved. There is no suffering of the servant without the suffering of God. It is the earthly side of this correspondence of suffering to which we now turn: the suffering of God is taken up and embodied in the life of "my servants, the prophets."

## SUMMARY

It is clear that human sin has not been without cost for God, and that cost is due in significant part to the fact that God has chosen to bear the people's sins rather than deal with them on strictly legal terms. For God to assume such a burden, for God to continue to bear the brunt of Israel's rejection, meant continued life for the people. Thus there is an explicit connection made between divine suffering and Israel's life; the former was necessary for the latter to occur. God's suffering made Israel's life possible.

What did such suffering mean for God? In some sense it meant the expending of life for God, expressed primarily in the image of weariness. God so gives of self for the sake of the relationship with the people that in some sense God's life can be said to be expended so that Israel's could be continued.

These concerns might in turn be related to the texts which speak of divine humiliation, of God immersing himself in the depths of Israel's troubles in order to make deliverance possible. In some sense God subjects himself to a humiliating situation, and thereby gives up something of what the divine life must be, for the purpose of Israel's salvation. It is only by entering deeply into the situation so fraught with death that the death-dealing forces are conquered and life is made possible once again.

Finally we note that God, in order to enable a new creation which transcends the present order of suffering and death, engages in such a giving of self that only one of the sharpest of human pains known can adequately portray what is involved for God. But such an event is not thought of solely in terms of the internal life of God. God's suffering is the heavenly counterpart to the suffering of the earthly servant of God. The suffering servant takes upon himself the suffering of God and does what is finally necessary for the forces of evil in this world to be overcome: suffering unto death.

# CHAPTER 10

Prophet, Theophany,
and the Suffering of God

## PROPHET AND MESSENGER

The prophet's life was reflective of the divine life. This became increasingly apparent to Israel. God is seen to be present not only in what the prophet has to say, but in the word as embodied in the prophet's life. To hear and see the prophet was to hear and see God, a God who was suffering on behalf of the people.

It has been commonly pointed out that, while the messenger plays an important role as mediator of the Word of God in premonarchical texts, this ceases from the time of Samuel on (2 Kings 1:3–4, 15 is an exception). The prophet constitutes a replacement and continuation of the line of divine messengers.[1] Then, as if to complete a circle, the prophet is succeeded by the angelic intermediaries of postexilic Judaism (e.g., in Daniel), though the messengers appear to become more obviously subordinate beings.

Differences between messenger and prophet may be seen. The prophet is a known individual, while the messenger is never named. The prophet lives and works for an extended period of time, while the "earthly life" of the messenger is confined to the time or times of the appearance. There is a distinctness of personality which the prophet has, independent of God, compared to the messenger.[2] The messenger almost always announces a word of favor, while the prophet more commonly proclaims a word of judgment. Nevertheless, because the Word of God is always spoken into the particularities of changing historical situations, this distinction may not be especially important.

Similarities may also be noted. Both are figures in human form.

Both are referred to as "man of God" (e.g., Judg. 13:8–9; 1 Sam. 2:27) and "messenger."[3] Both are announcers of the Word of God, and use the same language in specifying that purpose.[4] Both use the first person singular, as if God were speaking.[5] The redactors of both messenger narratives and prophetic oracles do interchange God and messenger/prophet, though much more directly in the former (e.g., Gen. 16:11, 13). In the prophetic materials, while God and "prophet" (or the name of the prophet) are not interchanged, it is often very difficult, if not impossible, to sort out explicit divine speech from prophetic speech; pronominal references do at times seem to be interchanged, particularly in Jeremiah.[6]

Further commonality could be present in connection with "membership in the divine council" (see Jer. 23:18–22; 1 Kings 22:19), though explicit divine council references for the messenger appear to be present only in later texts (e.g., Zech. 1:12; 3:1–8).[7] Though the meaning of the divine council is problematic, the fact that the prophets are said to be a part of this council indicates something of the intimate relationship they had with God. The prophet was somehow drawn up into the very presence of God; even more, the prophet was in some sense admitted into the history of God. The prophet becomes a party to the divine story; the heart and mind of God pass over into that of the prophet to such an extent that the prophet becomes a veritable embodiment of God.

The various similarities between messenger and prophet indicate a basic continuity between them, and suggest that we understand their relationship to God in comparable ways, albeit with the differences we have noted.

Other materials redactionally set in the preprophetic period may be helpful in explicating the relationship between prophet and God. Thus, some very striking language is used of Moses, as in Exod. 4:16 and 7:1:

> He [Aaron] shall speak for you to the people; and he shall be a mouth for you, and *you shall be to him as God.*

> And the Lord said to Moses, "See, *I make you as God* to Pharaoh; and Aaron your brother shall be your prophet."

While one must be careful not to read too much into these passages, they ought not be weakened to say, in effect, Moses is to God as

Aaron is to Moses. In some sense the Word of God becomes so embodied in Moses that in and through what Moses says (and does!) God himself becomes active in that situation. Moses becomes a vehicle for divine immanence.

Certain language used of the Spirit of God might also be helpful in this connection. Although it lies on the edges of the prophetic movement, it may have provided a conceptual framework within which the relationship between prophet and God was understood. Thus, for example, in Judg. 6:34, the action of the Spirit in taking possession of Gideon is described as putting him on like a garment; 1 Sam. 10:6 speaks of such action of the Spirit as turning Saul "into another man." The clothing imagery is also used in 1 Chron. 12:18 and 2 Chron. 24:20. Micah 3:8 and Isa. 61:1 (cf. 42:1) are perhaps to be understood in similar terms. In these cases, God becomes so active within the life of an individual that he can be said to be an embodiment of God. So completely does God become the power that energizes the person, that it is as if God himself were the one now speaking and acting.[8]

Decisive points of continuity with the older theophanic traditions are also evident in the calls of the prophets. As we have indicated, these calls are commonly connected with an appearance of God, with all the import that we have seen such appearances to have, particularly in terms of their personalistic and persuasive components (e.g., Amos 7:7; 9:1; Isaiah 6; Jeremiah 1; Ezekiel 1). It has been shown that there is a form-critical link between these calls and earlier appearances of God to Moses and Gideon.[9] At the same time, it would be a mistake to stop at this point in assessing the import of God's appearances to the prophets. They move beyond the older theophanies at one point in particular. God does not, as in the older theophanies, just appear, speak a word, and then leave. God leaves the word behind imbedded in the prophet. God calls the prophet to take the word received and embody that word from the moment of the call onward. The prophet, in effect, is called to function as an ongoing theophany. In the prophet we see a development from the more transient messenger of God to a more extended appearance of the Word of God in human form. One can thus now speak, not only of the participation of God in the appearance of the human, but also in the *history* of the human. The story of God is lived out in the story of the prophet.

How this understanding developed within prophecy can perhaps best be seen in terms of three concurrent movements: collapse of office and person; union of person and word; word/person becoming event. D. Robertson's study is of special help in this regard.[10] He states: "Because in the New Testament the word of God becomes a man, it is also, quite literally, an aspect of the Bible's plot"; thus his concern for tracing "the process by which spoken word becomes living person."

*Person and Office.*    As von Rad states regarding developments in prophecy: "Their office increasingly invaded their personal and spiritual lives."[11] While with Amos the distinction is clear, with Hosea and Isaiah prophetic office and private life begin to collapse. Both give names to their children which contain prophetic messages (cf. Hosea 1; Isa. 8:1–4), and Hosea marries at the command of God. With Jeremiah the distinction collapses altogether. He is set apart to be a prophet before his birth, indeed before his conception (1:5). Prophethood thus defines his person from the very beginning; it is the essence of his very being. He is decisively shaped by God not just to be a certain kind of speaker, but a certain kind of person. Thus, he no longer has a private life that can be truly called his own, having to do without wife or children and the normal run of social activities (Jer. 16:1–9; 15:17). While this is not so clear with Ezekiel, his life takes on a similar character (see 24:15–18).

*Person and Word.*    Again, it is with Jeremiah and Ezekiel that we see person becoming embodied Word of God. This shift is particularly evident in their call narratives. In Jer. 1:9 (cf. 15:16) the Word of God is placed by God's hand directly into Jeremiah's mouth. It is no longer necessary for the prophet to see or hear what he is to say; the word is transferred into his very being without having been spoken. This process is graphically portrayed in Ezek. 3:1–3:

> And he [God] said to me, "Son of man, eat what is offered to you; eat this scroll, and go, speak to the house of Israel." So I opened my mouth, and he gave me the scroll to eat. . . . Then I ate it; and it was in my mouth as sweet as honey.

The prophet thus ingests the Word of God; the Word of God is thereby enfleshed in the very person of the prophet. He embodies the Word of God; as a person the prophet becomes the Word of God. Von Rad warns against taking these passages "in too spiritual a way. . . . The entry of the message into their physical life brought about an important change in the self-understanding of these later prophets. (We may ask whether the entry of the word into a prophet's bodily life is not meant to approximate what the writer of the Fourth Gospel says about the word becoming flesh.)"[12] Terrien speaks of the "startlingly concrete terms of a quasi-sacramental absorption";[13] the prophet is a "living incarnator of divinity."[14] God cannot be separated from the word which he gives. In giving the word in such a way that it passes over into the very being of the prophet, God must be said to go with that word, so that in some sense God is *absorbed into* the very life of the prophet. The prophet becomes a vehicle of divine immanence. The prophet/God ambiguity of subject in many of Jeremiah's speeches is but one indication of the effects of this fact.

*Word, Person, and Event.*    That the Word is event is a generally acknowledged way of speaking of the proclamation of the Word of God. The Word of God is efficacious; it has the power to effect that which is articulated (see Isa. 55:10–11). Hence, the future of which the prophet speaks already begins to happen once the word has been spoken. By their response to that word, the people can, however, affect the *way* it is efficacious in their lives. For example, the word of judgment has power to bring about repentance and deflect the course of the spoken Word of God.

For the prophets, however, it is not only the words spoken which have effects; it is also the acts performed. Much has been written of the symbolic acts of the prophets (e.g., Isaiah 20; Jeremiah 19; Ezekiel 4—5).[15] It is clear that they were not intended to be merely illustrative of oral preaching, but—in a way similar to other symbolic actions, e.g., liturgical—the prophet thereby "prefigured as an event what he proclaimed through the word."[16] In this "intensified form" of prophetic speech, "Yahweh himself acts in the symbol, through the instrument of his prophet."[17] Again, it is not only a matter of hearing that is important for God and people, it is a matter of seeing.

Even more, not only are the words and symbolic acts of the proph-

ets efficacious but also the person of the prophet in his totality
becomes an event of God. Thus, regarding Ezekiel, W. Zimmerli can
say that "the person of the prophet himself is described as a 'sign' for
the people" (cf. 12:6, 11; 24:24, 27). "The *Bios* of the prophet is
recorded in his messages not as a matter of autobiographical interest,
but as that which is capable of expressing the Word of Yahweh."[18]
Passages such as Amos 9:1, "Smite the capitals until the thresholds
shake," and Jer. 25:15, "Make all the nations to whom I send you
drink" the cup of wrath, show the merging of divine and prophetic
events. It is, however, finally in the prophetic figure of the Suffering
Servant that we see how the person, in all that he is and does (though
apparently without speaking!), becomes a saving event.

Now it is certainly true that the prophet is not simply the reflex of
God, as if he never had anything of his own to say or do. The prophet
is a distinct personality from God, subject to all the foibles and flaws
of any human being. But, as we turn to the suffering of the prophet, it
is wise to remember that it is as a servant of God that he suffers. The
suffering emerges because of the service undertaken; hence the
prophet is not the suffering representative of the people, but one who
embodies the suffering of God.[19]

I will now examine each of the three categories of divine suffering
and see how they are paralleled in the life of the prophet.

## THE PROPHET'S SUFFERING
## BECAUSE OF BEING REJECTED

The prophets encountered resistance, and on a massive scale. They
were rejected as much as God. They were opposed by the powerful
and the common, kings and peasants. Because they themselves were
not figures of power, they could put up little resistance. They were not
in a position to impose their words on people. However much the
word they spoke was a hammer which broke the rocks in pieces (Jer.
23:29), it could be resisted and usually was. The people did not simply
reject the God whose word was being conveyed; they bore down on
the prophet himself. They made no distinction between person and
word; the prophets were rejected as persons. The result was that the
prophets often suffered at the hands of the people, even to the point
that their lives were put in danger (e.g., Jer. 26:10–24). But their
suffering was occasioned not only by overt persecution, but also

because of their lack of success, their awareness that the word they spoke was not being heeded (e.g., Jer. 20:7–10). We can see here decisive parallels between prophet and God, both in the fact that they were rejected and in the way in which they responded to that rejection. Moreover, the dual focus of God's suffering in this respect is paralleled in the prophets: the past/present reference with its focus on suffering because of rejection, and the present/future reference with its suffering because of the tension as to what to do with respect to the future. Material in Hosea and Jeremiah may serve to illustrate this point.

*Hosea.*[20]   Just as God is repudiated by the people (e.g., 4:10, 12) so is Hosea (9:7–8); just as God wonders what should be done to such a rebellious people (6:4), so does Hosea (9:14). But it is the marriage of Hosea in particular, however disputed its interpretation, that can be seen as a metaphor (in the fullest sense of that term) for God's marriage to Israel.

The fragments on Hosea's marriage in chapters 1 and 3 surround an introspective statement of God in chapter 2. But the statement of chapter 2 is remarkable in that "the language intermingles the prophet's own experience and the theological word. The prophetic consciousness is inseparable from the lover's introspection."[21] It is not always clear here what refers to the God who has been injured by Israel's harlotry and what applies to Hosea who has been dishonored by the harlotries of his wife (cf. vv. 2, 4–5, 7). Yet, while God's history with the people covers past (v. 15), present, and future (2:16–23), Hosea's marriage only correlates with that history with respect to present and future (3:1–5). Hosea's marriage to a wife of harlotry is, from the beginning, parallel to the people who "commit great harlotry by forsaking the Lord" (1:2). Hosea is thus asked by God to live out a married life that will correspond to the *present* situation in which God finds himself in relationship to the "wife of harlotry," which is Israel. "Both God and prophet have in common a bond which attaches them to similarly faithless partners."[22] The children of Hosea, whose startling names are given by God, embody before the society of which they are a part the message of God for Israel. Thus, God does not simply give the prophet a word to speak to the people; God commands him to be an embodiment of the divine life in the totality of his own life. By so participating in the realities of God's life, Hosea lives out before the people the life of God.

Hosea endures public dishonor as a societal outcast, not simply as an illustration of a God who is also dishonored and an outcast, but as a metaphor of God. It is not only that Hosea experiences in his own life what life is like for God, as true as that is; Hosea suffers in his own life the agony of *God* over what has happened. "The prophet has been invaded and permeated by the presence of Yahweh in such a way that he has become a living monstrance of the divine reality."[23] As such a metaphor, Hosea in his total person says something that cannot be reduced to statements, concepts, or speech; the Word of God as embodied conveys the Word "in person" in a way that no simple speaking or writing can. Moreover, because of the startling effect such an embodiment must have had on Hosea's society, such an embodied metaphor would have upset traditional ways of thinking about God and his relationship to the people. By characterizing the mingled sorrow and anger of God the lover, because of what has happened to the relationship, Hosea intended to move the people to repentance. The story of Hosea's marriage may be said to have a family resemblance to other symbolic acts of the prophets, whereby the Word of God is both spoken and embodied.

*Jeremiah.*[24]   It is often thought that Jeremiah is a prophet whose personal life is revealed to us in an especially full way. We not only have more biographical information (e.g., chapters 36—45), but we also are given a glimpse into his most intimate thoughts in his "Confessions" and other tension-filled materials (e.g., 4:10; 11:20). It is likely, however, that these materials are not introduced for biographical purposes; they are intended to reflect the nature of the Word which Jeremiah brings. He not only speaks the Word of God; he embodies it. And all the twists and turns of his own humanity are intended to portray for the people not simply his own life, but his own life as an enfleshment of the life of God.[25] Moreover, though it is often stated that Jeremiah serves as a representative of the people before God in some of this material, another direction of interpretation seems more likely for most texts.

In Jer. 15:17 he indicates that he did not sit with the merry-makers, nor rejoice, because God had filled him with indignation. It is God's own stance toward the people, now embodied in the prophet (15:16), that occasions this removal from the normal run of the life of the people. Jer. 16:1–9 contains the full story: The prophet is commanded not to take a wife or have children (v. 2), not to participate in mourning rites and to receive comfort therefrom (vv. 5–7), nor to join in feasting (vv. 8–9). These various activities are all indicative of what it means to live in a good relationship with a community. All of this participation is taken away from Jeremiah as a way of prefiguring the end of these activities in the life of the people. But is this forfeiture not also a picture of God's own relationship to the community? Does not the prophet here show forth what life with Israel is like for God? God, too, has "forsaken my house . . . abandoned my heritage" (12:7; cf. 11:15; Hos. 9:15), and has become "like a stranger in the land, like a wayfarer who turns aside to tarry for a night" (14:8). Israel was God's dwelling-place in the world (cf. 17:12). In this act Jeremiah is made into a profound witness to the homelessness of God. The foxes have holes and the birds have nests, but God is an alien in the land, with all the mingled anguish and anger involved in dispossession.

It is in this context that Jeremiah's "Confessions," better described as lament-accusations, are best understood (11:18—12:6; 15:10–18; 17:14–18; 18:19–23; 20:7–18). They are not to be understood as laments representative of the people, but rather, reflective of the life of God. Not only is Jeremiah cut off from all that goes by the name of home, he is falsely accused and persecuted by people from his hometown (11:21–23), his family (12:6), and "familiar friends" (20:10). The laments sometimes follow a notice of specific acts directed against him, as in Jer. 20:7–10 (cf. 18:18; 20:2):

> I have become a laughingstock all the day;
> every one mocks me. . . .
> The word of the Lord has become for me
> a reproach and derision all day long. . . .
> "Denounce him! Let us denounce him!"
> say all my familiar friends, watching for my fall.

These laments are most like those laments in the psalter where the psalmist is being falsely accused by enemies (e.g., Psalms 4; 9—10; 12; 17; 31). Although he sought good for the people (e.g., Jer. 17:16; 18:20), they have requited him with evil; it is only because he has been burdened with the word of the Lord that he speaks as he has. As with the psalmists, Jeremiah pleads his innocence and asks God to visit his persecutors with vengeance.

It is precisely this sort of lament-accusation that we have found in divine speech. Given the fact that the laments of prophet and God are so similar in their form and general orientation, in fact sometimes standing side-by-side, it is difficult to avoid the conclusion that the prophet's laments are a mirror of the laments of God. In and through the lamenting of the prophet one can hear the anguish of God over what has happened in his relationship with the people. As the people have rejected God, so have they rejected the prophet; as God responds, so does the prophet: they both complain against the accusations of the people; they both protest the charges that are brought; they both use "Why?" and "How long?" questions; they both move to a statement regarding the end such a people deserve. Regarding that last point, it is important to see Jeremiah's cry for vengeance on his persecutors as correspondent to God's announcement of judgment. What might seem to be a very personal vendetta is, in fact, a conformation of the prophet's words to the message of wrath of God.[26] If the "Confessions" of Jeremiah "lead step by step into ever greater despair,"[27] then this movement is also parallel to God's own progressive dismay over what has happened.

The basic point at which the laments differ is in the addressee: Jeremiah's are addressed to God and God's to the people (or the world, cf. Isa. 1:2; Mic. 6:1–2; Jer. 18:13). Yet, apart from the fact that the identity of the speaker necessitates this contrast, the placement of the "Confessions" within varying contexts of direct address to the people means that their *present* function is to speak to the people and not to God. And that word is, finally, a word about God and not about Jeremiah; the material is not biography, but proclamation. It is not that Jeremiah is identified with God. Jeremiah is indeed a person who had his own lament-accusations to voice, and there are peculiarities to his own situation compared to that of God. Yet, as the one who embodies the Word of God in the world, none of Jeremiah's words preserved to us is solely his own. The lamenting Jeremiah mirrors before the people the lamenting God.

Because the prophet so personally holds up the suffering of God before the people, the pain of God is seen to be no private matter.

Because it is the people who have called forth this movement in God, it is the people who should be confronted with the effects of their own rejection. Yet the motive is not to get them to feel sorry for God, but to startle them into repentance. The fact that in the prophet they are not only hearing but seeing, should make it a more persuasive word.

Jeremiah also suffers because of a God-like tension over what should be done with respect to the future of the people. We see this effect not least in his efforts to hold back the wrath of God (6:11; cf. 20:9): "Therefore I am full of the wrath of the Lord; I am weary of holding it in." Jeremiah experiences pain and weariness in this restraint (cf. 15:17–18), for he does not want the people to be visited with judgment any more than God does (15:11; 17:16; 18:20). Jeremiah's restraint, as well as the accompanying suffering, is thus parallel to the restraint of God, who has repented again and again (15:6). His entire life, indeed even his bones, are all broken up because of the Word of God which he embodies but holds back (23:9). "What convulsed the prophet's whole being was God. His condition was a state of suffering in sympathy with the divine pathos."[28] The tension in God over what to do with the people whom he loves has its earthly counterpart in the prophet.[29] As a member of the divine council, he incarnates the story of God in his own tension-filled life.

It is in this context that the two instances of God's rebuke of Jeremiah (12:5; 15:19–20) are to be understood. Jeremiah seeks to be relieved of this tension (15:18a); he has had enough of weariness (12:5). God continues to bear up under this tension, but Jeremiah cannot keep up with God, and so wants it all to end for the wicked right now, not least so that the land will cease to mourn (12:1–4; cf. 23:10). The fact that the wicked still live seems to Jeremiah to be due to the failure of God (15:18b). But God makes it clear in 15:19 that to seek to escape from such tension is to cease to be a prophet. Only if Jeremiah accepts this fact can he stand in the council and be as God's mouth. Thus, to be a true prophet is to be willing to stand in the same tension-filled situation as God himself and to endure weariness as long as God does.

## THE PROPHET'S SUFFERING
## WITH THE PEOPLE

As with God, the prophet suffers over what has happened to the people or in anticipation of what will happen. Examples from Jeremiah are particularly striking. The suffering of prophet and God are so interconnected that it is difficult to sort out who is speaking in many texts. Nor should one try to make too sharp a distinction. As if with one voice, prophet and God express their anguish over the suffering of the people.

It is not uncommon to interpret these materials in terms of the prophet's representative suffering on behalf of Israel.[30] But another approach seems preferable. These texts should be interpreted in terms of the prophet's embodiment of God's mourning. The prophet suffers in his capacity as a servant of God. It is true that Jeremiah's mourning parallels that of the people (e.g., 4:31), but so does God's. Thus, both God and prophet enter into the mourning of the people. In taking this approach, the prophet's mourning becomes a Word of *God* to the people and not a word of the people to God. In and through the prophet, the people should be able to see how God has entered into the anguish of their situation and made it his very own, as in Jer. 4:19:

> My anguish, my anguish! I writhe in pain!
>    Oh, the walls of my heart!
> My heart is beating wildly;
>    I cannot keep silent;
> for I hear the sound of the trumpet,
>    the alarm of war.

From the context of this passage we see that the anguished cries are anticipatory of the judgment to come, a devastation that suggests the effects of a nuclear holocaust (vv. 23–26). The vision of the future is so filled with terror that Jeremiah's entire being is wracked with pain. The passage is surrounded by what is clearly divine speech (vv. 17–18, 22), so that it is not altogether evident that it is Jeremiah himself speaking, or that he speaks only for himself. The point seems to be that this speech expresses more than his own empathy with the destroyed people and land; the prophet is an enfleshment of the emotions of God over what is about to occur. God and prophet speak with one voice.

Jer. 8:18—9:1 is even bolder:

> My grief is beyond healing,
>    my heart is sick within me.

Hark, the cry of the daughter of my people
    from the length and breadth of the land:
"Is the Lord not in Zion?
    Is her King not in her?"
Why have they provoked me to anger with their graven images
    and with their foreign idols?
The harvest is past, the summer is ended,
    and we are not saved."
For the wound of the daughter of my people is my heart wounded,
    I mourn, and dismay has taken hold on me.
Is there no balm in Gilead?
    Is there no physician there?
Why then has the health of the daughter of my people
    not been restored?
O that my head were waters,
    and my eyes a fountain of tears,
that I might weep day and night
    for the slain of the daughter of my people!

Again, the identity of the speakers is not certain, though one might suggest that the passage moves from divine speech (vv. 18–19) to the people (v. 20) to the prophet (8:21—9:1). Yet, it seems best to understand the mourning of God and prophet as so symbiotic that in everything we hear the anguish of both. The admixture of speakers, including the people, seems to portray a cacophany of mourning. All involved are caught up in expressing their dismay over what has happened. At the least, Jeremiah's mourning is an embodiment of the anguish of God, showing forth to the people the genuine pain God feels over the hurt that his people are experiencing. We see comparable mournings of Jeremiah in 10:19–20, 13:17–19, and 14:17–18, all reflective of God's own mourning.

In addition to Jeremiah, other prophetic materials are to be interpreted in comparable ways. Thus, Ezek. 21:6: "Sigh therefore, son of man; sigh with breaking heart and bitter grief before their eyes." Here Ezekiel is expressly commanded by God to take up wailing and sighing before the people. While this activity functions as a sign to the people of what is to come (v. 7), it also serves to reflect the divine mourning, as seems clear from the phrasing of v. 12: "Cry and wail, son of man, for it is against my people!" God's mourning is to be borne by the prophet in anticipation of what is to happen (cf. also Mic. 1:8; Isa. 22:4).

Finally, we note that God's mourning for nations other than Israel is taken up by the prophet, often at God's behest (e.g., Ezek. 27:1). In Isa. 21:3–4 we see how the prophet's mourning is extended to include Babylon. The prophet embodies the grief of God over what happens to any sufferer, whoever or wherever they might be.

In these various passages we have seen that the purpose of the prophet's mourning is not to hold up before God the distress of the people; it is to portray in living and personal fashion before the people the anguish of God. When it is anticipatory of the judgment which is to fall, it serves as a last-ditch vehicle for startling the people into repentance and avoidance of what is surely coming. Because God has this vision into the probabilities of the future in a way that the prophet does not, it is necessary for God to ask the prophet to take up such wailings. He thereby functions as servant of God. At the same time, because God sees that disaster is almost inevitable, such divine anguish is in fact lamentation. This lamentation of God and prophet then continues out beyond the times and places of judgment and enters into the actual sufferings of the people.

One other point of continuity between prophet and God should be cited in this connection. We have noted the failure of God in what he has attempted to accomplish in and through Israel (Jeremiah 45). In many ways the narratives in chapters 36—44 seem to make one major point, and that has to do with the failure of Jeremiah. The futility of his efforts is sketched out amid the swirl of events that portray the final tragedy of developments in Israel's life. "Jeremiah's path disappears in misery, and this without any dramatic accompaniments."[31] It is a story which ends with Jeremiah being forced to spend his final days in Egypt. Thus the homelessness of God is finally embodied in the homelessness of Jeremiah. The failure of Jeremiah matches the failure of God. That, too, is reason to mourn.

## THE PROPHET'S SUFFERING
## FOR THE PEOPLE

While this dimension of suffering in the prophets is less well developed than the other two, we get some glimpses of important developments. One such item is the fact that Jeremiah's restraint and resultant weariness, mirroring those of God, make for an expending of life which occasions continued life for the people of God; yet, while the potential for ongoing life is there, it turns out to be only a temporary reprieve. Even though Jeremiah pictures himself as a sacrificial victim, "a gentle lamb led to the slaughter" (11:19), there is nothing to suggest that either Jeremiah or the redactor of the book understands his suffering to be vicarious, that through his suffering Israel would be redeemed.

Some passages in Ezekiel push a little further in this direction. Von Rad considers three texts to be especially significant: Ezek. 13:4–5; 33:1–9; 4:4–6. In the first text, the true prophet is seen as one who, in a situation of battle, does not follow behind the troops collecting the spoils. He is in the front line trenches "in order to protect the people with his life,"[32] to prevent the brunt of the onslaught from being visited upon the people (cf. 3:16–21). This activity has primary reference to intercessory prayer on the people's behalf, and stands in the tradition of Moses (Ps. 106:23; cf. Exod. 32:10–14) and Jeremiah (18:20). We have seen how the work of the intercessor has occasioned divine repentance with respect to judgment. In Ezek. 33:1–9 the prophet is, in essence, said "to be answerable with his own life for those who were put in his care." Yet, while the prophet places his own life in danger by entering into this task on behalf of the people, his suffering as such is not understood to be vicarious.

Ezek. 4:4–6 takes us a bit further in its description of the prophet performing an act of suffering whereby he is to "bear the punishment [or guilt]" of the people. As we have seen, this language is also used of God himself, as well as the scapegoat (Leviticus 16) and the Suffering Servant (Isaiah 53). At one level this is a prefigurement of the suffering which the people are to endure in the days ahead;[33] while it may delay the judgment, it does not finally avert it. Yet, in the fact that all of the people's guilt is, as it were, gathered together and laid on him to endure, an important conceptual framework is provided for further developments.[34] That which has been characteristic of God's relationship to the people has now become characteristic of the prophet's life. The prophet so participates in the story of God for his people that he also bears the burden of their sins. This kind of thinking leads to the formulations in Isaiah 53 (cf. also Ezek. 3:26 with 53:7).

Contemporary at least in part with this material is one strand of tradition pertaining to Moses.[35] In Exod. 32:30–32, Moses is pictured as going to God to make atonement for the sins of the people, and offering to give his own life for their sake; "his own existence is offered for the redemption of the one threatened by the wrath of God."[36] In Deuteronomy this role of Moses is expanded. He intercedes for the people at great cost to himself (9:18–29), and finally suffers for the sins of the people by not being allowed to enter the promised land: God "was angry with me on your account" (Deut. 1:37; 3:26; 4:21). Here is given "the picture of a man who, while greatly afraid, took God's wrath on himself, and who was to die vicariously outside the promised land."[37] This idea of the one being recognized by God as the vehicle by which the many can be saved is evident also in other OT texts (e.g., Gen. 18:23–33; Jer. 5:1), but is exemplified supremely in the OT in the figure of the Suffering Servant.

A few remarks regarding the Servant Songs are in order (Isa. 42:1–7; 49:1–7; 50:4–9; 52:13—53:12).[38] However one resolves the identity of the servant, that he is a prophetic figure is generally recognized. He stands in the Moses-Jeremiah-Ezekiel tradition in particular, with important points of connection with the laments of the psalter.[39] Here the suffering of the prophet, while continuous in many ways with those who precede, is raised to a new key. His suffering is viewed explicitly in vocational terms, willingly taken up, to the death, for the sake of the many. His death is expressly vicarious, a personal sin-offering (53:10), recognized by God as effective for the redemption, not only of Israel, but of the whole world. This vicarious suffering is explicitly claimed to be the will of God (vv. 4, 6, 10); it is a means God has chosen to effect his salvific will for the world.

Yet one additional point needs to be made. We have seen how in Isa. 43:24 God himself plays the servant role that the prophetic servant here assumes. We have seen the earthly/heavenly correspondence in 2 Isaiah between the suffering of God and servant. Given the relationship we have witnessed between God and prophet, with the Word of God enfleshed in the very person of the prophet, do we not also have to assume something similar with the servant? This may in fact be expressed by the Spirit language of 42:1, and the fact that the effects of his work are those normally ascribed to God alone (e.g., 42:1, 4, 7). At the very least, we must say that the suffering of the servant is reflective of the suffering of God; in the giving up of the servant for the world, personal self-sacrifice is seen to define God's purpose here. But even more, as the servant is the vehicle for divine immanence, we should also say that God, too, experiences what the servant suffers. This consequence is something which God chooses to bring not only upon the servant but also upon himself. While God does not die, God experiences in a profound way what death is like in and through the servant. By so participating in the depths of the death-dealing forces of this world, God transforms the world from within; and a new creation thereby begins to be born.

As a way of summing up, we return to an earlier category we have used. There is an *intensification* of the divine presence in the prophet comparable to what we have seen to be the case in the theophany. Many of the observations we have made regarding theophany are applicable also to the prophet.

God is present and active not only in and through what the prophet speaks, but also in what he does and, indeed, in who he is. The prophet's life is an embodiment of the Word of God; the prophet is a vehicle for divine immanence. The prophet's life is thus theo-morphic.[40] By so participating in the story of God, his life is shaped into the image and likeness of God. The people thus not only hear the Word of God from the prophet, they *see* the Word enfleshed in their midst. In and through the suffering of the prophet, the people both hear and see God immersed in human experience. Through the prophet, Israel relates not only to a God who speaks, but also to a God who appears.

This sequence indicates something of the kind of Word of God with which Israel has to do. It is not a disembodied word; it is a wholly personal word spoken to the whole person. As such a word spoken "in person," it has the potential of being a more convincing word, of having an increased impact upon the people. Appearance makes a difference to words; seeing adds something to hearing. Further, it indicates something of the kind of word which is to be carried along by the people. They are not simply to speak that word or do it, but they are to reembody that word in the world.

Moreover, this phenomenon also indicates something of the kind of God with whom the people have to do. God is one who has sent such a personal Word, all in order to encounter them and communicate with them in as personal and effective a way as possible. God desires closeness; intimacy is God's goal. Further, God is one who chooses to be so present in the finitude and frailty of a human being—indeed, a powerless human being as power is usually conceived. He is one who startles the nations, for who would have believed that the arm of the Lord was revealed in such a one as this (Isa. 53:1)? In and through such individuals, God thereby identifies with frail people. And it is thereby shown that God is not a suffering-at-a-distance God; God enters into the suffering of all creatures and experiences their life. Moreover, this experience means entering into a death-filled situation with the people, not only so that God can experience it, but so that God can work creatively from within it and raise them up to be a part of a new world (cf. Ezekiel 37).

Finally, we should note that the prophet's life as embodied Word of God is partial and broken.[41] The OT does not finally come to the conclusion that God was incarnate in a human life in complete unbrokenness or in its entirety. While a prophet such as Jeremiah was set aside from the beginning of his life, the notion of the Word of God becoming flesh is associated only with his call. The Word of God enfleshed in an unbroken way in the totality of a human life must await a new day. Yet, in the prophet we see decisive continuities with what occurs in the Christ-event. God's act in Jesus Christ is the culmination of a longstanding relationship of God with the world that is much more widespread in the OT than is commonly recognized.

# Notes

PREFACE

1. On the important place of the suffering of God in the thought of Martin Luther, see especially M. Lienhard, *Luther: Witness to Jesus Christ* (Minneapolis: Augsburg Pub. House, 1982).

CHAPTER 1.   INTRODUCTION

1. I use the phrase "kind of God" in the same sense as in such common phrases as "What kind of person is Sarah?"

2. T. Matthews, *Under the Influence* (New York: Macmillan, 1977), 343.

3. Cf. the discussion of "Christomonism" in G. E. Wright, *The Old Testament and Theology* (New York: Harper & Row, 1969), 13–18.

4. There are many helpful studies of metaphor, too numerous to cite here. From the perspective of OT studies, see J. Barr, "Theophany and Anthropomorphism in the Old Testament," VTSup 7 (1959): 31–38; D. Clines, "Yahweh and the God of Christian Theology," *Theology* 83 (1980): 323–30; J. Hempel, "Die Grenzen des Anthropomorphismus Jahwes im AT," *ZAW* 57 (1939): 75–85; idem, "Yahwehgleichnisses der israelitischen Propheten," BZAW 81 (1961): 1–29; H. Kuitert, *Gott im Menschengestalt* (Munich: Chr. Kaiser Verlag, 1967); P. Trible, *God and the Rhetoric of Sexuality,* OBT 2 (Philadelphia: Fortress Press, 1978); W. Vischer, "Words and the Word: The Anthropomorphisms of the Biblical Revelation," *Int* 3 (1949): 3–18; cf. also the summary of U. Mauser's work in "Image of God and Incarnation," *Int* 24 (1970): 336–56; W. Wifall, "Models of God in the Old Testament," *BTB* 9 (1979): 179–86; B. Vawter, "The God of the Hebrew Scriptures," *BTB* 12 (1982): 3–7. From other perspectives, see S. McFague, *Metaphorical Theology: Models of God in Religious Language* (Philadelphia: Fortress Press, 1982); I. Ramsey, *Models and Mystery* (New York and London: Oxford Univ. Press, 1964); M. Black, *Models and Metaphors* (Ithaca, N.Y.: Cornell Univ. Press, 1962); D. Tracy, *The Analogical Imagination* (New York: Crossroad, 1981); M. Johnson, ed., *Philosophical Perspec-*

*tives on Metaphor* (Minneapolis: Univ. of Minnesota Press, 1981); A. Ortony, ed., *Metaphor and Thought* (New York and Cambridge: Cambridge Univ. Press, 1979); especially helpful is J. Martin, "The Use of Metaphor as a Conceptual Vehicle in Religious Language," (Ph.D. diss., Oxford, 1982).

5. Black, *Models and Metaphors,* 237. Contrast the discussion of Martin at some of these points (75ff., 133ff., 212ff.). She makes a strong case that the metaphor does not have a double meaning, literal and metaphorical, but a single meaning which results from the "interanimation" of two "networks of associations" (the tenor and the vehicle).

6. G. B. Caird, *The Language and Imagery of the Bible* (Philadelphia: Westminster Press, 1980), 17ff.

7. This more accurately states the kind of language with which we are dealing than anthropomorphism does. See the reservations regarding the latter term in A. Heschel, *The Prophets* (New York: Harper & Row, 1962), 268ff.

8. See especially Mauser, "Image of God"; Kuitert, *Gott im Menschengestalt;* Clines, "Yahweh." See n. 4 above.

9. Cited in Clines, "Yahweh," 324.

10. H. H. Rowley, *The Faith of Israel* (London: SCM Press, 1956), 75.

11. E. Jacob, *The Theology of the Old Testament* (New York: Harper & Row, 1958), 32.

12. See especially Hempel, "Die Grenzen."

13. This is emphasized in Mauser, "Image of God," and Kuitert, *Gott im Menschengestalt.*

14. See Barr, "Theophany," 33; see chap. 6 for further discussion.

15. J. Janzen, "Metaphor and Reality in Hosea 11," *Semeia* 24 (1982): 26.

16. See S. Ogden, *The Reality of God and Other Essays* (New York: Harper & Row, 1966), 171ff., 149ff.

17. Martin, "Use of Metaphor," 208ff.; cf. 111ff.

18. So Janzen, "Metaphor and Reality in Hosea 11," 19, 26.

19. E.g., W. Eichrodt, *Theology of the Old Testament* (Philadelphia: Westminster Press, 1961, 1967), I: 210ff. Eichrodt's suggestion that Israel understood the anthropomorphisms "in a quite literal way" goes beyond the evidence.

20. There is, of course, only a relative distinction between the psychical and physical anthropomorphic metaphors. There are times when scholars seem to argue that certain metaphors are truly revealing of God (e.g., love), while denying an essential continuity to others, perhaps especially when traditional understandings of God, such as immutability, are threatened by a metaphor such as divine repentance. All metaphors need to be probed for their insights, though not all are of equal value, as we shall see.

21. Caird, *Language and Imagery,* 153, Cf. Barr, "Theophany," 31, who distinguishes between anthropomorphisms and theophany; only the latter is a serious attempt to come to terms with the form of God.

22. Cf. Caird, *Language and Imagery,* 154ff.

23. Ibid., 176ff.

24. Ibid., 17ff.

25. G. von Rad, *Old Testament Theology* (New York: Harper & Row, 1962, 1965), I: 146.

26. Both Mauser ("Image of God") and Heschel *(Prophets)* also speak in these terms. See my discussion in chap. 6.

27. See especially Hempel, "Die Grenzen."

28. For an effort at a diachronic view, see J. S. Chesnut, *The Old Testament Understanding of God* (Philadelphia: Westminster Press, 1968). On origins, see the succinct summary and bibliography of C. L'Heureux, "Searching for the Origins of God," in *Traditions in Transformation,* ed. B. Halpern and J. Levenson (Winona Lake, Ind.: Eisenbrauns, 1981), 33–58.

29. R. Knierim, "Cosmos and History in Israel's Theology," *HBT* 3 (1981): 74, and the context of the statement.

30. The most obvious omission in these pages is a study of wisdom literature. We omit that, but not because of anticipated disjunctions with what we present here; in fact, an examination of wisdom should reveal fundamental continuities.

## CHAPTER 2.   GOD IN OLD TESTAMENT THEOLOGY

1. S. Ogden, *The Reality of God and Other Essays* (New York: Harper & Row, 1966), 1.

2. J. A. T. Robinson, *Honest to God* (Philadelphia: Westminster Press, 1963).

3. See, e.g., Trible, *God and the Rhetoric of Sexuality;* M. Daly, *Beyond God the Father* (Boston: Beacon Press, 1973); R. Ruether, *Religion and Sexism* (New York: Simon & Schuster, 1974); L. Russell, *Human Liberation in a Feminist Perspective* (Philadelphia: Westminster Press, 1974).

4. See, e.g., G. Gutierrez, *A Theology of Liberation* (Maryknoll, N.Y.: Orbis Books, 1973); J. Segundo, *The Liberation of Theology* (New York: Macmillan, 1977).

5. See the Anglican Church commissioned review of J. Mozley, *The Impassibility of God* (Cambridge: Cambridge Univ. Press, 1926); see also J. Moltmann, *The Trinity and the Kingdom of God* ((New York: Harper & Row, 1981), 30–36. Patripassionism, a modalistic heresy which does not distinguish between the Father and the Son, is not applicable to this discussion.

6. J. Moltmann, *The Crucified God* (New York: Harper & Row, 1968). On the Holocaust, see, P. Opsahl and M. Tannenbaum, eds., *Speaking of God Today: Jews and Lutherans in Conversation* (Philadelphia: Fortress Press, 1974); cf. also the review in "Jewish Faith After Nazism," *Judaism* 20 (1971): 263–94.

7. On the entrenchment side, one can cite the resurgence of fundamentalistic thought. On the experimental side, see P. van Buren, *The Secular*

*Meaning of the Gospel* (New York: Macmillan, 1963); Harvey Cox, *The Secular City* (New York: Macmillan, 1965).

8. Cf. S. Ogden, "What is Theology?" *JR* 52 (1972): 22–40. Cf. also D. Patrick, *The Rendering of God in the Old Testament,* OBT 10 (Philadelphia: Fortress Press, 1981), 46ff.

9. Contra the bifurcation in, e.g., C. Westermann, "The Role of the Lament in the Theology of the Old Testament," *Int* 28 (1974): 38. "The meaning of such talk about a God who laments and mourns lies not in its saying something about God in himself but about his relationship to his people. It enables those who are afflicted to hold on to an incomprehensible God." The same perspective pervades Heschel's *The Prophets;* cf. also P. D. Hanson, *Dynamic Transcendence* (Philadelphia: Fortress Press, 1978), 21.

10. See the last statement of such a perspective in R. H. Pfeiffer's *Religion in the Old Testament* (New York: Harper & Row, 1961).

11. See, e.g., W. F. Albright, *From the Stone Age to Christianity* (Baltimore: Johns Hopkins Univ. Press, 1940); idem, *Yahweh and the Gods of Canaan* (Garden City, N.Y.: Doubleday & Co., 1968).

12. Von Rad, *OT Theology.*

13. Cf., e.g., B. S. Childs, *An Introduction to the Old Testament as Scripture* (Philadelphia: Fortress Press, 1978).

14. Cf. the symposia in *Word and World* 1 (1981): 105–15; *JSOT* 16 (1980); *HBT* 2 (1980): 113–211.

15. Cf. the work of James Dunn, *Unity and Diversity in New Testament* (Philadelphia: Westminster Press, 1977), 81–102. For a comparable diversity in the Jewish tradition, cf. Heschel's *The Prophets* with E. Berkowitz's *Man and God: Studies in Biblical Theology* (Detroit: Wayne State Univ. Press, 1969).

16. E.g., H. H. Rowley, *The Faith of Israel.*

17. Ibid., 19; Rowley uses the criteria of distinctiveness and pervasiveness.

18. Cf. B. S. Childs, *Biblical Theology in Crisis* (Philadelphia: Westminster Press, 1970). Especially important articles giving impetus to this critical review were those of L. Gilkey, "Cosmology, Ontology and the Travail of Biblical Language," *JR* 41 (1941): 194–205; J. Barr, "Revelation Through History in the Old Testament and in Modern Theology," *Int* 17 (1963): 193–205.

19. The book by B. Albrektson (*History and the Gods* [Lund: C. W. K. Gleerup, 1967]) has been especially influential.

20. Cf., e.g., J. Barr, s. v. "Revelation in History," IDBSup; W. Lemke, "Revelation Through History in Recent Biblical Theology," *Int* 36 (1982): 34–46; Hanson, *Dynamic Transcendence.* Hanson's book may be viewed as a constructive effort to restate a more acceptable way of speaking of divine action in history from an OT perspective. The task is somewhat obscured, however, by the polemical language used to combat various forms of orthodoxy. Moreover, it is not made entirely clear what is entailed in speak-

ing of divine transcendence, and how such a God is, in fact, related to the world more generally, which would affect how God is to be perceived as related to history (cf. 21, 98–101). For an analysis of this issue from the perspective of systematic theology, see S. Ogden, *Reality of God*, 164–87.

21. For an especially important effort along these lines, see Knierim, "Cosmos and History."

22. Eichrodt, *Theology of the OT.*

23. Cf. R. C. Dentan, *The Knowledge of God in Ancient Israel* (New Haven: Seabury Press, 1968).

24. Von Rad, *OT Theology.*

25. Ibid. 1: 112.

26. E.g., ibid." The most essential subject of a theology of the Old Testament, the living Word of Yahweh coming on and on in Israel forever."

27. It is in fact so spoken of by a variety of scholars. Recently, see R. Clements, *Old Testament Theology: A Fresh Approach* (Atlanta: John Knox Press, 1978), 23: "The diversity of the biblical traditions find their unity only in the nature and being of God." Cf. also J. Barr, *The Bible in the Modern World* (London: SCM Press, 1973), 115.

28. C. Westermann, *Elements of Old Testament Theology* (Atlanta: John Knox Press, 1982).

29. For Westermann to use the tripartite canon to justify this particular division of central concerns is quite arbitrary; they bear no special relationship to the canonical division or its contents.

30. From an OT perspective in particular, cf. J. Barr, "Story and History in Biblical Theology," *JR* 56 (1976): 1–17.

31. Cf. Terence Fretheim, *Deuteronomic History* (Nashville: Abingdon Press, 1983), 38, for further discussion.

32. Cf. especially G. von Rad, *The Problem of the Hexateuch and Other Essays* (New York: McGraw-Hill, 1966), 1–78. Cf. also the review by J. I. Durham, s. v. "Credo, Ancient Israelite," IDBSup.

33. Cf. Westermann, *Elements of OT Theology,* 46.

34. For the most recent thorough discussion of this text, see R. Dentan, "The Literary Affinities of Exodus 34:6ff.," *VT* 13 (1963): 34–51. He cites the very small number of other studies.

35. See Num. 14:18; Neh. 9:17; Pss. 86:15; 103:8, 17; 145:8; Jer. 32:18–19; Joel 2:13; Jon. 4:2; Nah. 1:3.

36. E.g., Exod, 20:6; Deut. 5:9–10; 7:9; 1 Kings 3:6; 2 Chron. 30:9; Neh. 9:31; Pss. 106:45; 111:4; 112:4; Jer. 30:11; Lam. 3:32; Dan. 9:4.

37. See Dentan, "Literary Affinities," who is especially concerned to demonstrate affinities with wisdom literature. While predominantly literary, the parallels in the description of the figure of wisdom in Proverbs 8 should be noted. Dentan also shows that the material is pre-Deuteronomic.

38. The only real contender is the related sentence, "his steadfast love endures forever" (cf. Psalm 136).

39. The generalizations would not live, however, if there were no supports ever given in Israel's ongoing story.

40. See especially, von Rad, *OT Theology,* 2: 115–19.

41. Cf. Hanson, *Dynamic Transcendence,* 37.

42. It should be noted that there are additional reoccurring statements which could be drawn in here. For example, Deut. 6:4 and parallels in Second Isaiah and elsewhere. Cf. Fretheim, *Deuteronomic History,* 15–26, for the role of the first commandment in Deuteronomy.

43. See, e.g., P. Trible, *God and the Rhetoric of Sexuality;* W. Brueggemann, "Israel's Social Criticism and Yahweh's Sexuality," *JAAR Sup.* 45 (1977): 739–72; P. Bird, "Images of Women in the Old Testament," in *Religion and Sexism,* ed. R. Ruether (New York: Simon & Schuster, 1974), 41–88; N. Gottwald, *The Tribes of Yahweh* (Maryknoll, N.Y.: Orbis Books, 1979); P. Hanson, *The Diversity of Scripture,* OBT 11 (Philadelphia: Fortress Press, 1982).

44. Gottwald, *Tribes of Yahweh,* 912.

45. Cf. chap. 1 n. 7.

46. U. Mauser, *Gottesbild und Menschwerdung* (Tübingen: J. C. B. Mohr [Paul Siebeck], 1971), is one important book by an OT scholar who may be said to stand in the succession of Heschel.

47. See particularly the work of J. Crenshaw, e.g., "Popular Questioning of the Justice of God in Ancient Israel," *ZAW* 82 (1970): 380–95; idem (ed.), *Theodicy in the Old Testament,* IRT 4 (Philadelphia: Fortress Press, 1983). See also the considerations of the "dark side of God" in D. Gunn, *The Fate of King Saul* (Sheffield: JSOT Press, 1980).

48. Eichrodt, *Theology of OT* 2: 15ff.

49. See, e.g., W. Brueggemann, *In Man We Trust* (Atlanta: John Knox Press, 1972).

50. In addition to Westermann's *Elements of OT Theology,* see also *Blessing in the Bible and The Life of the Church,* OBT 3 (Philadelphia: Fortress Press, 1978).

51. Knierim, "Cosmos and History." The work of John Barton on natural theology is also of importance here; see his *Amos' Oracles Against the Nations* (New York and Cambridge: Cambridge Univ. Press, 1980).

52. Eichrodt, *Theology of OT* 2: 15.

53. See, e.g., Gottwald, *Tribes of Yahweh;* J. W. Rogerson, *Anthropology and the Old Testament* (Atlanta: John Knox Press, 1978).

54. See the review of A. Carr, "The God Who Is Involved," *TT* 38 (1981): 314–28.

55. See the work of D. Nicholls, e.g., "Images of God and the State: Political Analogy and Religious Discourse," *THST* 42 (1981): 195–215.

56. See J. G. Janzen, "Modes of Power and The Divine Relativity," *Encounter* 36 (1975): 379–406; idem, "Metaphor and Reality in Hosea 11," in *SBL Seminar Papers, 1976* (Missoula: Scholars Press, 1976), 412–45. This

latter article has been rewritten and included with others in the collection of essays, "Old Testament Interpretation from a Process Perspective," *Semeia* 24 (1982): 7–44. See also G. Coats, "The Kings' Loyal Opposition: Obedience and Authority in Exodus 32—34," in *Canon and Authority,* ed. G. W. Coats and B. O. Long (Philadelphia: Fortress Press, 1977), 91–109.

## CHAPTER 3.   GOD AND WORLD: BASIC PERSPECTIVES

1. Eichrodt's *Theology of the Old Testament* is divided into three major sections, one of which is entitled "God and World" (2:15–228). Yet, it is something of a catch-all section, fragmented in its discussion, with minimal attention to the relationship of this material to the whole of the work. See also G. von Rad, "Some Aspects of the Old Testament World-View," in *PHOE,* 144–65; R. Knierim, "Cosmos and History." W. Zimmerli (*The Old Testament and the World* [Atlanta: John Knox Press, 1976]) is concerned only incidentally with the relationship between God and world, but discusses in important ways a corollary of this, namely, the thisworldly orientation of a range of aspects of Israel's faith, life, and hope.

2. Cf. Eichrodt, *Theology of the OT* 2: 99; R. Knierim, "Cosmos and History," 75.

3. The phrase is Heschel's; cf. *Prophets,* 9. Covenantal language might be helpful in probing the OT perspective at this point. I avoid that language because modern scholarship associates it with a monarchical image of God's relationship to Israel and the world. Those who interpret covenant in terms of reciprocity (e.g., Brueggemann) stand in some tension with this general understanding. Covenant may be evidence for a monarchical image, but other possibilities are available for exploration.

4. See Knierim, "Cosmos and History"; L. Stadelmann, *The Hebrew Conception of the World* (Rome: Biblical Institute Press, 1970).

5. See Stadelmann, *Hebrew Conception of World,* 3; Knierim, "Cosmos and History," 74–76; Eichrodt, *Theology of the OT* 2: 112.

6. Knierim, "Cosmos and History," 76.

7. Ibid., 78. See Eichrodt, *Theology of the OT* 2: 186–94, for a discussion of earlier scholarly views regarding a possible spatial limitation of God to specific earthly places in some OT texts.

8. Ibid., 71.

9. Ibid., 86. For Knierim, a "god without a world" is "an inconceivable idea for the Old Testament." I agree, but would further say that a god outside of the world is also inconceivable.

10. The verb "they will perish" ('*ābad*) is used only once elsewhere for the earth (Jer. 9:12), where it refers to ruin and not annihilation. The verb "pass away" ('*ābar*) often carries the sense of "pass on" (see Isa. 8:8) and may even mean "be renewed," as in Ps. 90:5–6.

11. Translation and interpretive issues in the latter suggest another approach. Isa. 34:4 (cf. 24:21) would seem to have reference to God's enemies rather than cosmology. In Isa. 51:6, the translation of the phrase, "vanish like

smoke" is problematic. Also, as C. R. North, *The Second Isaiah* (Oxford: At the Clarendon Press, 1964), 210, suggests, we may have to do here with a concessive-conditional clause, "though the heavens should vanish . . . , yet, my salvation. . . ." Both Ps. 102:28 and the last phrases of Isa. 51:6 would seem to entail an earthly existence. On the new creation, see Knierim, "Cosmos and History," 101–3.

12. Stadelmann, *Hebrew Conception of World*, 54.

13. Knierim, "Cosmos and History," 79ff.

14. Ibid., 81, 85. Cf. P. Santmire, *Brother Earth* (New York: Thomas Nelson, 1970), 192–200.

15. Ibid., 85. Stadelmann, *Hebrew Conception of World*, 8, observes: "Certainly we have here more than a poetical personification of the cosmos."

16. Ibid., 78.

17. See ibid., 63–65, for a discussion of various reasons why these matters have not played a very important theological role in OT scholarship.

18. See ibid., 66. Bonhoeffer's understanding of the God-world relationship is a contemporary statement that correlates well with this Old Testament perspective. On this, see the fine summary of J. Burtness, "As Though God Were Not Given," *Dialog* 19 (1980): 249–55.

19. Knierim, "Cosmos and History," 85–88. Knierim does not seem to recognize sufficiently the effect that human sin has on the cosmic order.

20. Ibid., 86. An exception is D. Clines, "Yahweh and the God of Christian Theology," *Theology* 83 (1980): 326. For the basic theological issues, see N. Pike, *God and Timelessness* (London: Routledge & Kegan Paul, 1970); S. Ogden, *The Reality of God*, 144ff.

21. On these issues, see especially J. Barr, *Biblical Words for Time*, rev. ed. (London: SCM Press, 1969).

22. See ibid., 151ff. It might be noted that even if time itself were created, this does not necessarily mean that eternity *remains* a reality other than time. One could say that, since the creation, eternity has been integrated into time. Eternity is probably best defined in terms of God's distinctive experience of time.

23. Ibid., 154ff.

24. See D. Patrick, *The Rendering of God*, 50–51. Patrick, however, operates with a monarchical image in his understanding of the God-world relationship.

25. Cf. A. Weiser, *The Psalms: A Commentary*, OTL (Philadelphia: Westminster Press, 1962), 597ff. There are numerous other passages which could be cited to reinforce this understanding of God and time, e.g., those materials which speak of times when God is present or absent.

## CHAPTER 4.   GOD AND WORLD: FOREKNOWLEDGE

1. An exception is Eichrodt, *Theology of the OT* 2: 183ff.

2. Cf. *BDB*, 19. See Luke 20:13.

3. See also Num. 23:3; 1 Sam. 14:6; 2 Sam. 16:12; Jer. 21:2; Jon. 1:6;

Zeph. 2:3. Cf. also the use of *mî yōdê*, "who knows," in 2 Sam. 12:22; Joel 2:14; Jon. 3:9. For a brief treatment of the latter, cf. my "Jonah and Theodicy," *ZAW* 90 (1978): 228–29.

4. Jer. 51:8 and Isa. 47:2 are somewhat different constructions and concern Babylon. The divine uncertainty is thus seen to prevail across a wider world than Israel.

5. The bulk of the pertinent instances are to be found in biblical literature from the 7th and 6th centuries B.C. This is due in part to the fact that divine speech is presented in a more sustained fashion in this material. Cf. n. 8.

6. See E. Kautzsch, *Gesenius' Hebrew Grammar*, 2d. ed. (Oxford: At the Clarendon Press, 1910), Par. 159; H. Ferguson, "An Examination of the Use of Tenses in Conditional Sentences in Hebrew," *JBL* 1 (1882): 40–94. *'im* with the imperfect, or equivalent, is used where the condition possibly or probably will occur in the present or future.

7. Comparable conditional sentences in divine speech may be located in 1 Kings 9:4–6; Ps. 132:12; Isa. 1:19–20; Jer. 4:1–2; 17:24–27; 38:17–18; 42:10–16 (cf. Gen. 18:26–30; Exod. 19:5). Passages such as Jer. 12:16–17 and 18:7–10 (no conditional particle is used) are not as certainly applicable in this context, for they are general statements as to what God will do if this or that action is taken on the part of a variety of peoples (cf. Ezek. 2:5–7). God knows what God will do, but the conditionality of the references still needs attention in this regard.

8. It may be too hasty to extrapolate from these passages from the seventh through sixth centuries to a general statement about the perspective of the OT. The absence of OT perspectives to the contrary, however, suggests that here we have to do with at least greater explicitness about the matter, and perhaps a new development in Israel's thinking about God. If the latter is the case, it is a testimony to Israel's conceiving of God in increasingly personal categories, rather than a development in the direction of removing God from the life of the world.

9. It is generally recognized that the last phrase was deliberately changed from this to the way it reads in translations like the RSV, "But Abraham still stood before the Lord," to avoid any suggestion of God's waiting on Abraham.

10. We are indebted in this discussion to suggestive comments made on Genesis 18 by J. G. Janzen, "Metaphor and Reality in Hosea 11," 19–20. For a persuasive attempt to place this passage in the context of the fall of Jerusalem and the theological issues addressed at that time, see J. Blenkinsopp, "Abraham and the Righteous of Sodom," *JJS* 33 (1982): 119–32. Our discussion might well be used to supplement his case.

11. Contra G. von Rad, *Genesis: A Commentary*, rev. ed., OTL (Philadelphia: Westminster Press, 1973), 210, v. 17 does not consider the judgment "as already fixed, indeed as already executed." One might say that God has decided what to do, but the decision is preliminary, not irrevocable, as v. 21

indicates. Jer. 20:16 uses repentance language to refer to the *execution* of the divine decision.

12. Cf. ibid., 211.

13. This also needs to be related to the phrase, "to keep the way of the Lord by doing righteousness and justice" (v. 19). The point is that "the way of the Lord" *is* righteousness and justice, and if Abraham and his descendents are going to be expected to walk in this way, then there needs to be no uncertainty with respect to the matter.

14. Contra von Rad, *Genesis,* 212, the integrity of the conversation would be compromised if "both Yahweh and Abraham knew what the results of the investigation will be and what the consequences will be for Sodom."

15. Speculation regarding why Abraham's count stopped with ten who were righteous is irrelevant, for the issue of the justice of God's decision had by then been established beyond the shadow of a doubt (see n. 19 below). This, contra Blenkinsopp, "Abraham," 130, that "the conversation moves towards the definition of the minimum necessary" for God's decision to be reversed. I use the language of decision throughout for a decision which is preliminary. It might be better to use the word "plan" in line with the use of the verbs *hāšab* (Jer. 18:11; 26:3; 36:3; cf. the nominal usage in 51:29; Mic. 4:12) and *zāmam* (Jer. 4:28; 51:12; Lam. 2:17; Zech. 1:6: 8:14). Generally, there is a distinction made in these passages between plan and execution.

16. B. S. Childs, *The Book of Exodus,* OTL (Philadelphia: Westminster Press, 1974), 567.

17. Ps. 106:23 reports on this future-affecting activity of Moses vis-à-vis the decisions of God (cf. Jer. 18:20). Cf. G. W. Coats, "The King's Loyal Opposition: Obedience and Authority in Exodus 32—34," in *Canon and Authority,* 97–106.

18. For further discussion of the significance of the divine lament, see chaps. 7–8.

19. The fact that Amos does not respond in 7:7–9 probably indicates that Amos realizes that he can make no further contribution to the discussion; judgment is inevitable. God's actions are just. Amos's refrainment from further comment is thus parallel to Abraham's halt at the number ten in Gen. 18:32.

20. This verse is commonly recognized as a Deuteronomic(?) intrusion. Cf. H. W. Wolff, *Joel and Amos,* Hermeneia (Philadelphia: Fortress Press, 1977), 181–82.

21. This interpretation would suggest that the word for "secret," *sôd,* contains an indirect reference to another meaning of the word *sôd,* namely, the council of Yahweh (Jer. 23:18, 22; cf. Gen. 49:6; Ps. 55:14) as the context where Yahweh and prophet "consult with one another in a spirit of intimacy and trust." Contra Wolff, ibid., 187. On the deliberative character of the divine council, see N. Whybray, *The Heavenly Counsellor in Isaiah xl 13–14* (New York and Cambridge: Cambridge Univ. Press, 1971), especially pp. 48–

53, and 1 Kings 22:19–22; Job 1—2; Isaiah 6. Whybray makes clear that Isa. 40:13–14 refers, not to consultation in general, but in relationship to the act of creation.

22. Cf. J. L. Mays, *Hosea: A Commentary,* OTL (Philadelphia: Westminster Press, 1969), 61–62. H. W. Wolff, *Hosea,* Hermeneia (Philadelphia: Fortress Press, 1974), 187–88. This could be profitably related to certain divine experiments, such as in the matter of "helpmeet" in Genesis 2. Cf. Patrick, *The Rendering of God,* 18.

23. Cf. the discussion of Janzen, "Metaphor and Reality," 20–21.

24. This probably explains the fluidity in the announcement that God will not hear either him (7:16c) or them (11:14; 14:12). Cf. R. Carroll, *From Chaos to Covenant* (New York: Crossroad, 1981), 114ff.

25. U. Mauser, *Gottesbild und Menschwerdung,* 109–10.

26. Ibid., 100. It may be important to stress that it is *not* God's will to save which is diminished; that will remain intact, though judgment must now fall. Cf. also the use of *māšak* in Ezek. 12:25, 28.

27. For further discussion, see especially Janzen; T. Raitt, *A Theology of Exile* (Philadelphia: Fortress Press, 1977), 87ff.; cf. W. Brueggemann, "Jeremiah's Use of Rhetorical Questions," *JBL* 92 (1973): 358–74.

28. Wolff, *Hosea,* 119, 156; cf. 141.

29. Mays, *Hosea,* 96ff.

30. Janzen, "Metaphor and Reality," 10. Janzen has carefully laid out a somewhat different interpretation of the nature of some of these questions, seeing them more in terms of the life of Yahweh, rather than the life of Israel. The divine questions are existential questions, involving a decision-making process in response to possibilities presented to him. Such questions do not provide answers in the sense of information, but enable the move from possibility to actuality within the divine life; thus, they are "to be *lived toward,* in such a way that, in time, the self which one has become is 'the answer' " (p. 12).

31. F. Andersen and D. Freedman, *Hosea,* Anchor Bible (Garden City, N.Y.: Doubleday & Co., 1980), 51, 426, 431, 588ff.

32. Cf. Mays, *Hosea,* 157: "Hosea's many anthropomorphisms are meant as interpretive analogies, not as essential definitions."

33. See our discussion in the Introduction.

34. Cf. Janzen, "Metaphor and Reality," 24–25.

35. Cf. ibid., 15–16.

36. Cf. especially the discussion in Raitt, *A Theology of Exile,* 95ff.

37. A. Jepsen, "Warum? Eine lexikalische und theologische Studie," in *Das Ferne und Nahe Wort,* BZAW 105 (1967): 106–13, seeks to make a distinction in usage between *Maddûaʿ* and *lāmāh,* with the former used in information gathering and expressing amazement, while the latter is used in complaints and reproaches. This is too simple, however, as the use of the former in Jer. 36:29 and the latter in Jer. 2:29 shows.

38. A passage like 1 Sam. 23:10–13 might be cited in support, except that we have insufficient knowledge of the situation to determine the nature of God's accessibility to the knowledge. It may only entail God's thoroughgoing knowledge of the present on the basis of which reasonably certain judgments about the future might be made.

39. Most commentators on the Psalms make reference to the omniscience of God in connection with this passage, e.g., Weiser, *Psalms*, 801–2, who does not define what he means by the idea, as is the case with most. A. A. Andersen, *The Book of Psalms* (London: Oliphants, 1972), 906, suggests that the passage has to do with practical rather than theoretical omniscience, a distinction which escapes me.

40. For a clear and helpful discussion of these issues from the perspective of the philosophy of religion, see B. L. Hebblethwaite, "Some Reflections on Predestination, Providence and Divine Foreknowledge," *RS* 15 (1979): 433–48.

## CHAPTER 5.   GOD AND WORLD: PRESENCE AND POWER

1. See especially W. Brueggemann, s. v. "Presence of God, Cultic," IDBSup; idem, "The Crisis and Promise of Presence in Israel," *HBT* 1 (1980): 47–86; R. Clements, *God and Temple* (Philadelphia: Fortress Press, 1965); H. J. Kraus, *Worship in Israel* (Richmond: John Knox Press, 1966); H. H. Rowley, *Worship in Ancient Israel* (Philadelphia: Fortress Press, 1967); S. Terrien, *The Elusive Presence* (New York: Harper & Row, 1978). See also the bibliography cited in chap. 6 n. 2.

2. Not unlike distinctions Christians commonly make when they speak of the "real presence" in the Lord's Supper, or "where two or three are gathered in my name, there am I in the midst of them." The failure to recognize such distinctions has led both to forced harmonization (e.g., Clements, *God and Temple*, 63ff., speaks of divine presence as an extrapolation of his continual coming) and to unnecessary traditio-historical conclusions (e.g., von Rad, *OT Theology* 1: 235–37, separates tent and ark on the basis of incompatible notions of presence).

3. Brueggemann ("Presence of God") speaks of four categories: the coming God; the God who leads (under which he includes theophanies to individuals); the abiding God; the hidden God. He tends to see these categories in terms of four periods in Israel's history, rather than in theological relationship to one another in terms of intensifications of presence.

4. See W. Lemke, "The Near and the Distant God: A Study of Jer. 23:23–24 in its Biblical Theological Context," *JBL* 100 (1981): 541–55.

5. See von Rad, *OT Theology* 1: 136.

6. See H. H. Schmid, "Schopfung, Gerechtigkeit und Heil," *ZTK* (1973): 1–20.

7. See Clements, *God and Temple*, 1–16.

8. On ark and temple, see especially Clements, *God and Temple;* Terrien *Elusive Presence;* and the bibliography in the footnotes of the latter.

9. The theological focus here, and in the Deuteronomic history as a whole, is on the first commandment. See Fretheim, *Deuteronomic History*, 15–26.

10. See especially G. von Rad, *Studies in Deuteronomy* (London: SCM Press, 1953); M. Weinfeld, *Deuteronomy and the Deuteronomic School* (Oxford: At the Clarendon Press, 1972). Interestingly, Deuteronomy has little interest in heaven as God's dwelling.

11. See M. Weinfeld, "kābôd," *ThWAT* 5 (1982): 23–40; Eichrodt, *Theology of the OT* 2: 32. Strangely, von Rad, *Theology*, 1: 239 n. 115, considers the dwelling references in the Priestly writing to be of "no importance."

12. Cf. C. Westermann, *Isaiah 40—66: A Commentary*, OTL (Philadelphia: Westminster Press, 1969), 170. Here hiddenness has to do with God's special presence in lowly Israel as over against the "men of stature" (v. 14) in the world (cf. 1 Cor. 1:27).

13. The specific language of hiddenness only rarely has an epistemological focus, mostly in Job ('*lm*, 11:6, 28:21; *spn*, 10:13; 17:4) and in Deut. 29:29; Prov. 25:2 (*str*). Even the silence of God in the laments (e.g., Ps. 83:2; 109:1) has a focus in deliverance, not revelation (see Pss. 22:24; 27:7–10). Of course, God's hiddenness *in* his revelation is presented in other ways (e.g., Isa. 55:6–11). Still other language is used to express the idea of structural distance with respect to presence, and will be dealt with below. The hidden/revealed God issue needs to be distinguished from that of the hidden/present God. On the hiddenness of God, see L. Perlitt, "Die Verborgenheit Gottes," in *Probleme Biblischer Theologie*, ed. H. W. Wolff (Munich: Chr. Kaiser, 1971), 367–82. G. Wehmeier, "str," *THAT* 2 (1976): 174–81.

14. See Brueggemann, particularly in "Presence of God"; W. Zimmerli, *Old Testament Theology in Outline* (Atlanta: John Knox Press, 1978), 70–81; Terrien, *Elusive Presence,* uses other language, but is concerned essentially with the same issue throughout. His blending of the hidden/present and hidden/revealed issues makes for some lack of clarity. On divine freedom, see S. H. Blank, "Doest Thou Well To Be Angry: A Study in Self Pity," HUCA 26 (1955): 36ff.; J. J. M. Roberts, "Divine Freedom and Cultic Manipulation in Israel and Mesopotamia," in *Unity and Diversity,* ed. H. Goedicke and J. Roberts (Baltimore: Johns Hopkins Univ. Press, 1975), 181–90; cf. also J. J. Collins, "The Biblical Precedent for Natural Theology," JAARSup 45/1 (1977): 39–40.

15. I believe this to be true of the considerations of both Zimmerli and Brueggemann, where the preponderance of freedom language tilts the discussion in that direction.

16. This may also be seen in Ezek. 10:1–19; 11:22–25, of which Eichrodt, *Theology of the OT* 2: 33ff., says: The Glory "abandons this its dwelling-place only with reluctance, withdrawing hesitantly first from the Temple area and finally from the holy city."

17. On divine necessity, see Blank, "Doest Thou Well To Be Angry?"

40ff., and the divine constraint in view of promise. From a NT perspective, cf. the use of *dei,* "it is necessary," in the synoptic Gospels.

18. On the use of these categories, see, e.g., R. Clements, *God and Temple.* The Deuteronomic reform is commonly spoken of in these terms.

19. Brueggemann rightly stresses the importance of this formula in Israel's thinking about presence.

20. Cf. Eichrodt, *Theology of the OT* 1: 275–79, who connects holiness with a "profound sense of the *opposition* between the worlds of divine and human existence" (italics mine). The stress should, rather, be on the *difference;* whatever opposition between the two "worlds" arises, is due not to some structure of things, but because of the sinfulness of the people. Eichrodt, 279, sees this properly when, in commenting upon Isa. 6:3, he says, "what overwhelmed him was not that separation from the divine realm which is the common lot of man, but the contradiction between his own sinful nature and that of the Thrice-Holy" (cf. Isa. 10:17).

21. From the perspective of systematic theology, cf. the discussion of P. Sponheim, "Transcendence in Relationship," *Dialog* 12 (1973): 264–71; R. Hazelton, "Relocating Transcendence," *USQR* 30 (1975): 101–9; R. H. King, *The Meaning of God* (Philadelphia: Fortress Press, 1973).

22. Cf. also the close relationship between redemption and the activity of the holy God in 2 Isaiah (41:14; 43:3, 14; 47:4). Contra Eichrodt *Theology of the OT* 1: 281, this would seem not to have reference to the "marvel of his mode of being," but to the way in which the holiness of God is manifested on behalf of Israel.

23. So Eichrodt, *Theology of the OT* 1: 273, and von Rad, *OT Theology* 1: 205.

24. Cf. this emphasized statement of Eichrodt, *Theology of the OT* 1: 273 (cf. p. 275): " . . . this [holy] means *him who is unapproachable because of his complete 'otherness' and perfection when compared with all created things."* See the helpful statements about holiness in connection with Ps. 51:11 in Terrien, *Elusive Presence,* 325.

25. So von Rad, *OT Theology* 1: 205–6.

26. The phrase is Sponheim's, "Transcendence in Relationship."

27. So Heschel, *Prophets,* 486.

28. Literature dealing explicitly with OT views of divine power is comparatively rare, though the issue is often on the edges of other discussions. See especially, J. G. Janzen, "Modes of Power and the Divine Relativity," *Encounter* 36 (1975): 379–406; D. Griffin, "Relativism, Divine Causation and Biblical Theology," *Encounter* 36 (1975): 342–60; W. Brueggemann, " 'Impossibility' and Epistemology in the Faith Tradition of Abraham and Sarah (Gen. 18:1–15)," *ZAW* 94 (1982): 615–34.

29. See, e.g., Eichrodt, *Theology of the OT* 2: 161–79. It is uncertain what Eichrodt means by the phrase, "flat determinism" (p. 179). There seems to be some lack of coherence in Eichrodt at this point, speaking correctly here as

he does of "God's *effective* action in all things," while elsewhere speaking of God's action and sovereignty as sufficient, absolute, and controlling (pp. 164, 174, 177). See also G. von Rad, "Some Aspects," 152.

30. Brueggemann, " 'Impossibility' and Epistemology." The translation of *pele'* remains something of a problem here.

31. Ibid., 616, 619.

32. Ibid., 627.

33. See chaps. 6–7.

34. Westermann, *Essentials of OT Theology*, 120, nearly gets to this point when he states that the flood story is a witness to the "patient tolerance of man in spite of his inclination to evil; God will not in every case intervene as judge against the evil doing of a person or a group. He can also bear it, tolerate it without intervening." The problem phrase is "in every case," for it suggests an occasionalism that is finally morally incoherent. The text simply affirms that God has made a promise, which entails a limitation in the use of power against evil.

35. See Knierim, "Cosmos and History," 78.

36. On Genesis 1 and creation, see Knierim, ibid., and the literature he reviews on pp. 71–73; cf. also W. Brueggemann, *Genesis* (Atlanta: John Knox Press, 1982). An earlier form of this perspective was given in my paper, "Creation Thought and the Absence of God," in the Old Testament Theology Seminar at the 1977 SBL Convention.

37. Cf., e.g., Eichrodt, *Theology of the OT* 2: 98ff.

38. While one might use the language of tension with ibid., 179, it seems likely that contextual issues determined whether the divine or creaturely causation was focused upon. One could profitably compare doxological language, ancient and contemporary, where the activity of God typically, and rightly, fills the scene; but, if pressed, one would not be saying that God is the sole causative factor in a whole range of things for which God is being praised. On nature as a living, responsive reality, see Eichrodt, *Theology of the OT* 2: 152–53; Stadelmann, *Hebrew Conception of World*, 8. On dual agency, see A. Farrer, *Faith and Speculation* (New York: Oxford Univ. Press, 1967); King, *Meaning of God*, 76ff.

39. M. Noth, *The History of Israel* (New York: Harper & Row, 1958), 1–2. Italics mine. This statement is striking, for it would seem to affirm our perspective (except for the word "superficial"), namely, that God does not use power by interfering with natural and human causes, but works alongside of them as another, though especially significant, causal factor. The implication is that God's activity is as much an objective factor in, say, the Exodus, as the strong east wind or the leadership of Moses, though it is nowhere unambiguous (cf. systemic distance). In any analysis of an event, therefore, faith and history need to be kept together. Far from distorting the "objective" facts, faith is a presupposition, like any other used by historians, which finally allows the event to be fully reconstructed. While apart from faith an intelligi-

ble account can be given of events for a variety of purposes (e.g., historical research), a full account would not be possible. See D. Griffin, "Relativism," 359.

40. Even the more "miraculous" events reported in the OT would seem not to be free from such causes, and hence not totally determined by God. Given the likelihood that Israel conceived of even such events from within what was then believed to be normal cause and effect relationships (cf. Eichrodt, *Theology of the OT* 2: 167 n. 4), it is better to speak of special *intensifications* of divine presence or activity rather than interruptions or interventions. This approach would also help to avoid the occasionalism so common in discussions of these matters. See n. 34 above.

41. On seemingly unprovoked divine action, see Eichrodt, *Theology of the OT* 2: 179–80. See the development of these issues in my study of selected texts from Joshua and Judges in *Deuteronomic History,* 49ff.; cf. also R. Polzin, *Moses and the Deuteronomist* (New York: Seabury Press, 1980).

42. See especially Brueggemann, *In Man We Trust;* Coats, "King's Loyal Opposition."

43. To put the issue in terms of coercive vs. persuasive power is not helpful. See especially Janzen, "Modes of Power." Cf. also N. Frankenberry, "Some Problems in Process Theodicy," *RS* 17 (1981): 179–97; articles by G. Coats and L. Ford in *Semeia,* 24 (1982): 53–87.

44. See Eichrodt, *Theology of the OT* 2: 78–79.

45. Janzen, "Modes of Power," helpfully reminds us that, only if the productive powers within nature and history can be understood *both* as inhering in the world *and* as coming from God, will historicism, scientism, and naturalism be avoided—and we might add, fatalism. If this is not understood, as Hosea so long ago recognized (e.g., Hos. 2:8), the way is open to a new polytheism. On divine retribution, see K. Koch, "Is There a Doctrine of Retribution in the Old Testament?", in *Theodicy in the Old Testament,* 27–87. See also, P. D. Miller, Jr., *Sin and Judgment in the Prophets* (Chico, Calif.: Scholars Press, 1982).

46. Eschatological issues lie outside the purview of our discussion, e.g., God's *ultimate* control of the world or the Resurrection.

47. One thinks in particular of wisdom literature.

## CHAPTER 6.   GOD IN HUMAN FORM

1. Eichrodt, *Theology of the OT* 2: 15.

2. On theophany, see especially J. Jeremias, *Theophanie* (Neukirchen-Vluyn: Neukirchener Verlag, 1965); IDBSup, s.v. "Theophany in the Old Testament"; J. Kuntz, *The Self-Revelation of God* (Philadelphia: Westminster Press, 1967); F. Cross, *Canaanite Myth and Hebrew Epic* (Cambridge: Harvard Univ. Press, 1973); J. Barr, "Theophany and Anthropomorphism in the Old Testament," VTSup 7 (1959), 31–38; T. W. Mann, *Divine Presence and Guidance in Israelite Tradition: The Typology of Exaltation* (Baltimore: Johns Hopkins Univ. Press, 1977); R. Rendtorff, "The Concept of Revelation in

Ancient Israel," in *Revelation as History,* ed. W. Pannenberg (New York: Macmillan, 1968), 23–53.

3. See the discussion in Terrien, *Elusive Presence,* 68–71.

4. See Kuntz, *Self-Revelation.*

5. Jeremias ("Theophany") makes a distinction between two basic types, and is followed here in the most basic sense, though the second clearly has a variety of subtypes. Terrien (*Elusive Presence,* 69–71) speaks of at least three different types, isolating the patriarchal narratives as a "sui generis" type, "epiphanic visitations." Strangely, Terrien does not deal with the parallels in Judges 6 and 13. The OT uses the word "appear" (Niphal of *rā'āh*) for a variety of the second major type of theophanies; they can be distinguished in some ways, but the word "appearance" is perhaps the most appropriate word for all.

6. See in particular the study of Cross, *Hebrew Epic,* 91ff., 147ff.

7. See Jeremias, "Theophany."

8. Words of judgment are occasionally found, e.g., Numbers 12, 14, 16; 1 Samuel 3; Ps. 50:1–7.

9. See above, n. 2. For a clear and succinct summary of the scholarly discussion, see especially T. Mann, *Divine Presence,* 2–17.

10. See especially W. Beyerlin, *Origins and History of the Oldest Sinaitic Traditions* (Oxford: Basil Blackwell, 1965). Rendtorff ("Concept of Revelation") denies that there is such a phenomenon as a regularized cultic theophany in the Priestly writer, claiming only specific historical ones. Yet, this can be achieved only by treating certain texts as secondary and ignoring such passages as Lev. 9:4–6.

11. God rarely appears to non-Israelites; cf. Genesis 16; Numbers 22—24.

12. See especially Brueggemann, "Crisis and Promise," for the importance of this language in Exodus 33 in particular. See also J. Muilenburg, "The Intercession of the Covenant Mediator (Exod. 33:1a, 12–17)," in *Words and Meanings* (Cambridge: At the Univ. Press, 1968), 159–81.

13. The distinction between "natural pheomena" and the appearance of the form of a human being may be made (see Terrien, *Elusive Presence,* 70), but they also have in common their empirical base, a very important consideration. In those few instances where only the word "appear" is used (Gen. 12:7; 17:1; 26:2, 24; 35:9), some empirical reference must be assumed for such a word to have any meaning.

14. So von Rad, *OT Theology* 2: 19. Cf. also Brueggemann, s. v. "Presence of God," IDBSup, 681: "There is no interest in any form of appearance." Terrien is similarly concerned to give a positive evaluation of the "hearing of the ear" and a devaluation of any references to the "seeing of the eye" (e.g., *Elusive Presence,* 112). Contrast T. Vriezen, *An Outline of Old Testament Theology* (Oxford: Basil Blackwell, 1958), 185, 188.

15. It is important to make a differentiation between the OT and certain NT and Christian realities (e.g., Luke 16:31; Heb. 11:1), where the concern

for the empirical in the life of faith seems to diminish. A distinction should be made between the constitutive era, when the faith was being established among the people of God (this would include the appearance of the Messiah in the flesh), and the importance of the empirical element for doing just that, and the subsequent history of the people of God. Yet the concern for the empirical remains an important concern in the life of faith. The use of the visible element in the sacraments serves many of the same purposes we have seen for the empirical phenomena in the theophanies. The spoken word alone is not deemed sufficient for the life of faith.

16. J. Barr, "Theophany," 33.

17. The common distinction made between the J and E sources at this point must not be overdrawn. Even if one follows the source division to the letter, there may be less directness involved, but without any lessening of the anthropomorphic language. Terrien gives (*Elusive Presence,* 121ff., 131ff.) higher valuation to the northern traditions, on grounds that appear to have no basis in the texts themselves.

18. The distinction between meteorological and volcanic activity drawn by Westermann (*The Praise of God in the Psalms* [Richmond: John Knox Press, 1965], 93ff.) is now generally denied, with all the phenomena seen in terms of meteorology. See Terrien, *Elusive Presence,* 153.

19. They are probably one pillar, showing up differently during night and day. See Mann, *Divine Presence.*

20. The connection in Exod. 14:24 with a battle shows some continuity with the theophanies of God as Warrior.

21. Eichrodt suggests this in *Theology of the OT* 2: 16.

22. A partial exception would be Exodus 3, which combines the messenger form with appearance in a flame of fire. Both are also present in Judg. 13:20 (cf. 6:21; Gen. 15:17). See also Judg. 2:4 and the exceptional use of the messenger to speak to the community (though see Exod. 23:21). Elsewhere the messenger is used in connection with the community in accompanying presence contexts (e.g., Exod. 14:19; 23:20–23; 33:2), another point of continuity between accompanying and theophanic presence.

23. See, e.g., Barr, "Theophany," 34–36. He speaks of "practical accommodation" in disagreeing with Eichrodt's suggestion that this is a weakening of the "sensible perceptibilities of God." Barr also objects to talk of these phenomena as being "mere symbols" of presence (so Eichrodt), and would agree that the visibility of God is not placed into question; it is just that no precise delineaments of form can be discerned.

24. This is extended to hearing God in Deut. 4:32–36; 5:24–26.

25. Brueggemann's discussion of Exodus 33 in "Crisis and Promise" seeks to be balanced in a concern for assurance of presence (vv. 12–17) and divine freedom (vv. 18–23). Generally speaking, however, it would seem that Brueggemann's overarching concern is to protect the freedom and sovereignty of God. The more prominent theological issue is that of having a

divine presence *at all* (the issue with which Exodus 33 begins), not that of the abuse of the divine presence. Cf. G. W. Coats, "The King's Loyal Opposition," 100–103.

26. Here we touch base with Brueggemann's concerns once more.

27. Cf. Terrien's discussion, *Elusive Presence,* 70.

28. See C. Westermann, *God's Angels Need No Wings* (Philadelphia: Fortress Press, 1978), 8.

29. R. Boling (*Judges,* Anchor Bible [Garden City, N.Y.: Doubleday & Co., 1975], 131) speaks of a three-way conversation in which Gideon is involved, with both angel and God, but that he does not realize it. To appeal to Mal. 3:1–2 for a separation between angel and God here fails to consider developments in the understanding of messenger.

30. Von Rad, *Genesis,* 206.

31. Hos. 12:4E identifies the "man" as a "messenger," who in turn is identified with "God."

32. Verbs for "standing" also assist us in making connections with a human figure. Thus, the language of "stationing oneself" *(yāšav)* for God in Exod. 34:5 and 1 Sam. 3:10, and for the messenger in Num. 23:22, along with verbs for coming, descending, or passing by, also suggest a human figure. See also the use of *'āmad,* "stand," for "man" or God or "messenger" in Num. 12:5; 22:24, 26; Josh. 5:13; Gen. 18:22; and *nāṣav,* "stand," in Gen. 28:13 and Amos 7:7; 9:1 for God, in Gen. 18:2 for "man" and in Num. 22:23, 31, 34 for messenger.

33. See Vriezen, *Outline of OT Theology,* 186.

34. A comparable perspective seems to be present in Exod. 23:20–23, where there is an interchange between the "messenger" and the divine subject, "I." Such is also the case in Judg. 2:1; Gen. 48:15–16 and Gen. 24 (cf. vv. 7, 40 with 27, 48). It is difficult to determine from these passages, however, whether the messenger is understood to have a form which is visible. It seems unlikely, though the pillar could be assumed in Exodus 23, and the messenger could be addressed in Gen. 24:12–14. In any case, given the use of messenger language in the larger contexts of these passages, it is likely that the messenger, at least, is understood to be actually present in invisible form. Gen. 48:15–16, makes no apparent distinction between messenger and God.

35. Cf. Barr, "Theophany," 37. Eichrodt *(Theology of the OT* 2: 24–25), speaks of three stages of development, climaxing in the angelic intermediaries so familiar from later Judaism. For an intermediate stage, see the role of messenger as protector (1 Kings 19:5), destroyer (2 Sam. 24:26; 2 Kings 19:35), judge (2 Sam. 14:17, 20; 19:27). See also n. 66 below.

36. See Eichrodt, *Theology of the OT* 2: 21–29. He speaks effectively against the various efforts to soften the impact of these passages.

37. Cf. also Judg. 6:21 and 13:20; Gen. 15:17. Terrien's suggestion (*Elusive Presence,* 110) that the messenger in Exodus 3 should not be taken

literally may or may not be true. It is sufficient here to say that the text does thereby insist that the appearance is not formless (cf. v. 6).

38. Contra G. Mendenhall, *The Tenth Generation* (Baltimore: Johns Hopkins Univ. Press, 1973), 57–59. Our interpretation would also be consistent with those theophanic passages which speak of God as "rider of the clouds" (e.g., Pss. 18:10–12; 68:4; 104:3; Isa. 19:1).

39. Regarding the Priestly materials, Rendtorff ("The Concept of Revelation," 36) states that the *kābôd* here "represents God in a much more massive sense, so that Yahweh himself is in it," and the glory in turn is "in a cloud" (p. 35).

40. Eichrodt (*Theology of the OT* 2: 37) speaks of a "heightened metaphor." While its primary force may be "directly, without mediation," and may entail no seeing (so Terrien, *Elusive Presence,* 91), the choice of this metaphor needs careful consideration in view of what we have seen to be the essential relationship which a metaphor bears to that to which it refers. Cf. also "mouth to mouth" in Num. 12:8, in a context concerned with form.

41. So Eichrodt, *Theology of the OT* 2: 37.

42. The reference in Exod. 33:23 to the "back" of God might also be appealed to here. This suggests, not only that even Moses was granted less than a full sensorial view of God, but that what he was given had the lineaments of a human form.

43. Barr, "Theophany," 36.

44. E. Jacob (*Theology,* 74) states that in the prophets "God always appears in human form." Terrien (*Elusive Presence,* 229) certainly overstates the difference. We have seen above that it is irrelevant for our purposes whether we have to do with a dream/vision or not; the human form is still present. Cf. also 1 Kings 22:19. On the similarities of 1 Kings 22 and Isaiah 6, see Zimmerli, *Ezekiel 1,* Hermeneia (Philadelphia: Fortress Press, 1979), 98, who finds further parallels in Ezekiel 1. See also N. Habel, "The Form and Significance of the Call Narratives," *ZAW* 77 (1965): 297–323, for parallels between the theophanies of Exodus 3 and Judges 6 and those of the prophets.

45. See Jeremias, "Theophany"; Kuntz, *Self-Revelation,* 58–59; Terrien, *Elusive Presence,* 71–72; J. Muilenburg, "The Speech of Theophany," *Harvard Divinity Bulletin* 28 (Jan., 1964): 35–47.

46. See Zimmerli, *I Am Yahweh* (Atlanta: John Knox Press, 1983); Rendtorff, 38–41. Ties to the NT may be observed in the "I am" sayings of Jesus in the Gospel of John in particular.

47. See H. Preuss, " ' . . . ich will mit dir sein,' " *ZAW* 80 (1968): 139–73.

48. See A. Thiselton, "The Supposed Power of Words in the Biblical Writings," *JTS* 25 (1974): 283–99. Cf. J. Barr, *The Semantics of Biblical Language* (Oxford: At the Clarendon Press, 1961), 129–40.

49. It is striking that Zimmerli (*OT Theology in Outline,* 18) can speak of vulnerability when speaking of the giving of names more generally, but in no way follows through on this when dealing with the name of God; in essence

he denies it in his discussion of Exodus 3 (p. 21). For important guidelines and limitations in the discussion of the significance of names, see J. Barr, "The Symbolism of Names in the Old Testament," *BJRL* 52 (1969): 11–29.

50. Cf. Lev. 18:21; 20:3; 21:6; 22:2, 32, and the repetition of the phrase "I am the Lord," throughout this section of Leviticus. Tying the name of God so closely to the commandments indicates that there were certain expectations placed on those who know the name.

51. While it is sometimes suggested that naming has a greater significance for ancient peoples, including Israel, as over against the contemporary world, this seems difficult to sustain to any great extent. Most of what is said would be true of the significance of naming in at least some segments of modern society.

52. Cf. Barr, "The Symbolism of Names." The lack of any one-to-one correspondence between name and nature means that one cannot draw inferences necessarily from name to nature, and at best, only in a partial way.

53. Contra Zimmerli, *OT Theology in Outline,* 20. Even if there is a certain lack of final *definition* in the name Yahweh in Exod. 3:14–15, just by virtue of the gift of the name, God places God's ownself at the disposal of those who can name it. The lack of final definition is not a qualification of the giving of oneself, but, as with all names, a recognition of the limitation in the possibility of drawing inferences from name regarding nature.

54. Seeing is given a largely negative valuation in Terrien (*Elusive Presence,* 152) where he speaks of the tendency "to lull worshippers into the delights of passive spirituality and the loss of social responsibility." See also Brueggemann, "Crisis and Promise," 60. He speaks of making God "an object of adoration, visibility, observation, veneration, an object of the human subject." The crucial importance of seeing for ethics must not be discounted because of the dangers involved. The opposite danger, of course, is a retreat into spirituality, with even greater dangers for the ethical life.

55. So Eichrodt, *Theology of the OT* 2: 27. Given the larger context of Eichrodt's discussion of this matter, it is uncertain what he means by such phrases as the "quasi-human" form of the messenger, or (p. 28) that God "is in no sense present in a human body." There is nothing in these texts, with the possible exception of Judg. 13:6, where the countenance of the messenger is said to be "very terrible," which would suggest that any other than a normal human form was perceived by theophanic recipients. Moreover, the "likeness as it were" of Ezek. 1:26, especially in view of the use of "likeness" elsewhere in the chapter (e.g., v. 16), makes no suggestion that the form perceived might be set off from the human form as otherwise known. The concern is to guard against precision in delineation, not to suggest a form which was in some way other than human. See von Rad, *OT Theology* 1: 146.

56. See Eichrodt, *Theology of the OT* 2: 31.

57. See Barr, "Theophany," 38; Eichrodt, *Theology of the OT* 1: 211–16; 2: 21.

58. Eichrodt's concern (*Theology of the OT* 1: 213; 2: 21) that such language is not "subjecting God to human limitations," needs to be qualified, however. Any appearance is a limitation, though it does not qualify God's Godness. Even more, one of the essential points of significance in the theophanies has to do with the fact that they are witnesses to divine limitation.

59. Eichrodt, *Theology of the OT* 1: 215. See p. 212: "A doctrine of God as spirit in the philosophical sense will be sought in vain in the pages of the Old Testament." He goes on, however, to suggest that John 4:24 might be able to bear such an interpretation; but this is extremely doubtful. See R. Brown, *The Gospel According to St. John,* Anchor Bible (Garden City, N.Y.: Doubleday & Co., 1966), 1: 172.

60. L. Koehler, *Old Testament Theology* (Philadelphia: Westminster Press, 1957), 119–20.

61. E. Jacob, *Theology of the OT,* 76–77; cf. Eichrodt, *Theology of the OT* 2: 27–28.

62. A. R. Johnson, *The One and the Many in the Israelite Conception of God* (Cardiff: Univ. of Wales Press, 1961), 28–33.

63. Cf. the language of Koehler, *OT Theology,* 120–21: "His whole nature is not brought to bear" in the appearance, but "in order to represent Himself intimately to man He turns only one side or operation of His nature towards him by entering a certain condition." Such equivocation, and even suggestion that God can somehow be partially God, seems unnecessary and confusing.

64. So Eichrodt, *Theology of the OT* 2: 15ff., and the title of the section.

65. Westermann (*Basic Forms of Prophetic Speech* [Philadelphia: Westminster Press, 1967], 100) prefers to speak of stages here, with a movement from a directness of God's revelation, to the use of the messenger form. The texts are too interwoven, however, to permit talk of stages; besides, it is a matter of degrees of indirectness for all appearances. Moreover, some of the more direct appearances are in the Priestly writing (Gen. 17:1; 35:9), so that it is difficult to see this staging in terms of God's "withdrawal into the distance."

66. One could conceivably understand even the later uses of messenger in these terms. Thus, for God to "send" a messenger (Mal. 3:1–2) is not necessarily to send some subordinate being, but to send God's ownself in a certain form.

67. Even Eichrodt tends in this direction, speaking of "defects" in early Israel's understanding of God (*Theology of the OT* 1: 213) or "naive notions" (2: 21, 23). See Jacob, *Theology of the OT* (74) on "crude realism." Eichrodt (*Theology of the OT* 2: 28) sets these passages apart from Christian pre-existent logos interpretations, though his arguments are largely beside the point. It is certainly correct not to ascribe such notions to the OT authors; it is another matter altogether, however, whether there are continuities at this point with later Christian theology. It is certainly not a case of radical

discontinuity. The NT makes the connection explicit in its use of Exod. 14:19 in 1 Cor. 10:4. Jacob says that in the light of the NT, we must see these passages, "not as vain speculations, but as approaches to the biblical solution of the divine presence, that of God become man in Jesus Christ" (*Theology of the OT*, 74). See von Rad's almost passing reference to the "divine kenosis" (*OT Theology* 1: 367).

68. For a helpful discussion of the idea of progressive revelation, see J. W. Rogerson, "Progressive Revelation: Its History and Its Value as a Key to Old Testament Interpretation," *Epworth Review* 9 (1982): 73–86.

69. Eichrodt, *Theology of the OT* 2: 21. He uses the language of "mask," p. 27.

70. Von Rad, *OT Theology* 1: 145. Cf. also Barr, "Theophany," 38. Von Rad even includes such references as Exod. 15:3 and Mic. 1:2–3 as evidence that "Yahweh has the form of man."

71. Von Rad, *OT Theology* 1: 146.

72. See Barr, "Theophany," 38. R. P. Carroll, "The Aniconic God and the Cult of Images," *Studia Theologica* 31 (1977): 51–64, makes it clear that the ban on images has nothing to do with either the invisibility or the formlessness of God.

73. Cited in Eichrodt, *Theology of the OT* 1: 212 n. 1.

74. Further development of the theophanic motif as it relates to the prophet will be taken up in chap. 10.

## CHAPTER 7.    GOD SUFFERS BECAUSE

1. Heschel, *Prophets;* Mauser, *Gottesbild und Menschwerdung.* Commentaries on Hosea often contain some helpful, if brief comments relative to God's suffering.

2. Westermann, *Basic Forms,* 202–3; idem, *Elements of OT Theology,* 174; "The Role of the Lament in the Theology of the Old Testament," *Int* 28 (1974): 37–38.

3. See Westermann, *Basic Forms,* 202–203.

4. See H. W. Robinson, *The Cross in the Old Testament* (London: SCM Press, 1955); idem, *Suffering Human and Divine* (New York: Macmillan, 1939).

5. E.g., W. Janzen, *Mourning Cry and Woe Oracle* (Berlin: Walter de Gruyter, 1972); T. Raitt, *A Theology of Exile;* J. Scharbert, *Der Schmerz im AT* (Bonn: Peter Hanstein, 1955); S. Blank, "Doest Thou Well To Be Angry?"; L. Kuyper, "The Suffering and Repentance of God," *SJT* 22 (1969): 257–77.

6. See especially articles by W. Brueggemann, "From Hurt to Joy; From Death to Life," *Int* 28 (1974): 3–19; idem, "The Formfulness of Grief," *Int* 31 (1977): 263–75.

7. Westermann, *Basic Forms,* 203.

8. Raitt, *A Theology of Exile,* 86ff.

9. The verb used here, *tāwāh,* is a *hapax*; given the parallelism with v. 40,

it should be translated "pained," as the various English versions suggest in one way or another.

10. For a recent review of the issues of Psalm 78, see A. Campbell, "Psalm 78: A Contribution to the Theology of Tenth Century Israel," *CBQ* 41 (1979): 51–79.

11. The bulk of the material on Genesis 6—9 is taken from my paper, "Creation Thought and the Absence of God," delivered to the OT Theology Seminar of the SBL at its 1977 convention. See also W. Brueggemann, *Genesis,* 73–88. Westermann ( *Elements of OT Theology,* 120) chooses not to speak of eternal divine self-limitation, only selective nonaction.

12. On Isaiah 1, see the commentaries of O. Kaiser and J. Mauchline in particular, and S. Niditch, "The Composition of Isaiah 1," *Biblica* 61 (1980): 509–29.

13. Heschel, *Prophets,* 80.

14. On Jeremiah 2, see now T. Overholdt, "Jeremiah 2 and the Problem of 'Audience Reaction,' " *CBQ* 41 (1979): 262–73; cf. Brueggemann, "Jeremiah's Use of Rhetorical Questions."

15. See Westermann, "The Role of the Lament," 37–38.

16. On the psalms and prophecy, see A. R. Johnson, *The Cultic Prophet in Ancient Israel* (Cardiff: Univ. of Wales Press, 1962).

17. See Terrien, *Elusive Presence,* 266.

18. Heschel, *Prophets,* 48.

19. Raitt ( *A Theology of Exile,* 84–89) includes certain exilic psalms along with Jeremiah and Ezekiel passages in isolating accusatory comments made by the people regarding God. But, at least from the perspective of the final redactors, the psalm laments are considered to be statements from faith, and hence would receive a different response from God from those which we find in the wilderness and prophetic texts. Raitt, however, does demonstrate that the various questions and God's response to them do not commonly fit into a special disputation speech genre.

20. So Eichrodt, *Theology of the OT* 2: 427.

## CHAPTER 8.   GOD SUFFERS WITH

1. See my study of Judges 2—3 in *Deuteronomic History,* 87–98.

2. For a recent study of the translation issues, see R. Haak, "A Study and New Interpretation of QṢR NPŠ," *JBL* 101 (1982): 161–67.

3. H. W. Wolff, *Joel and Amos,* 231.

4. J. L. Mays, *Amos: A Commentary,* OTL (Philadelphia: Westminster Press, 1969), 85.

5. For redactional issues here, cf. Wolff, *Joel and Amos,* 236–39.

6. Ibid., 249.

7. The accusation normally precedes the lamentation (e.g., Ezekiel 17). There is an unusual admixture of lamentation and announcement of judgment in Ezek. 32:1–16. This might be related to the lament-accusation

pattern discerned in the first section, though the perspective is more oriented to the future. On redactional issues, see Eichrodt, *Ezekiel,* 431–32.

8. On the oracles against the nations, see J. Barton, *Amos' Oracles Against the Nations.*

9. Zimmerli, *Ezekiel,* 397.

10. Ibid.

11. Most commentators give little recognition to the fact that God is speaking in these texts.

12. The RSV emends unnecessarily here. See the JB and the translation of J. Bright, who believes Jeremiah to be speaking here (Bright, *Jeremiah,* 68, 72). Westermann (*Elements of OT Theology,* 142) speaks of God's lament.

13. Heschel, *Prophets,* 112. For extrabiblical parallels regarding the mourning for the dying and rising God, which may be reflected in certain Old Testament texts, see F. Hvidberg, *Weeping and Laughter in the Old Testament* (Leiden: E. J. Brill, 1962).

14. See P. Trible, *God and the Rhetoric of Sexuality,* 40ff.

15. See especially W. Janzen, *Mourning Cry and Woe Oracle.*

16. Ibid., 82.

17. Ibid., 22–23.

## CHAPTER 9.   GOD SUFFERS FOR

1. See von Rad, *OT Theology,* 1: 270–71. Because the priests are representatives of God himself, through whom God acts (cf. Lev. 6:24–30; 10:16–20), God too may be said to bear the sins of the people.

2. See Zimmerli, *Ezekiel,* 2: 163–65.

3. Both the Septuagint and the Targumim have difficulty with this verse, translating it in less anthropomorphic terms.

4. See S. Blank, "Doest Thou Well To Be Angry?" 30ff. The remarks of H. W. Robinson, *The Cross in the Old Testament,* 185, are striking: In Jeremiah 45 "we see comfort brought to the sorrow of man by the realization of the sorrow of God. Baruch is overwhelmed by the sense of the failure of the prophet's work and of his own, and the prophet recalls him to the thought of the failure of God . . . . There is hardly a passage in the Old Testament which gives us a more impressive glimpse of the eternal cross in the heart of God."

5. Janzen, "Metaphor and Reality," 22.

6. See especially the commentaries of Wolff, Mays, and Andersen/Freedman, as well as the contributions of Janzen, Mays, and Collins in "Old Testament Interpretation from a Process Perspective," *Semeia* 24 (1982).

7. We essentially follow the translation of J. L. Mays in "Response to Janzen: Metaphor and Reality in Hos. 11," *Semeia* 24 (1982): 47.

8. See above, p. 55.

9. Divine repentance and anger are commonly interwoven themes, e.g., Exod. 32:10–14; Jon. 3:9–10.

10. One could also compare Exod. 32:14 with 32:34–35 in terms of the divine repentance followed by a partial judgment. In this text it is Moses who reminds God (v. 13), while in Hosea 11 God remembers. In either case it is the memory of God which is the crucial factor.

11. See Mays, "Response to Janzen," 47; Janzen, "Metaphor and Reality," 40 nn. 5, 7.

12. In the present redaction, including Hos. 13:9–16, this is not only an intermediate, but apparently a temporary response of God, though return is still an open possibility at the end of the book. See the discussion of J. Collins in *Semeia* 24 (1982): 110ff.

13. Terrien (*Elusive Presence,* 265) also calls attention to Ezek. 21:8–17 in a striking way, where God's wielding of the sword against Israel contains the theme of divine "self-immolation."

14. Weiser, *Psalms,* 195.

15. Terrien, *Elusive Presence,* 289. This passage has also been a part of rabbinic discussion of God's self-humiliation. See J. Moltmann, *Trinity and the Kingdom,* 27ff. He also notes connections with the doctrine of the Shekinah.

16. See the discussion of J. Muilenburg, "Isaiah 40—66," *Interpreter's Bible* 5 (1956): 731ff.

17. For a brief review, see R. Mason, *The Books of Haggai, Zechariah and Malachi* (New York and Cambridge: Cambridge Univ. Press, 1977), 118–19.

18. See S. Blank, "Doest Thou Well To Be Angry?" 29ff.; H. Wolff, *Studien zum Jonabuch* (Neukirchen-Vluyn: Neukirkener Verlag, 1965).

19. See Trible, *God and the Rhetoric of Sexuality,* 64; Muilenburg, "Isaiah 40—66," 472.

20. The attempt on the part of a few scholars (e.g., A. Schoors, *I Am God Your Savior* [Leiden: E. J. Brill, 1973], 91) to avoid the full force of the metaphoric language is unfortunate. Cf. Muilenburg, "Isaiah 40—66," 473.

## CHAPTER 10.    PROPHET, THEOPHANY, AND THE SUFFERING OF GOD

1. See J. Ross, "The Prophet as Yahweh's Messenger," in *Israel's Prophetic Heritage,* ed. B. W. Anderson and W. Harrelson (New York: Harper & Row, 1962), 105–6; E. Jacob, *Theology of OT,* 77; Westermann, *Basic Forms,* 100.

2. Jacob, *Theology of OT,* 77, speaks of the messenger as a "distinct personality," but as one who "exists and functions by virtue of God's free decision." Vriezen (*Outline of OT Theology,* 209) speaks of the "unity of this particularization with the divine being," while at the same time recognizing that the messenger could act independently. Cf. our discussion above with respect to the relationship of messenger and God (chap. 6).

3. Ross ("The Prophet," 106) notes that the specific messenger language for the prophet is late (Hag. 1:13; 2 Chron. 36:15–16; Malachi; cf. Isa. 42:19; 44:26; 66:1–2), and that, except for Hos. 12:4E, no reference is made to the

messengers in the earlier prophets, though messenger language forms are used. He suggests that this may have to do with their message of judgment and the need to separate themselves from the peace-speaking prophets (cf. Jer. 6:14); when the later prophets' message turns toward peace, there is no further need for such caution. However, given the terminological and self-reference problems for the prophet (cf. Amos 7:14; 1 Sam. 9:9), this development may have had more to do with the fact that prophets were only later recognized by the community to be what they in fact were. Cf. also Westermann (*Basic Forms,* 115) who ascribes the late appearance of the messenger language for the prophets to the fact that early ideas about divine messengers were such that only a god or divine creature could be such a messenger.

4. The only non-prophetic use of the formula *ne'um yhwh* is by the messenger in Gen. 22:16, while *kōh 'āmar yhwh* is used by the messenger in 1 Kings 1:4, 15.

5. Cf. Hosea 11, though in the light of the unique Gen. 31:13, the reference in the prophets may have been less direct.

6. Cf. Jer. 8:18—9:3. One might also note here the apparent interchange of God and Davidic king in Ps. 45:6, and the use of "messenger" for the priest in Mal. 2:7.

7. There is no evidence to suggest that the plural forms in divine speech in Genesis 1, 3, 11; Isaiah 6, or the "sons of God" (e.g., Gen. 6:4; Job 1) are references to the messenger; the angelic intermediaries of the later literature may be a convergence of what were originally separate conceptions.

8. In the Judges context, one might also cite the juxtaposition of Judg. 6:7–10 and 6:11–24, and the connections with Judg. 2:1–5. There are striking similarities of content between the word of the messenger in 2:1–5 and that of the prophet in 6:7–10 (cf. 10:11–14). Given this unique appearance of the prophet in Judges, this appears to be a later attempt to identify the messenger of 2:1–5 and 6:11–24 with a prophetic figure, or at least to indicate that the prophet and the messenger are seen to have a comparable relationship to God.

9. See N. Habel, "Form and Significance," 297–323. See also J. Crenshaw, "Amos and the Theophanic Tradition," *ZAW* 80 (1968): 203–15.

10. D. Robertson, *The Old Testament and the Literary Critic* (Philadelphia: Fortress Press, 1977), 71–81.

11. Von Rad, *OT Theology* 2: 274.

12. Ibid., 91–92.

13. Terrien, *Elusive Presence,* 255.

14. Ibid., 241.

15. See, e.g., von Rad, *OT Theology* 2: 95–98.

16. Zimmerli, *Ezekiel,* 156.

17. Von Rad, *OT Theology* 2: 96.

18. Zimmerli, *Ezekiel,* 54. Cf. also von Rad, *OT Theology* 2: 233, 275; Mauser, *Gottesbild und Menschwerdung,* 86.

19. Cf. Westermann, *Elements of OT Theology,* 173.

20. In addition to the commentaries, see especially Mauser, "Image of God," and Terrien, *Elusive Presence,* 241ff.

21. Ibid., 244.

22. Mauser, "Image of God," 353.

23. Terrien, *Elusive Presence,* 246.

24. See especially Mauser, *Gottesbild und Menschwerdung,* 78ff.; Heschel, *Prophets,* 103ff.

25. See Mauser, *Gottesbild und Menschwerdung,* 89ff.

26. Ibid., 111.

27. Von Rad, *OT Theology* 2: 204.

28. Heschel, *Prophets,* 118.

29. See Mauser, *Gottesbild und Menschwerdung,* 108ff.

30. E.g., Heschel, *Prophets,* 119–22.

31. Von Rad, *OT Theology* 2: 207. His discussion of these chapters is representative of the current discussion. For a different view, see E. Nicholson, *Preaching to the Exiles* (Oxford: Basil Blackwell, 1970).

32. See von Rad, *OT Theology* 2: 233, 275, 403ff.

33. See Zimmerli, *Ezekiel,* 164–65, for discussion.

34. Von Rad, *OT Theology* 2: 233, 404, seems to be of two minds as to whether a vicarious bearing of guilt is involved here.

35. Cf. von Rad, *OT Theology* 2: 261, 276ff.

36. Eichrodt, *Theology of the OT* 2: 450.

37. Von Rad, *OT Theology* 2: 276.

38. See especially the commentaries of Westermann, Muilenburg, and the study of von Rad, *OT Theology* 2: 250–62, 273–77.

39. The connection with laments is emphasized by Westermann in particular; cf. *Isaiah 40—66,* 265.

40. This is language used both by Heschel, *Prophets,* 319, and Mauser, *Gottesbild und Menschwerdung,* 76, 115ff.

41. See Mauser, "Image of God," 355ff.

# Indexes

## SCRIPTURE

195

## AUTHORS